D1594845

General John Sedgwick

General
John Sedgwick

The Story of a
Union Corps Commander

Richard Elliott Winslow III

PRESIDIO

Published by Presidio Press, 31 Pamaron Way, Novato, CA 94947

Library of Congress Cataloging in Publication Data

Winslow, Richard Elliott, 1934-
    General John Sedgwick, the story of a Union corps
commander.

    Bibliography: p.
    Includes index.
    1. Sedgwick, John, 1813-1864. 2.   United
States — History — Civil War, 1861-1865 — Campaigns
and battles. 3.   Generals — United States — Biography.
4. United States.   Army — Biography.   I.   Title.
E467.1.S4W54   973.7'41 [B]   80-26960
ISBN 0-89141-030-9

Cover design by Kathleen A. Jaeger
Maps by Gary Creighton
Printed in the United States of America

To my father,
Richard E. Winslow, Jr.,
whose lifelong interest in
and affection for history
has helped me in writing this book.

CONTENTS

Acknowledgments

I am indebted to many people for their assistance in the preparation of this book. Dr. Warren W. Hassler, Jr., of the Pennsylvania State University originally suggested this topic and guided its evolution from a seminar paper to a completed dissertation. The Chicago Civil War Round Table awarded a grant for my project.

For my research, I visited many libraries whose staffs cheerfully provided books, newspapers, and manuscripts. The institutions include: the university libraries of Penn State, New Hampshire, Maryland, Kentucky, Harvard, Yale, Brown, and Bowdoin; the state historical societies of all six New England states, New York, New Jersey, and Pennsylvania; the Library of Congress; the National Archives; the public libraries of Boston, Massachusetts; Cornwall and Litchfield, Connecticut; the Litchfield County (Connecticut) Historical Society; and the Connecticut State Library, Hartford. I enjoyed the hospitality of the citizens of Cornwall Hollow, Connecticut, who showed me around, and explained various aspects of the John Sedgwick story.

Recognizing the need for a Sedgwick biography, Dr. James I. Robertson, Jr. of the Virginia Polytechnic Institute and State University, Blacksburg, Virginia, showed an interest in my work and encouraged its publication.

The suggestions of Joan Griffin and Rain Blockley, editors at Presidio Press, materially improved the content, organization, and style of my manuscript through successive drafts to press copy. Gary Creighton, a cartographer with the Kentucky Geological Survey, drafted the excellent maps.

Finally I thank my parents, relatives, and friends for their unfaltering support during the writing of this book.

Lexington, Kentucky
September 1980

ix

Preface

John Sedgwick was perhaps destined for a military career. His grandfather, bearing the same name, had served as a major during the American War of Revolution. Born in 1813 at Cornwall Hollow, Connecticut, young Sedgwick taught school and worked on the family farm. But these professions held no allurement for him. He entered the United States Military Academy, graduating in 1837, twenty-fourth in a class of fifty. Commissioned as a second lieutenant, Sedgwick embarked upon a lifelong career in the army.

His service paralleled the military history of the United States for the next two decades. Seeing action in the Seminole War, the Mexican War, and various expeditions against the Plains Indians, Sedgwick was a major in 1860. At that time he was seriously contemplating retirement.

But this personal hope was dashed. Upon the outbreak of the American Civil War, Sedgwick's many years of proven ability were badly needed by the Union. He remained in the army. Rapidly promoted as the war continued, Sedgwick became a major general. As a corps commander, he fought in many of the fiercest battles of the East. On occasion, he was acting commander of the Army of the Potomac.

At the height of his fame and reputation, Sedgwick was killed in action near Spotsylvania Court House, Virginia, in May 1864. The nation mourned his death. John Sedgwick was remembered by his contemporaries and peers as a steadfast soldier who contributed much to ultimate Union victory.

Despite Sedgwick's crucial role during the Civil War, no one has fully examined his remarkable career. The general discouraged during his lifetime any effort to write his biography. After the conflict, writers and journalists chose other personalities and overlooked

Sedgwick's accomplishments. Today the once-popular general is remembered by Civil War buffs and students of military history, but forgotten by the public.

This neglect may be attributed to several factors. Since Sedgwick did not survive the war, he obviously did not write his memoirs, collect and organize his papers, or grant interviews to newspapermen. Sedgwick's staff officers and army acquaintances, busy establishing postwar careers or fighting Indians during the 1870s and 1880s, never got around to writing the general's biography. The overall paucity of his personal papers, as well the thin and scattered reminiscences of the general's associates has hampered and discouraged prospective researchers. Civil War historians have turned instead to Grant, Lee, Sherman, Sheridan, and others for their biographies.

Some work on Sedgwick, nevertheless, was done. Patriotic citizens and veterans' organizations erected statues and monuments to his memory; dedicatory addresses were often preserved as souvenir pamphlets. Sedgwick's former assistant adjutant general and chief of staff, Martin T. McMahon, was in demand as a speaker at veterans' reunions and encampments; his reminiscences were printed up as booklets. Thomas W. Hyde, the general's aide-de-camp, wrote an eulogistic memoir, *Following the Greek Cross*, published in 1895, which includes much valuable material. Sedgwick's sister, Emily S. Welch, privately published her own brief remembrances. To the great service of present-day scholars, Carl and Ellen Battelle Stoeckel gathered together the most important Sedgwick papers and subsidized their publication in 1902–1903. This two-volume work, *Correspondence of John Sedgwick, Major-General*, is by far the best single source relating to the general's life. These pioneering efforts represent the foundation for modern study.

While using many standard works on this period, I have also examined many neglected manuscript collections. Private letters and diaries of Sedgwick and his officers and men reveal the grim atmosphere of war, providing a graphic day-by-day account of the many rumors, frustrations, and anxieties. Newspapers and regimental histories also have yielded significant information.

In this book, I am interested in Sedgwick himself — the man's character and actions. Many Civil War military biographies virtually paraphrase the orders and reports of the *Official Records of the Union and Confederate Armies* in a confusing recital of names, units, times, geographical locations, numbers, and losses. Such studies become a mental exercise in moving little blue and red pins around on an imaginary map. Such an approach is not my intention.

John Sedgwick lived in the midst of momentous times. He engaged in consequential historic activities. This study, focused on Sedgwick's pivotal Civil War years, fills an omission in this period's historiography. For too long a time, Sedgwick has been mentioned in footnotes, tucked away in an index, or relegated to a portion of the Chancellorsville campaign. A modest person, he would not have cared. But the modern Civil War enthusiast is curious and feels otherwise. Now over a century after his death, Sedgwick rightly deserves his own biography. His life is indeed a rich and fascinating story.

CHAPTER 1

FROM THE PLAINS
TO THE PENINSULA

AT FORT WISE during December 1860, Maj. John Sedgwick, commanding the 1st Cavalry, finally received the news of Abraham Lincoln's election to the presidency of the United States. Mail from the East usually required several weeks to arrive at this recently constructed fort on the plains east of Pikes Peak in the Kansas Territory. Although far removed from the sectional controversies and political turmoil of the East, Sedgwick was disturbed, explaining in a letter to his sister, Emily, that he had heard of the "probable difficulty he [Lincoln] will experience, if not direct opposition, to his inauguration. It seems lamentable that this Union that we have boasted of and glorified so much should be broken up."[1]

"Uncle John," as he was affectionately known to his soldiers, was in a quandary. "How a disruption will affect me I cannot foresee; probably would result in my leaving the service at once," the veteran soldier confided to his sister. "I do not feel quite ready to do this, but when I am ready I want to. . . . if I have any cause of regret, have no one to blame but myself."[2]

Sedgwick was often slow to make a decision, but once he did, he was resolute. For several years, he had seriously contemplated resigning from the army. An 1837 graduate from the U.S. Military Academy at West Point, he had devoted his life to an army career and had seen action in the Florida War against the Seminole Indians, the Mexican War, and, most recently, against the Kiowa

1

and Comanche Indians on the Great Plains. A lifelong bachelor, now forty-seven years old, he anticipated an early retirement to his boyhood home and farm at Cornwall Hollow, Connecticut. The last Indian campaign and all the hardships endured while constructing the fort were so exasperating that he was determined to resign his commission the following spring. He had lived frugally throughout his years of service and could afford retirement. This sectional crisis could upset his plans.[3]

To compound Sedgwick's difficulties, his superior officer, Col. Edwin V. Sumner, went on leave that January. As the only field officer with the regiment, Sedgwick remained in charge at Fort Wise and could not go on furlough.

Sedgwick felt during January 1861 that "a remedy will be found to forge the links of the Union stronger than ever. All other evils compared with disunion are light";[4] but as the months passed, the news from the East became more and more alarming. South Carolina had already seceded from the Union in December 1860. Other Southern states followed and eventually formed the Confederate States of America.

While awaiting a decision on his application for a leave of absence, Sedgwick was busy with the many administrative details at the fort and had little time to worry about the momentous events in the East. During February, he met with 3,000 Indians who were "all collected for the purpose of receiving presents, and making a treaty, relinquishing their claims to the gold regions." When the news reached Fort Wise of the April 12 Confederate bombardment of Fort Sumter, South Carolina, Sedgwick made an immediate decision. Being a man of honor, the major "felt that, educated at his country's expense, he could not desert her in her hour of need."[5]

Such a patriotic stand was characteristic of John Sedgwick. He was a solid man. Soldiers responded to his open nature, modesty, and blunt, straightforward manner. Heavy, short, and muscular, he weighed over 200 pounds. He had a magnificent profile, curly chestnut hair, and a full beard, cut short and with some gray in it. His personal appearance was unpretentious. A careless dresser, he frequently wore plain clothes without an insignia of rank, and he was often mistaken for a common soldier. His trademark was a round straw hat. Simple in his habits, Sedgwick preferred to have his headquarters in his tent rather than in a house, and he rode the same horse, "Tom," that he had owned for ten years.

With the government's need for qualified, experienced officers, the Civil War offered advancement for career army men. On March 25, President Abraham Lincoln and Secretary of War Simon Cameron had signed Sedgwick's commission of lieutenant colonel of the 2d Cavalry, to rank from March 16. Two months later, on May 29, Sedgwick was directed by Brig. Gen. William S. Harney, commanding the Department of the West at St. Louis, to report to Fort Leavenworth, Kansas, and await further orders. The major then journeyed to the East and briefly saw his cousin, Judge John Sedgwick III. The judge felt that professionally the war would be a great opportunity for the modest soldier who himself believed that he might be promoted to colonel. Conscientious about his decision, Sedgwick said to his cousin, "I had hoped to leave military life, but this cannot be now, for my country needs my services."[6]

On arrival at the national capital in June, Sedgwick was assigned to duty in the defenses of Washington. He entered into the utter confusion that almost overwhelmed the Lincoln administration during the early days of the war.

During the early spring of 1861, Col. Robert E. Lee and Lt. Col. William J. Hardee were commanding the 1st Cavalry, and upon their defection to the Confederacy, Sedgwick filled this vacated post. But severe illness — perhaps an attack of the cholera then raging in the capital — prevented Sedgwick from active field duty with his unit. While the disastrous battle of Bull Run was being fought during late July, he was still confined to his sickbed. The Union defeat affected him deeply; he wrote home, "We have lost everything, even our honour. . . . if the enemy had not suffered severely . . . they could have marched into Washington last night."[7]

On his recovery, Sedgwick was not sent to the field, but was appointed to a court of inquiry. On August 10, the assistant adjutant general, James B. Fry, detailed Sedgwick and two other officers to meet at Alexandria, Virginia, for a court-martial case. For such an active individual as Sedgwick, this desk job was undoubtedly exasperating.

After the Bull Run defeat, the Lincoln administration realized the necessity for a complete army reorganization and adequate defenses for the city of Washington. Maj. Gen. George B. McClellan, fresh from his victories in western Virginia, arrived in the capital during late July to assume these responsibilities. Sedgwick was given a brigade in the defenses of Washington on August 12; two weeks later he was promoted to full colonel, to rank from April 25. His complete command of about 3,300 men was stationed at Camp Sackett near Alexandria, Virginia.[8]

The remainder of 1861 and early 1862 was a time of preparation for both sides. Old service friendships were broken as Southern officers resigned their commissions from the U.S. Army. During September, Sedgwick received a solemn letter from William N. R. Beall of Kentucky, who wrote, "I very much regretted that things came to a state that caused me to feel it my *duty* to leave the Army."[9]

As Sedgwick began organizing his personal staff, he received a note from an uncle, Charles Sedgwick, asking that he use his influence to secure a place on McClellan's staff for William Dwight Sedgwick, Charles's son. The colonel was assured that his cousin was "a gentleman with the strong frame of a peasant. I take it for granted that he has not white feathers to show."[10] McClellan could not use William, but John Sedgwick was happy to assign his cousin to his own staff. Young Sedgwick was a graduate of Harvard University, a practicing lawyer, and had left a wife and three children to volunteer his services for the Union cause. Although nepotism often resulted in inefficient men on Union army staffs, young Sedgwick proved a competent assistant to his high-ranking cousin.

There was little for the officers and men to do at Camp Sackett that winter except apply for leaves, maneuver for promotions, or request transfers. Lt. Abner R. Small of the 3d Maine desired a transfer and, when Sedgwick did not grant it, groused about his commander:

> Our first impressions of Sedgwick were not happy. I have heard that a smile occasionally invaded his scrubby beard, but I never saw one there. . . . He was an old bachelor with oddities; addicted to practical jokes and endless games of solitaire.[11]

During the long wait for the spring campaign, Sedgwick spent most of the time at his brigade headquarters, except when assigned again to temporary court duty in Washington. The machinations of the politicians disgusted him: "They are doing nothing in Congress except scrambling after contracts, and other things of less importance."[12] Although Sedgwick wanted to return to his hometown in

Connecticut for a few days, he avoided pressing McClellan for a leave, as hundreds of other officers were constantly beseeching him.

Uncle John's patience was rewarded. During February 1862, McClellan relieved Brig. Gen. Charles P. Stone of his command. Discredited by a terrible Union defeat at Ball's Bluff the previous October, Stone was later placed under arrest. Having become acquainted with Sedgwick's fine qualities, "Little Mac," as McClellan was nicknamed, assigned him to lead Stone's division. McClellan thought John Sedgwick was "one of the best and most modest soldiers we had."[13]

To command this division, Sedgwick was advanced to a brigadier general of volunteers on February 6, 1862, to rank from August 31, 1861. This promotion marked his rise from relative obscurity and strengthened his admiration and friendship for McClellan. To his sister, Sedgwick admitted, "I enter upon the duties with a great deal of diffidence. It is a large command (thirteen thousand men), occupying an important position, and I fear, above my capacity; however, I shall do my best."[14]

On or about February 18, Sedgwick embarked on a small steam tug on the Chesapeake and Ohio Canal for Poolesville, Maryland, to join his command. This division was composed of three brigades, led by Brigadier Generals Willis A. Gorman, Napoleon J. T. Dana, and William W. Burns, with an artillery complement commanded by Col. Charles H. Tompkins. The men had been badly demoralized by Stone's failure.

Before the end of the month, McClellan entrusted an important military operation to his new brigadier general. McClellan saw the strategic importance of reopening the Baltimore and Ohio Railroad to the west of Washington, and "regarded the possession of Winchester and Strasburg as necessary to cover the railway in the rear." These two towns were near the northern or lower end of the Shenandoah Valley, which was being guarded by Union Maj. Gen. Nathaniel P. Banks against the maneuvers of the wily Confederate major general, Thomas J. "Stonewall" Jackson. To aid and support the harassed Banks, McClellan temporarily assigned Sedgwick to Banks's Mountain Department and ordered him to move up the Potomac River to Harpers Ferry. One of his brigades was to remain behind to "observe and guard the Potomac from Great Falls to the mouth of the Monocacy." The war now began in earnest for the veteran general.[15]

On February 24, Sedgwick's division was subjected to gale-force winds, which blew all day and continued into the night. At least half the tents were blown down and the troops shivered through a cold night. In the midst of the storm, the general received his orders to pack up and be ready to march. The bulk of his division started westward at daybreak. In their haste, many soldiers left behind their tents and most of their baggage. They did not know their destination. Many fell from exhaustion; others threw away some of their equipment. One soldier, who carried over fifty pounds on his back, remarked, "Just try it and travel off two miles or more without stopping; perhaps you would enjoy it."[16] Sedgwick led the march, but a few lucky regiments boarded freight cars.

Four days later, both contingents arrived at Harpers Ferry. The following morning, the men were enthusiastic tourists and visited Fort John Brown. They looked out from the same hole through which the abolitionist had fired, and they chipped pieces of wood from the window sash for souvenirs.

The luxury of sightseeing soon ended. On March 2, some of Sedgwick's units marched out of Harpers Ferry, in a severe snowstorm, to occupy Bolivar Heights and gain the strategic ground overlooking the confluence of the Potomac and Shenandoah rivers. The next day, four companies crossed the Shenandoah River on a rope ferry and occupied Loudon Heights. Meanwhile, engineers were working to complete a railroad bridge across the Potomac. Sedgwick always coordinated the activities of his specialized units.

Banks then advanced southward to clear the Confederates from the valley in an attempt to prevent Jackson from striking at Washington through the Blue Ridge passes. Sedgwick was ordered to march westward toward Winchester in support. He withdrew his outpost troops and tramped to Berryville on March 11. Two days later, the soldiers heard the booming of artillery in the distance. They marched six miles toward Winchester, but before they could smell gunpowder Uncle John turned his men around. The Southerners had fallen back toward Strasburg without a fight; Banks no longer needed additional support and had countermanded his orders for Sedgwick.

Leading his men back toward Berryville for an overnight bivouac, Sedgwick picked up another of his regiments, the 20th Massachusetts, which had just come up from Poolesville by canal boats and quick marches. Resting troops filled the woods and fields for miles around.

sensitive ✓

On the march back to the Potomac, an incident occurred that endeared Uncle John to his men. Standing on the road and watching the column of men pass by, the general saw an excited hatless officer approach, calling, "General! General!" The officer breathlessly explained that "the troops yonder are tearing out a sutler!" Knowing that this sutler was dishonest and often cheated his men, Sedgwick mounted his horse and rode deliberately in the opposite direction. Shouts of laughter from the men followed the officer who volunteered the information. Uncle John had demonstrated to his new command that he understood and sympathized with the common soldier.[17]

By March 15, Sedgwick and his division had arrived back at their original encampment at Harpers Ferry. The general immediately telegraphed Washington, expecting to be withdrawn. The citizens in the area were hostile toward his troops, and Sedgwick commented, "I am disgusted at the depredations our men are committing, stealing everything they can lay their hands on. I am sorry to say they are supported in it by many of their officers."[18]

Actually, new orders were already on their way to Sedgwick. General McClellan, President Lincoln, and Edwin M. Stanton, the new secretary of war who replaced the corrupt Simon Cameron in January, had completed preparations for the spring offensive and had reorganized the Army of the Potomac into four corps. The 2d Corps, numbering about 21,500 men, was divided into three divisions and placed under the command of Maj. Gen. Edwin V. Sumner. Sedgwick was assigned to the 1st Division and was reunited with "Old Bull" Sumner, his superior officer and friend during their years together on the Great Plains. Brig. Gen. Israel B. Richardson was given the 2d Division, while the 3d was commanded by Brig. Gen. Louis Blenker.

On March 13, McClellan's chief of staff, Maj. Randolph B. Marcy, notified Banks that Sedgwick's division was to be detached from Banks's command. McClellan wanted this division for an amphibious operation to Fort Monroe, Virginia, on the tip of a long peninsula bordered by the York and James rivers. From Fort Monroe, McClellan would execute his bold plan — to march his proposed force of 155,000 men up the Yorktown Peninsula seventy miles to capture the Confederate capital of Richmond.[19]

Sedgwick waited impatiently for army officials in Washington to decide where they wanted his division. With Banks in apparent control of the situation in the Shenandoah Valley, there was nothing to do except conduct daily drills. Finally, on March 21, Marcy advised Sedgwick to arrange for transportation to Washington via the Baltimore and Ohio Railroad. Three days later, Sedgwick reported to Marcy that "General Banks telegraphs that Jackson is in full retreat and that I may leave as soon as transportation arrives." On March 27, the day the majority of Sedgwick's troops left Harpers Ferry, Maj. Gen. David Hunter wrote to Secretary of War Stanton, hoping to pluck these soldiers for his own force. Hunter, who was leading an expedition to recapture Charleston, South Carolina, explained, "If you could send me General Sedgwick's division . . . I . . . would almost guarantee to have our flag waving over Fort Sumter by the anniversary of its capture." Hunter's request went unheeded. On the same day, McClellan notified Stanton, "Some two brigades of Sedgwick's Division will embark to-day. . . . We are pushing it as rapidly as transports arrive and are coaled."[20]

Sedgwick's regiments marched over the rebuilt railroad bridge and continued downriver to Sandy Hook and Point of Rocks. The division boarded railroad cars for the trip to Washington, which they soon departed for Alexandria, Virginia, for embarkation. The general secrecy and last-minute arrangements produced an atmosphere of confusion.

To move his large command on the steamer trip to the Yorktown Peninsula, Sedgwick had to split his division. The general himself arrived at Fort Monroe on March 29, in advance of most of his men, and went into camp at Hampton. There he consulted with the many corps and division commanders. Maj. Gen. Samuel P. Heintzelman noted, "There is utter confusion on the wharves."[21] He and Sedgwick had a brief altercation, but the matter was apparently settled. Some of Uncle John's regiments encountered equally aggravating problems: bad weather and leaky, crowded steamers.

Finally arriving at Hampton, Sedgwick's reassembled division indulged for several days in catching oysters and shellfish for food and sport. The men were waiting for McClellan's whole army to arrive. As there was no immediate urgency, the kindly Sedgwick allowed his men to enjoy themselves.

To McClellan's disappointment and dismay, his proposed total force of 155,000 never arrived. Lincoln had detached Blenker's division, some 10,000 men from Sumner's 2d Corps, for transfer to the Shenandoah Valley. Other detachments and changes, together with soldiers on sick leave, left McClellan with about 85,000 men, of which some 67,000 were ready for battle. To oppose McClellan's invasion, the Confederate general, Joseph E. Johnston, had about 56,000, with 47,000 present for duty.

Sedgwick was optimistic about the Union chances for success. On April 3, after examining the Union encampment, he wrote, "We march at daylight, sixty thousand men and the finest artillery in the world. I do not think we can be whipped. General McClellan . . . told me today we should probably have a fight to-morrow; if not, he did not expect one before reaching Richmond."[22] The largest military operation up to this time in American history was about to begin.

The Army of the Potomac was now poised for its advance up the Peninsula. McClellan's initial military objective was the reduction of the Confederate works, held by some 15,000 troops at Yorktown, some twenty-five miles away.

On April 4, Sedgwick's buglers sounded reveille at daylight; at 6 o'clock, he moved his division forward. Marching through Little Bethel and Big Bethel, he noticed the extensive earthworks and barracks that had been deserted by the Confederate forces. After months of winter camp and occupation duty, the men sensed that they soon would be engaged in their first fighting of the war. Toward the late afternoon of April 5, amidst an almost constant rain and cannonading booming at intervals in the distance, Sedgwick's troops struck the enemy's lines south of Yorktown. There Sedgwick pitched his camp in a low muddy flat about two miles south of the village. The rains created knee-deep mud. The men called the place Camp Misery.[23]

But the quick pace continued. Regiments went on reconnaissance, others began throwing up breastworks, and heavy siege guns were being hurried to the front. After a reconnaissance on April 7, Lt. Oliver Wendell Holmes, Jr., of the 20th Massachusetts, noted, "It's a campaign now & no mistake — no tents, no trunks, — no nothing."[24]

On April 11, the entire division moved a mile to Camp Winfield Scott near the banks of the Warwick River. Sumner's corps now occupied the center of the Union line. A civil engineering team of the 1st Minnesota drew valuable sketches of the roads, positions of headquarters, and batteries along the front, which greatly aided Sedgwick's intelligence of the military situation.

Although McClellan had enjoyed an early initiative, he now became cautious. Swampy ground, an incorrect map, and a strong Confederate force convinced him to halt his advance. Throughout early April, Sedgwick's soldiers entrenched. Soldier E. J. Russell, of the 15th Massachusetts, wrote, "Just now six hundred men passed me, everyone of whom had either a shovel, axe, or pick, for fatigue duty. So you see it takes back-bone to be a soldier in McClellan's army."[25] McClellan's offensive bogged down into being a siege operation. For Sedgwick's division, the anticipation of capturing Richmond was gone.

Days passed, giving the Confederates valuable time. Sedgwick's division lay along the lines and earthworks thrown up by the Revolutionary Army. Uncle John's tent was pitched in a clump of peach trees near the spot George Washington had made his headquarters eighty years before. Sedgwick paused for orders; he explained, "We are patiently waiting for the siege-train to be put in position before anything can be done, and the roads are such that is as much as can be done to bring up supplies. . . . Everyone is impatient for a move, and none more so than the General himself."[26]

Supplies ran low, and even the 3,000 men at work daily could not transport everything. One day a self-appointed committee of a Rhode Island artillery battery exhibited its meager rations to Sedgwick and asked if he thought that was enough for men to live on. Uncle John answered, "No! It is almost impossible to get them, but I will see that you get more very soon." The unit sent four drivers to Shipping Point for rations; when they returned the next day, the general asked if they were getting more to eat. Pvt. Thomas Aldrich said they were but that they were working for it. Sedgwick and his staff laughed. As the general rode away, he remarked, "That's right; bring up all you can; it is the only way we can get anything up here."[27]

To add to the difficulties of rain, mud, and boredom, McClellan was unhappy. He felt that the Lincoln administration — especially Secretary of War Stanton — was not providing the Army of the Potomac with sufficient troops and yet was urging an immediate advance to break the enemy's line at Yorktown. McClellan's gloom influenced subordinates and fellow officers: Capt. William F. Biddle, his aide-de-camp, wrote angrily to his father, "If anything can be put before the people to show the treatment McClellan has received at the hands of the administration, or rather of Stanton, it should be done . . . the treachery of Stanton ought to be exposed." Sedgwick felt the same pessimism, exclaiming, "I mean to stand or fall with McClellan. . . . I believe they are determined to crush him."[28]

As the siege of Yorktown continued, daily skirmishes kept the Union forces on edge. Sharp picket fighting was incessant day and night. McClellan notified one of Sedgwick's brigade commanders to "waste no ammunition." No music or calls were allowed in camp. The troops were awakened every morning at three o'clock and kept ready under arms until daylight. During the night, Southern pickets showed lights to decoy the Union troops to fire and thus betray their approximate size and location. On April 18, soon after midnight, Gorman's pickets in Sedgwick's division accidentally began firing at each other. The alarm spread to the reserves and other regiments as musketry and artillery blazed away, awakening most of the Army of the Potomac. The abrupt firing ended without casualties, however.[29]

All the Yankee soldiers complained about the continual rain, and many became sick from exposure. Morale dropped. Col. Francis Channing Barlow, an officer in Richardson's division and commander of the 61st New York Regiment, grumbled, "I have bites from some mysterious animals or insects which we never see, but know only from their bites. Food as before — no meat for several days, only bean soup and rice. . . . Horrible smells environ our dwelling."[30] A Union advance was needed, if only to improve morale and attempt to occupy higher ground free from disease-breeding swamps.

Sedgwick's men corduroyed every road and bridged every creek around their camp; the artillery dragged guns and mortars into position. By May 3, McClellan had constructed sixteen batteries and several redoubts, and had armed them with over a hundred guns. The Army of the Potomac was finally ready to end the siege and capture Yorktown.[31]

McClellan planned to complete all his preparations by May 5 and to begin a bombardment the following morning. After constant shelling exchanges throughout the previous day and night, Sedgwick's outposts reported quietness the morning of May 4. Believing the Confederates had left their works, Lieutenant Hume of the 19th Massachusetts started to cross the field. No gun was fired. He continued on. The regiment advanced and placed its flag on the fortifications. The 20th Massachusetts advanced at about the same time and also raised its flag. The news of the Confederate evacuation caught the Union forces by surprise. The cry arose, "The rebels have gone!"[32]

Sedgwick's forces moved into the fort, stacked arms, and rested on the large parade ground within. Bands started to play. Men wandered around to see what they could find. Portholes had been filled with logs of wood, known as "Quaker guns," and men of straw had been stationed as gunners. All signs indicated that the enemy had retreated hastily: tents were left standing with guns and ammunition abandoned. Finding fires and breakfast smoking hot, Sedgwick's troops ate the food. Relic seekers discovered newspapers, letters, and reports, and mailed them home. The initial enthusiasm for souvenirs vanished when hidden Confederate land mines — called torpedoes — suddenly exploded. They had been buried in the ground near various objects. One man was killed. All these Confederate ploys and ruses had served their purpose in gaining time for their retreat, as General Johnston, in delaying the Union advance for a month, wanted to avoid exposure of his troops to powerful Union artillery fire.[33]

During that afternoon and the following day, McClellan sent forth two infantry divisions and the Union cavalry under Maj. Gen. George Stoneman. In this attempt to cut off the Confederate retreat, the Battle of Williamsburg was fought. The troops of the 2d Corps were not involved; Sumner's men were awaiting steamer transportation farther up the York River. On hearing of the heavy Union casualties — over 2,200 compared to the Confederate loss of 1,700 — McClellan ordered Sedgwick's division to move immediately toward Williamsburg, taking two days' rations. However, after making a personal assessment at the battlefield and learning that the Southerners were retreating, McClellan countermanded his orders.

Sedgwick turned his columns around and headed back to Yorktown. With rain falling, the half-mile tramp in knee-deep mud took eleven hours; the men dared not step out of line as the ground was full of torpedoes. The three roads leading into Yorktown were jammed with troops, and McClellan's aides attempted to get them all on board ship at the same time. Mass confusion resulted, and Sedgwick's division was forced to endure exposure to heavy rain throughout the night. At 8 A.M. on Tuesday, May 6, Sedgwick's first regiments climbed aboard the steamers at Yorktown for the twenty-five-mile trip upriver to West Point. Most of the soldiers slept during the slow voyage. It took two days to transport Sedgwick's entire division in this second attempt to cut off Johnston's retreating forces.

Fighting broke out as the Federal soldiers were landing at West Point. Union soldiers wading ashore were supported by the firing of their gunboats. Sedgwick arrived safely and wrote, "Upon our arrival here, the enemy attempted to dislodge us, but we had landed too many troops for them. The skirmish was quite lively for two hours."[34] The Union loss was thirty-nine killed and thirty-five wounded. The Confederate casualties are unknown.

While at West Point, Sedgwick set up unique communications to his headquarters: a human telegraph. A line of men, some twenty feet apart, extended from the battle line to headquarters. The men at the front would start the message, and it would be repeated by each turning his head to the rear as he spoke. Sedgwick's years of improvisations on the Plains aided his inventiveness in the Civil War.[35]

For the next several weeks, the Union advance continued with almost no opposition. The Southern military strategy devised by General Johnston was to fall back to the outskirts of Richmond, gather together his retreating army, and obtain additional forces from other parts of the Confederacy for a defense of its capital. As the Federals marched westward, Sedgwick followed the general direction of the Richmond and York River Railroad and occasionally crossed the track. Optimism that they were going to capture Richmond gripped every Union soldier. At Cumberland on May 17, Sedgwick wrote, "General McClellan is acting with much prudence and caution. . . . Six weeks will tell the story, in that time we will beat them badly or be beaten ourselves, which must settle the question." He expressed hope that he might be home "in a few months at least."[36]

The march continued through New Kent Court House, Bottom's Bridge, and finally to Camp Tyler, named for ex-president John Tyler, whose magnificent estate was close by. Sedgwick's division was now just fourteen miles from Richmond. On May 27, he felt even more confident about the possibility of an early victory, writing his sister, "I did [do?] not expect to write again till after reaching Richmond unless we received some repulse."[37]

Many soldiers believed the war was almost over. Never were spirits so high. McClellan's aide-de-camp, Capt. William F. Biddle, thought, "We may get Richmond without a fight."[38] Rumors had it that "Stonewall" Jackson might join the main Confederate army in front of Richmond; many Union soldiers believed that they could take Richmond and destroy Jackson too.

Before McClellan launched his final offensive drive to capture Richmond, he beseeched the Lincoln administration to transfer to his command the 38,000 Union troops under Maj. Gen. Irwin McDowell in the Fredericksburg area. Believing that all precautions should be taken to contain Jackson in the Valley, however, the president sent McDowell westward to aid the fumbling General Banks in pinning down Stonewall and preventing any possible juncture with Johnston.

The maneuvering and altercations between Lincoln and McClellan were of little concern to Sedgwick, who was virtually overwhelmed with the problems of his own division. The health of his troops was of vital concern. Many were sick with malaria, contracted during the early weeks of the campaign. The situation had improved slightly on arriving at higher ground at Camp Tyler. Fresh vegetables and fruit, however, were difficult to obtain because the local people refused to sell their produce. But this inconvenience was no problem; Uncle John slyly remarked, "Our men have a way of getting them."[39]

The physical duress on his division was reflected in other ways. Discipline began to break down. When two captains of a New York regiment refused to bring out their companies at parade, giving the petty excuse of their companies' rearrangement and displacement from their previous positions in the regimental line, Sedgwick acted decisively. He had no patience for mutinous conduct — an all too common occurrence in some Federal units — which if left unchecked would undermine his command. Without hesitation, as he had done several years earlier on the Great Plains in Kansas Territory when some members of his cavalry regiment threatened to desert in response to rumors of gold in the Rockies, Sedgwick stood firm. He sent these officers to McClellan's headquarters for court-martial.[40]

An unsolved strategic dilemma for the Army of the Potomac was the presence and condition of the Chickahominy River. This treacherous river had split McClellan's army in two during his advance, with Sumner's corps on the left or north bank. One of Sedgwick's officers, Lt. Col. Francis W. Palfrey of the 20th Massachusetts, described the river: "It was hard to say at the best of times where its banks were, and of which no man could say to-day where its banks would be to-morrow."[41] The Chickahominy was ordinarily a creek that varied in width from 200 to 300 feet. During the heavy rains of May the stream often widely overflowed its muddy banks, making troop movements hazardous.

To anticipate any emergency, Sumner began building two

bridges across the river. Sumner's Lower Bridge was built by Richardson's division, while the more famous "Grapevine," or Sumner's Upper Bridge, was constructed by Sedgwick's 1st Minnesota Regiment. The Grapevine bridge was built with logs — an arduous ordeal for the engineers, who worked in waist-deep water, mud, and tangled underbrush. Hoping to hasten the work, Sumner gave each bridge-building crew a barrel of whiskey. His generous act had a practical purpose, as the drinking water in the area was very bad; malaria, fever, and diarrhea affected many. Whiskey, or "commissary," as the soldiers called it, counteracted the effect of bad water.

The work of the Upper Bridge was supervised by army engineers and executed by experienced woodsmen of the Minnesota regiment. Finding grapevines growing in abundance along the stream, the men used them together with ropes to bind the cross logs of the bridge. The logs were suspended by ropes tied to the trunks of trees on the banks. The Grapevine bridge swayed back and forth. Both bridges with long corduroy approaches were finished about May 28. Had the favorable weather and the lull in military action continued a few more days, Sedgwick undoubtedly would have improved the stability of these bridges.

Duing the night of May 30, however, a violent rainstorm swelled the Chickahominy into a deep and rushing torrent. Saturday, May 31, was warm and cloudy, but the freshlet had virtually washed away Sumner's Lower Bridge; the Grapevine remained in position, although half adrift. It was at this critical moment — with the two wings of the Federal army connected by a single bridge threatening to collapse at any time — that Confederate Gen. Joseph Johnston struck.

McClellan was sick in bed with malaria and neuralgia, so the command of the Union left wing fell to Gen. Samuel Heintzelman. Johnston's attack on the exposed Union 3d and 4th corps was successful and drove back Heintzelman's soldiers to the vicinity of the Fair Oaks railroad station. The sounds of heavy, sustained firing alerted Sedgwick and his staff at their headquarters at about 1:30 P.M. Everyone knew a crisis was at hand. The long lull was over; the Battle of Fair Oaks had begun.

After an interchange of dispatches between Heintzelman and Sumner, and from Sumner to the Army of the Potomac headquarters, the 2d Corps received its orders from the incapacitated

McClellan "to be in readiness to move . . . at a moment's notice." The soldiers fell in, each with sixty rounds of ammunition and one day's rations. Sumner sent Sedgwick and Richardson forward to the bridges. At 2:30 P.M. McClellan issued orders to cross. Sumner was with Sedgwick at the Grapevine and commanded his men to move forward. An engineering officer protested, "General Sumner, you cannot cross this bridge," and argued that it was impossible. Sumner declared, "Impossible! I tell you I can cross. I am ordered."[42] Sedgwick's opinion was that the weight of the men would steady the creaking logs and hold the structure in place.

Led by General Gorman, the 1st Brigade crossed the bridge without excessive difficulty, with Col. Alfred Sully's 1st Minnesota in the lead. Farther downstream, Richardson's battered bridge held together momentarily to allow a few troops to walk across, but the remaining brigades were compelled to march upstream to use the still-intact Grapevine.

Once on the south bank of the Chickahominy, Sedgwick directed Gorman to hasten to the battle raging four miles ahead. Pushing on through knee-deep mud to the front, Colonel Sully formed the extreme right wing of the engaged forces. It was now 4:30 P.M. Sully's position near the Fair Oaks railroad station defended Courteney's house and the edge of a woods. The Southern forces opened up a steady fire, but it was aimed too high. The prompt arrival of Sedgwick's men during the height of the battle stopped General Johnston's advance and foiled his attempt to outflank Heintzelman's lines.

In a calculated risk, Sedgwick ordered the 1st Artillery, commanded by Lt. Edmund Kirby, to cross the Grapevine to support Gorman's troops. Sedgwick later learned from Confederate prisoners of war that their generals considered such a military feat impossible and made their attack plans accordingly. For some minutes the Southern assessment seemed correct. As Kirby's men approached the Grapevine, they discovered the corduroy road was in terrible condition, with some logs washed away. In this soft swampy section, cannoneers went in up to their waists as horses floundered and fell down. At one place a small bridge over a gully collapsed under the weight of a gun, and infantrymen stopped to help carry the piece up to solid ground. Finally the battery was ready to move again. Three artillery pieces, twelve-pound Napoleons, were somehow dragged across the Grapevine bridge and hauled up to the front. Once there, Kirby's guns opened a terrible fire to break and scatter the enemy.[43]

During the afternoon's fighting, Confederate Brig. Gen. John B. Magruder recognized his old battery, Light Company I, First U.S. Artillery, which he had commanded in the regular army before resigning his commission. Declaring, "That's my own battery, and I am going to have it or sleep to-night in hell," Magruder ordered charge after charge to take it. Sedgwick was in this immediate area with two infantry regiments that had come to Kirby's support. At one point, Magruder's soldiers almost overran Kirby's position. One Southern officer put his hand on a piece and said, "This is my gun." Kirby replied, "Not yet," as one of his cannoneers felled the attacker.[44]

With the exception of one regiment left guarding the bridge, Sedgwick's infantry brigades arrived at the battlefield in the late afternoon. The general's division occupied the crest of high ground near the Adams house, and by 5 P.M. his whole line was blazing. Perhaps Maj. Paul Joseph Revere of the 20th Massachusetts best expressed the spirit of the day: as his column halted to load rifles near the battle lines, he exclaimed to his men, "We are in luck to-day. We are not left in the rear to guard the river."[45]

Everywhere Sedgwick went, he was pleased with the performance of his troops. On being directed by Sumner to proceed to the right and take command of that flank, Sedgwick found Colonel Sully's troops "so well posted and so judiciously supported by General Burns that little remained for me to do."[46] Checking his lines with his chief aide, Capt. William Sedgwick, he rode into and through showers of bullets as imperturbably as if they were hailstones.

As daylight faded, there was a brief lull in the fighting. Sully's regiment moved farther to the right and occupied a wheatfield. Sumner gave Sully strict orders not to fire unless attacked, as it would expose his position. Concealed in the wheatfield, the Union soldiers saw a group of fifty horsemen appear at the front, not less than two hundred yards away. After observing the position for twenty minutes, they rode off. Sully knew he could have annihilated them easily, but he obeyed Sumner's orders. Shortly afterward, Sully became engaged with the enemy and learned from prisoners just brought in that the party on horseback had included the Confederate president, Jefferson Davis, members of his cabinet, other high officials, and Gen. Robert E. Lee. If Sedgwick's soldiers had fired, they would have annihilated the entire Confederate high command, crippling the Southern war effort.[47]

It was now almost dark. Sedgwick remained in charge of the extreme right wing; Sumner assumed direct personal command of the troops on the left side of the Adams house and ordered a charge in his sector. Lt. Oliver Wendell Holmes, Jr., of the 20th Massachusetts, threatened to shoot any man who ran; he gave one cowering individual a smart rap on the back with the edge of his sword to head the skulker in the right direction. Tearing down fences and running across a muddy field, the men charged with bayonets and drove the Confederates into the woods. The attack succeeded brilliantly. Dana's brigade killed one Confederate general, wounded two others, and captured a fourth. General Johnston was severely wounded, evidently by the rifle fire and artillery shelling from Sedgwick's division. After chasing the Southerners into the woods for about a hundred yards, Dana's brigade halted. It was so dark that the men could not see each other's faces.

At about 8 P.M., the fighting was over for the day. "Well, we licked 'em," wrote Holmes, "and this time there was the maneuvering of a battle to be seen — splendid and awful to behold."[48]

During the night, Sedgwick's regiments slept on their arms. Gen. Israel Richardson's troops arrived on the field and were placed on the general's left. At Sedgwick's headquarters, many Southern prisoners were afraid they would be butchered; they believed the Richmond newspaper accounts of alleged Union cruelties. But the general treated them kindly and convinced them that the press reports were false. From these prisoners, the general learned that the Confederates had attacked thinking that the Chickahominy was so high that the Union forces would be cut off from their supplies. One piece of news amused everybody at headquarters: another Northern division fighting alongside Sedgwick had "captured an omnibus and some buggies in which some ladies of Richmond had driven out to see the Yankees whipped."[49] But Sedgwick's timely march and superior fighting had changed the tide of the battle.

After an overnight bivouac under a tree, Sedgwick and his staff were expecting an early morning attack. Sunday, June 1, broke gray and misty; with the growing light, Uncle John's veterans saw the Confederate dead everywhere, and in the distance, a half mile to the west, they spotted the enemy. At 7:30 A.M., fighting broke out again, a clash probably brought about by overly excited troops on both sides who were within half-musket range of each other, rather than by intent of their commanding generals. Richardson's division fought most of the battle for the 2d Corps in this engagement; Sedgwick committed only a few units. After two hours of fighting, the Union line drove the Confederates back. By noon all was quiet.

Confederate Maj. Gen. Gustavus W. Smith had replaced the wounded Johnston. By that afternoon, Smith himself was replaced in a move whose significance was quickly realized as the war continued: Gen. Robert E. Lee became the new commander of the Army of Northern Virginia. (Sedgwick and Lee had known each other slightly in the Mexican War.) McClellan appeared on the field and received hearty cheers. He had risen from his sickbed and crossed the Chickahominy at Bottom's Bridge, as the Grapevine was practically washed away. He told Sumner and Sedgwick that "he had no changes to make; that he was satisfied with what had been done."[50]

The Battle of Fair Oaks, or Seven Pines, had ended. Both armies had committed approximately 42,000 men. The Federal forces suffered 4,384 casualties; the Confederates lost 5,729. The punishment inflicted on the 2d Corps was quite high: 1,223 casualties, with Sedgwick's division accounting for 347. To people in the North, the fall of Richmond seemed imminent. War correspondents had fed them overly optimistic reports from the battlefield. On June 2, the *New York Times* reported: "The end cannot now be delayed. General McClellan will probably at once follow up the already repulsed rebel army, and reinforced by General McDowell, will push on to Richmond."[51]

For the Federal troops in the field, however, the newspaper prediction was dashed by bad weather. The Union drive toward Richmond bogged down at the beginning of June when it rained for three days straight. The flooding of the Chickahominy cut off the Army of the Potomac from the north bank. Even Bottom's Bridge was considered impracticable to cross. The railroad bridge and trestlework were threatened with destruction. The ground — reddish clay and quicksand — became a vast swamp, and heavy guns sank into the earth by their own weight. Sedgwick made out his battle report on June 4 and sent the rough draft to his sister. Warning her not to "let it go out of your hands" for fear the press might print it, he complained, "The stream is still so high that it is impossible to get over our heavy artillery, and as much as we can do, to bring up supplies."[52]

In the days after the battle, Sedgwick's soldiers were not moved back across the Chickahominy. They remained in position opposite the enemy and threw up earthworks. The troops were not able to take off their filthy uniforms, not even their boots, and to change into clean clothes. The severely wounded were sent by rail to the White House Landing on the Pamunkey River, but many mangled and torn bodies remained and were decomposing. One of Sedgwick's chaplains, William G. Scandlin, recorded in his diary for June 1, "Men lay in all conceivable positions, just as they fell. I went down to gather our dead together and had men bury them, marking their graves with some boards bearing their names."[53]

The health of his division constituted a serious problem for Sedgwick; there were more losses by disease than in battle. Constant exposure, filthy conditions, poor diet, and various epidemics all combined to diminish the effective strength of his corps. Scores of Sedgwick's men became sick with typhoid fever, typhoid pneumonia, dysentery, and malarial fever. The diet of the soldiers consisted of hardtack and pork and beans, varied only by leaving the pork and beans for supper. After weeks of a steady regimen of salt provisions, some men developed scurvy. Sedgwick was older than his average soldier, and the ordeal was much more difficult for him. He wrote home, "I am now suffering in front of Richmond."[54]

Finally on June 11, Sedgwick was relieved from the front line and marched his division to high ground along the railroad. From Fair Oaks, Lt. Henry Ropes of the 20th Massachusetts exclaimed, "We have just been withdrawn . . . and are camped in comparative ease and comfort after 10 days of the hardest work soldiers can endure."[55] To counteract the dampness, many soldiers received a ration of whiskey every morning. For those stricken with scurvy, doctors prescribed lemons or a concoction of raw potatoes mashed in vinegar. Still, it was not a time of rest. The troops were constantly engaged in reconnaissances, skirmishes, and picket duty. During the very early morning of June 12, the division was called to arms by an attack of Confederate pickets. While waiting for the sun to rise, the soldiers had witnessed a total and perhaps frightening eclipse of the moon. The strain experienced by the division resulted in utter exhaustion for the men.

While the 2d Corps remained in position and ignorant of the

overall military developments, both McClellan and Lee worked out new strategies. McClellan requested reinforcements from Washington, but instead of receiving McDowell's corps, as he had hoped, he received only 9,000 additional troops. Much more successful in his efforts to increase troop strength, Lee welcomed the arrival on June 27 of Stonewall Jackson and his 25,000 men, who had slipped away from Banks and Brig. Gen. John C. Fremont in the Valley. Jackson's reinforcements and other additions built up Lee's army to 90,000 men; McClellan commanded approximately the same number.

The general lull continued into late June. Sumner's corps occupied the central position in the Federal line facing Richmond. Sedgwick's headquarters remained at Camp Fair Oaks on the south side of the Chickahominy. Heintzelman's 3d Corps held down the left flank. On the right wing, the Union line was anchored by Brig. Gen. FitzJohn Porter's 5th Corps on the north bank, with Brig. Gen. William B. Franklin's 6th Corps on the south bank of the Chickahominy. McClellan kept Brig. Gen. Erasmus D. Keyes in reserve.

At last McClellan was ready. Alarmed by a Confederate deserter's report that Jackson was fast approaching to join Lee's main army but satisfied that the Union bridges and entrenchments were at last completed, he acted. On Wednesday, June 25 — now known as the first of the Seven Days' Battles — McClellan sent an advance picket line westward preparatory to a general movement on Richmond. Sedgwick's 19th Massachusetts Regiment participated in this action. The action cost the Union army some 500 casualties, but accomplished McClellan's objective of a probe in force. Now he knew the nature of the ground for his anticipated attack on Old Tavern.

The next day, however, Lee struck first. Throughout the day, Sedgwick's division heard artillery firing far to its right; Porter's 5th Corps was engaged in heavy fighting. Sumner kept his corps in readiness but did not move. The news eventually arrived that the Union forces had fought and won at Mechanicsville, but no one along Sedgwick's and Richardson's lines knew the exact circumstances.

Sounds of a battle on Sedgwick's right were heard again on June 27. After a fusillade, quietness would return, only to be broken by another sharp exchange in the distance. As night approached, the soldiers of the 2d Corps climbed trees and saw the quick flashes of guns.

During these days of anxious waiting, Sedgwick became ill. Evidently stricken with the prevailing camp fever, he was unable to sit up in his saddle as he attempted to look over his lines. He should have been in a hospital, but he insisted on remaining with his division.

Meanwhile, two miles eastward on the Richmond and York River Railroad, McClellan grappled with the situation at his headquarters at Savage's Station, the location of many field hospitals and the chief supply depot. During the evening of June 27, he met with his corps commanders. The outlook, he decided, was not good. During the day, the newly arrived Jackson had fallen on Porter's exposed right wing, routed it, and won the Battle of Gaines's Mills. This action had occurred four miles to the northwest on the north bank of the Chickahominy, threatening the bulk of the Union army on the opposite bank. Although McClellan's army was about equal numerically to that of Lee, McClellan had been convinced by incompetent Union civilian spies that he was outnumbered almost two to one. These circumstances caused him to abandon any hopes of a swing into Richmond with his left wing. He therefore ordered his generals to prepare for a move through White Oak Swamp to a new base at the James River, fifteen miles to the south. The meeting broke up at 2 A.M.

The day of June 28 was needed, McClellan indicated, to evacuate the Army of the Potomac's line of supply wagons and herds of beef cattle across White Oak Bridge. As part of a covering force for this retreat, Sedgwick's troops remained in place. They enjoyed a day of relative quiet, as Lee was baffled by McClellan's move. There were now no doubts in the ranks of the 2d Corps about recent developments; stragglers from Porter's corps, beaten back from Gaines's Mills, brought in the news of defeat.

The problem of breaking camp occupied Sedgwick's complete attention during this critical day. Hospitals were closed, and the sick and wounded were transferred to Savage's Station. The quartermasters sent all extra clothing and spare supplies to the rear in wagons. Rations and ammunition were also being hauled away. Sedgwick was compelled to destroy all that he could not transport. At the principal depot at Orchard Station, men broke up barrels of flour, sugar, and meat and buried them in the mud. The soldiers helped themselves to new clothing and cut up and tore their old uniforms to pieces. Hardtack in a pile the size of a large building was set afire. With axes, the troops cut up iron kettles, canteens, cups, tents, and muskets. Commissary whiskey barrels were knocked apart, and the liquor ran in streams. The whiskey was set on fire, and some men burned themselves trying to drink it. Although much was destroyed, the corps took enough food and supplies to last another week.

At daybreak on June 29, Sumner's corps abandoned its lines and headed south. After assigning a few men to complete the destructive work at Fair Oaks and Orchard Station, Uncle John, still sick and feeble, mounted his horse and rode away in front of his troops. His determined character kept him from asking to be relieved from duty.

Retreating eastward along the Richmond and York River Railroad, Sedgwick halted his division at Allen's Farm and deployed his forces across the railroad. A rear-guard action was conducted under Gen. William Franklin to protect Savage's Station, some two miles farther east. The 2d Corps was ready and in good position to make a stand against the advancing Confederates. After waiting an hour, the general and his soldiers heard the Southerners cheering as they took possession of the deserted Fair Oaks works and camps. Led by Magruder, the Confederates attacked at 9 A.M. with artillery and musketry. Brisk fighting continued for two hours; the Union line beat off the assaults. Finding his artillery in an exposed position, Lt. Edmund Kirby advanced nearly one hundred yards to obtain the cover of a hill. From this protected spot, he fired rounds of shell and shot. By noon, the Battle of Allen's Farm was over. Sumner and Sedgwick succeeded in blunting the Southern drive and gained valuable time for the Union evacuation.

After this temporary stand, Sedgwick prepared to retreat again. General Franklin, finding a good defensive position at Savage's Station, meanwhile discovered that his lines did not overlap the 2d Corps and immediately notified Sumner that it would be sound strategy to combine their forces. Sumner agreed. Sedgwick's soldiers marched double-quick along the Williamsburg Road, suffering terribly in the heat of the day. The men quickly threw aside everything they did not need, and the side of the road was strewn with knapsacks, blankets, and overcoats. No one wasted time destroying them — instead each member of the division put forth

every effort to keep up, knowing that to fall out meant certain capture. After arriving at Savage's Station at about three o'clock,
Sedgwick deployed his brigades on the high ground to the south.
Regimental commanders sent one or two men over to a large field
hospital to get ice for the sunstruck victims of the march.

With the expected arrival of General Heintzelman, who had
also agreed to Franklin's plan to consolidate forces on a defensive
line at this location, the Union position would be very strong. At
4 P.M., while his men rested under the trees, Sedgwick accompanied
Franklin to a hospital to visit some wounded friends. The two
generals then continued on with their staffs to Heintzelman's sup-
posed position. As they rode out into an open field, they saw men
come out of the woods. Franklin thought they were Heintzelman's
soldiers. Sedgwick looked at them more closely, stopped, and cried
out, "Why, these men are rebels!" Franklin recalled, "We then
turned back in as dignified a manner as the circumstances would
permit."[56] Within seconds, the Confederate artillery opened up with
a field piece, and shells tore over the generals' heads. Franklin and
Sedgwick narrowly escaped death, but the incident did prevent a
Confederate surprise attack. The Union batteries quickly returned
the fire. Later the two generals learned that Heintzelman had
misunderstood his orders and had never arrived.

As the fighting began at 5 P.M., the exhausted Sumner was
awakened from a sound sleep; he immediately ordered Sedgwick's
troops to attack. A shower of shells snapped the branches of the trees
above the advancing men. Kirby's battery obtained the range of the
Confederates coming down the Williamsburg Road. Skirmishers of
Brig. Gen. William W. Burns's 2d Brigade, as they pushed through
a belt of trees between this road and the Richmond and York River
Railroad, spotted General Lee's "railroad battery," a thirty-two-
pound rifled cannon, with a sloping iron shield, mounted on a flat-
car. This "Land Merrimac" was pulled by a locomotive on the
railroad track.

After informing Sumner and Sedgwick, Burns received reinforcements, advanced northward to the railroad line, and began
firing. Burns's right flank raked and swept the big gun, causing it to
be run back. At the height of the fighting, Burns was wounded in
the face by a minie ball. He bandaged his wound with a handkerchief. Clotted blood covered his beard and clothes, but he refused to
leave the field. Magruder's attackers attempted to break through

the center, but Burns's brigade fought on in a hand-to-hand encounter. The wounded general's tenacity paid off. As he later wrote, "Our men showed their superiority, and the victory can be fairly claimed by us. [Magruder] was the attacking party, and was not only checked, but repulsed and driven from the ground."[57]

The fighting ceased at nightfall — about 7 P.M. On hearing of Burns's success, Sedgwick exclaimed to another officer, "That was Burns's fight. He showed himself a splendid soldier."[58] Uncle John appreciated his officers and men, and was always generous in his praise.

The Union victory at Savage's Station cost the Northern forces 3,000 casualties out of 20,000 men who made the stand. The Confederates determined their own loss at 4,000. About a half hour after the fighting ended, Franklin told Sumner of McClellan's orders to withdraw their forces across the White Oak Swamp on their way to the James River. Dumbfounded that the Union retreat should continue after this success, Sumner nevertheless consented when he read his superior's dispatch by the light of a candle. At about 11 P.M. and with great reluctance, he began his painful duty, leading his divisions southward on the road to White Oak Bridge. Part of the field was lighted by the still-burning railroad cars. It was a sad moment for all as the Army of the Potomac abandoned to the enemy 2,500 sick and wounded men in the field hospitals.

Sedgwick marched all night, bringing up the rear of the corps. He crossed White Oak Bridge at daybreak and allowed a short rest. The enemy did not press him. Sedgwick obeyed orders throughout the long retreat; he did not comment publicly or privately on the Union strategy. Sumner had been a long-time friend and superior officer, and McClellan had given him promotions and a division. Perhaps Sedgwick believed his best course in the controversy over the retreat would be served by passivity. The concept of a chain of command hierarchy instilled in him as a cadet at West Point may account for his silence; at any rate, the overriding objective now was saving the Army of the Potomac rather than destroying it by internecine disputes among the high command.

The sun rose on the morning of June 30, creating a stifling heat that grew throughout the day. Sedgwick's division had caught up with the main body of the Army of the Potomac; after a brief rest near the bridge, they marched southward along the Quaker Road and finally stopped at Nelson's farm, "Glendale." Troops posted west of and parallel to the road formed a second line of defense. Farther to the west beyond some woods, Brig. Gen. George A. McCall arranged his division to constitute a first line against likely Confederate attacks.

Sedgwick still could not permit his exhausted men the luxury of a long rest or relaxation. Many of his thirsty soldiers found the shade of trees but were unable to find water. To help defend the bridge where Franklin remained with artillery, Sedgwick was ordered at 2 P.M. to send back Dana's and Gorman's brigades double-quick along the same dusty road to White Oak Swamp. Under the overall command of General Dana, these brigades helped fight off Stonewall Jackson's advance from the north.

The major Southern attack, led by Lieutenant Generals James Longstreet and Ambrose Powell Hill, assaulted McCall's line at 3 P.M. If the enemy broke through both Union defense lines, they would sever the vital Union link along Quaker Road and cut McClellan's army in two. To Sedgwick's horror, this possibility seemed imminent: after initial resistance, part of McCall's division broke and fled before the Confederate assaults. Panic-stricken Union soldiers ran through Sedgwick's line to the rear. Sedgwick had available only Burns's brigade; desperate, he sent these troops forward. They crowned the crest of the hill and manned McCall's abandoned guns.

During these hectic moments, the general requested that his two detached brigades at White Oak Swamp immediately be sent back to where they were most needed. Running back as fast as they could — with many men collapsing along the road — the two brigades were faced right into line and sent into the woods. The soldiers arrived most propitiously. After his brigade had recovered its wind, Dana led them forward, and said to Sumner, "I will place my old regiment, general." As the 1st Minnesota passed, Old Bull called out, "Boys, I may not see all of you again, but I know you will hold that line." With muskets and artillery, Sedgwick's reunited division poured in "a most severe and murderous fire." Kirby's battery fired into the woods and succeeded in exploding an enemy caisson. As the muskets overheated from the rapid firing, men set their ramrods against trees in order to force charges into the heated barrels. Holmes noted, "The guns got so hot & dirty we couldn't load or fire more than ⅔ of them."[59]

Sedgwick paid no attention to his personal safety during these critical moments. Shells and balls fell about him. Struck on the arm by a ball, he discovered that he was not injured. A piece of shell hit Tom, his old horse, on the leg. Within a minute the general's own leg was grazed by a bullet, which went on through the horse. Tom groaned and died shortly thereafter. Mounting another horse, the slightly wounded Sedgwick refused to leave the field; he again escaped injury when his second horse was hit. Uncle John's personal example inspired his men, and they held on and saved the line.

The firing continued after dark. To Sumner's disappointment, he was again ordered to retreat after a victorious day. At 11 P.M. Sedgwick pulled together his command and continued his march southward along Quaker Road. Soldiers kept going, existing on pieces of hard bread. At daybreak on July 1, the troops reached Malvern Hill, where the whole Army of the Potomac was assembled.

Malvern Hill is an open amphitheater, about a mile wide and three-quarters of a mile deep. Swamps and ravines at its base aided the Federal defense. At the rear, the ground falls away abruptly to the James River. McClellan selected a superb defensive position and arranged a semicircular battle line several miles long, with the two flanks extended back in the direction of the river. The line bristled with batteries, while a vast artillery reserve was placed behind. Sumner's corps took its position to the rear of Heintzelman's troops, which in turn backed up the front-line division of Brig. Gen. Darius N. Couch. With Couch facing north against the anticipated route of the Confederate advance, Sumner's position represented the third line of defense, which also curved toward the east to protect the ground overlooking the ravine of Western Run. Sedgwick commanded this exposed right wing of the 2d Corps. Acting as reserves during the day, Sedgwick's division managed to secure some much needed rest as they awaited the next Confederate move. All was ready.

At 9 A.M., one of Stonewall Jackson's batteries began shelling Malvern Hill and opened fire on Sedgwick's exposed position. Union batteries silenced it almost immediately. Three other Confederate artillery pieces moved up and fired until noon when the ammunition was exhausted. Despite the heavy Confederate bombardment, Sedgwick suffered surprisingly few casualties. Although in readiness all day to meet the enemy on his front or to give reinforcement to other parts of the line, the general's division was not needed. He changed his position once or twice during the day. Sedgwick's men had earned their well-deserved rest.

The enemy concentrated the attack on the left side of the

Union line, and every attempt was repulsed with tremendous loss to the Confederates. Night fell, but cannon still boomed. Through the darkness, Sedgwick and his men tracked shells by their burning fuses and watched the explosions. At 9 P.M., the shelling on both sides ended.

The Battle of Malvern Hill was a complete Union victory. McClellan, however, became alarmed with the exhaustion of supplies — food, forage, and ammunition. He felt the necessity to fall back to his new supply base at Harrison's Landing, ten miles south on the James River. There his army could be resupplied from Federal transports. He ordered an immediate retreat.

During the early morning of July 2, Sedgwick's troops prepared to withdraw. Pickets came in from their posts. The 69th Pennsylvania left in advance of the division to march rapidly and push through any obstruction that might be encountered. Sedgwick then led his column down the River Road in a heavy rainstorm to Harrison's Landing. They arrived shortly after daylight and encamped in a plowed field of sticky mud. The Seven Days' Battles were over. That week the Union army of 91,169 effectives had suffered 15,849 casualties, including 2,420 in the 2d Corps. Lee's army of 95,481 men lost 20,614.

As written about by McClellan and many Union officers years after the event, the Peninsular Campaign took on a sense of romantic and magnificent failure. McClellan wrote:

> Exhausted, depleted in numbers, bleeding at every pore, but still proud and defiant, and strong in the consciousness of a great feat of arms heroically accomplished, it [the Army of the Potomac] stood ready to renew the struggle with undiminished ardor whenever its commander should give the word.[60]

Criticism of McClellan and his campaign began immediately at Harrison's Landing by Sedgwick's own soldiers, however, and continues to the present day by respected historians. One of Sedgwick's officers, Francis W. Palfrey, noted, "I regard McClellan as a failure. He was not only a disappointment, but his 'tall talk' made him an aggravating disappointment."[61]

The morale of Sumner's 2d Corps was shattered; many felt a loss of confidence in their army. This sour feeling extended to Col. Francis Channing Barlow, an acquaintance of Sedgwick and a rising officer in the Army of the Potomac, who was completely candid as he wrote home on July 4:

> It is considered generally that McClellan has been completely outwitted and that our present safety is owing more to the severe fighting of some of the Divisions than to any skill of our General. . . .
> McClellan rode along the crowd with only one attendant and no one noticed him. I think the whole army feels that it was left to take care of itself and was saved only by its own brave fighting. I think all confidence in McClellan is gone with the majority of the Army.[62]

Several days later, Barlow explained that he was amazed at the inaccuracy of the newspaper accounts and editorials about the Seven Days' Battles and the false impression given to the Northern people. He stated:

> We are surprised to learn from the New York papers that we gained a great victory. We thought here that we had made a disastrous retreat leaving all our dead and wounded and many prisoners and material and munitions of war in the hands of the enemy.[63]

Surely Sedgwick, with his many years' service in the army, recognized the disgruntled mood of his troops. Regarding his experience during the Seven Days, Sedgwick admitted, "Our men were without rations and without blankets, and in one of the severest of storms." He wrote home, "Rumors speak of changes in the cabinet and in the army."[64]

His fighting in the Shenandoah Valley and on the Peninsula did not bring an occupation of Richmond, only a rude encampment on the James River. Sedgwick felt pride for his division, sympathy for McClellan, and relief that he had survived the ordeal. But the Confederate capital remained untaken. A new plan or a new commanding general was needed for Union victory. He and his division had either to retrace their steps or find a new route to Richmond.

CHAPTER 2

AGONY AT ANTIETAM

AFTER THE TERRIBLE Seven Days' Battles, Gen. John Sedgwick and his men gradually regained their physical strength. During July 1862, the Army of the Potomac rested at Harrison's Landing, just fifteen miles from Richmond. After throwing up heavy fortifications, the men settled down in anticipation of a long stay on the high, rolling banks of the James River.

The men avoided the intense heat as much as possible, and many soldiers went swimming twice a day in the river or nearby creeks. Most built little platforms to elevate their tents and ensure circulation of air. Enterprising soldiers dug wells to obtain cold, clear drinking water and sold the surplus to regiments too lazy to dig their own. Sedgwick's troops recovered their spirits. One correspondent exclaimed, "Most of our wounded express a desire to recover speedily that they can again return to their regiments. All seem anxious to be present when Richmond is taken."[1]

Sedgwick's confidence rose during early July. The *New York Times* congratulated him and other Union officers, remarking, "the historian of this war and this movement [the Peninsular Campaign] will give such need of praise as to satisfy the ambition of the most ambitious."[2]

On July 4, Sedgwick was promoted to major general of U.S. Volunteers. As the vast bulk of the Union forces were U.S. Volunteers, or a national emergency army which kept expanding as the war continued, Sedgwick knew his rank was a temporary one. Once the war ended, the Union volunteer army would be mustered out. When that time arrived, Sedgwick's volunteer commission would expire, with his permanent rank reverting to that of colonel in the regular army. But honorary or not, Sedgwick was pleased. Undoubtedly his excellent fighting record, a larger army coupled with the thinning out of other Northern commanders in the recent campaign, made Sedgwick's elevation to major general a logical choice.

On July 8, the entire army was "taken by surprise by a most unexpected visit by President Lincoln. At 3:00 P.M., a rumor spread through the encampment that 'Uncle Abraham' had arrived." A salute of twenty-two guns awakened officers, many of whom at first believed the shots signaled an enemy attack. Lincoln later rode in review of the cheering soldiers. With McClellan at his side, the president began his inspection tour with Sumner's corps. Sedgwick wrote home, "General McClellan paid me and my division a high compliment in presenting us to the President. I believe he has recommended me for a Brevet Brigadier in the regular army. I know General Sumner has." It was after 9 P.M. when Lincoln completed his review. A newspaperman noted, "The whole thing tended visibly to elevate the spirits of the army."[3]

The weeks passed quietly and uneventfully. Sedgwick felt both a sense of relief from the active campaigning and an uneasy apprehension about forthcoming military operations. He noted, "No reinforcements have arrived. . . . The enemy have withdrawn and returned to the vicinity of Richmond. What our future movements are to be is quite uncertain."[4] After his men completed the construction of breastworks and clearing away trees, only one problem remained: disease. Both the Union and Confederate armies in Virginia were overwhelmed by fevers, scurvy, and diarrhea. Despite the Northern soldiers' efforts at sanitation, hundreds were taken ill in the epidemics that raged through the camps. After being carried to hospitals, many were carried out dead in a few days. The steady diet of "McClellan pies," as soldiers nicknamed the hard bread, undermined their physical constitution. McClellan had fresh vegetables shipped to Harrison's Landing to improve the health of his army, but they did not arrive until early August.

On July 11, Sedgwick wrote a letter of recommendation in support of his aide-de-camp, Maj. Richard F. Halsted, formerly of the 40th New York Volunteers, for the appointment of a colonelcy to a regiment. After a month's wait, Sedgwick finally received a reply from William Hillhouse, the adjutant general of New York.

Hillhouse reported that Gov. Edwin D. Morgan refused, as Halsted had "been dismissed from the service on sentence of a court martial."[5] Sedgwick nevertheless retained Halsted as a civilian aide.

During mid-July, Sedgwick learned that the Lincoln administration had altered the leadership and command structure of the Union army. Bowing to political pressure, the president appointed Maj. Gen. Henry W. Halleck to the vacated position of general in chief, or in effect, the commander of all the land forces in the United States. Lincoln needed Halleck as well as a personal military advisor in Washington for emergency conferences, and could not depend on a general absent in the fields. Although McClellan once held both jobs as commander of the Army of the Potomac and as general in chief, the latter post had not been filled for four months. Now McClellan retained his field post, but was subjected to Halleck's power, as "Old Brains" directed the concerted Union war effort from a map in Washington. Along with this indication of Lincoln's loss of confidence in McClellan's abilities, the president's telegrams to him displayed increasing irritation with McClellan's prolonged inactivity. The situation worsened, and there were rumors that McClellan would resign.

Sumner and Sedgwick kept their troops busy with inspections, drills, and parades. After one grand review of the 2d Corps on July 22, a reporter asserted, "Now mark the bearing of the men. There is a gunpowdery grimness about it not seen in unfought men. It is the touch which, added to the soldier, makes the veteran."[6] But Sumner and Sedgwick, both known as fighting generals, could do nothing with their seasoned troops, because McClellan issued no order to advance.

New military objectives of the Lincoln administration prevented reinforcements from being sent to McClellan. Considering Washington vulnerable to attack, Stanton and Halleck began to build up the strength of Maj. Gen. John Pope's newly created Union Army of Virginia. Originally numbering 38,000 upon its creation in late June, reinforcements arrived throughout July and August. Pope operated in the area of Manassas Junction, about twenty-five miles west of the capital. As the days and weeks passed, the Confederates under Lee massed their forces together to the west of this vital railroad junction, to a peak strength of about 49,000. Pope's augmented army swelled to 76,000. Washington must be defended.

In addition to these strategic reasons, though, Lincoln's advisors distrusted McClellan because he was a Democrat. The ill feeling between Washington and Harrison's Landing was not lost on Maj. Gen. Samuel Heintzelman, as he waited at that sweltering landing on the James River. He wrote: "There is hard pressure about withdrawing this army. If it is done, the country is ruined. It will ruin this army. All we want is the reinforcements that are within reach & we will advance. It is sad to see the country ruined by the imbecility in Washington."[7] Sedgwick remained silent in this crisis.

On August 1, McClellan received important dispatches from Halleck. Learning from Pope that "deserters report that the enemy is moving south of James River, and that the force in Richmond is very small," Halleck urged McClellan to make an immediate reconnaissance. To carry out this order, McClellan called on Maj. Gen. Joseph Hooker, who was dubbed "Fighting Joe" during the Peninsular Campaign.[8] After starting out during the late afternoon of August 2, Hooker was compelled to return for lack of good guides. The expedition set out again the next day and was joined a day later by Sedgwick's division.

Now commanding some 16,000 troops, Hooker sought to surprise the Confederates at Malvern Hill. Members of the 20th Massachusetts Regiment left their encampment at 6 P.M. and marched until 3 A.M. With his own division in advance of Sedgwick's men, Hooker issued strict orders against the use of fires or the making of loud noises. To increase the chances of success, Hooker approached Malvern Hill from the north and then turned around. Encountering little Confederate resistance, Hooker reoccupied the hill, with Sedgwick's troops serving in the rear to guard the approaches from Glendale and the north. The Second Battle of Malvern Hill cost the Union fifty-three casualties, while the Confederates lost over a hundred men, most of them prisoners of war. A reporter exclaimed, "The men are immensely elated at regaining old battlefields."[9]

During August 5 and 6, some of Sedgwick's troops encamped on top of Malvern Hill. Four of his stragglers, roaming in the woods, came across six mounted Confederates and took them prisoners; the four rode the captured horses to the 2d Division bivouac. Trying to make themselves comfortable in the intense heat, Sedgwick's veterans stretched their rubber blankets on stakes above their heads for shade. As they looked around the old battlefield, they discovered pits where the dead had been buried in piles — the ground had sunk and bones were protruding.

After the position was secured, McClellan arrived and rode over the field with Hooker. Many of the men were expecting a major battle, as Lee had sent three divisions to this area. However, during the early morning of August 7, Sedgwick's division received orders to fall back. After a four-hour tramp, they returned to their old encampment at Harrison's Landing.

Sedgwick and his troops soon learned the circumstances surrounding their withdrawal. On August 4, while the 2d Division was marching to Malvern Hill, McClellan had received a momentous telegram from Halleck: "Withdraw your army from the Peninsula to Aquia Creek."[10] The decision by Lincoln and Halleck to abandon the Peninsula greatly improved Lee's strategic position: now the Confederate commander could concentrate on overpowering Pope without diverting troops to hold McClellan to his position on the James River. Learning of this Union shift, Lee left on August 15 for northern Virginia, as his army began moving to confront Pope. As Lincoln's order to McClellan played into Lee's hands, McClellan, astonished and enraged by his instructions from Washington, nevertheless complied and called Hooker and Sedgwick back to Harrison's Landing.

It was impossible to abandon the Peninsula without some preliminary work. Many days were required for evacuation of the sick, the trains, and the artillery to Fort Monroe, some seventy miles away. The wharf facilities at Harrison's Landing were inadequate to handle the volume of men and supplies being loaded on the steamers for the voyage down the James River. Although the men worked incessantly, McClellan's efforts did not satisfy the impatient Halleck.

Sedgwick paid his men and made all preparations for the withdrawal. Several prisoners of war released from Richmond and many of his wounded men rejoined his division. A *New York Tribune* reporter captured the mood of the Army of the Potomac: "Suspense never brooded more terribly over a mass of men than over this army now. . . . What is next with this army? We have been disappointed. We are doing nothing."[11]

On August 16, Sedgwick began his march down the Peninsula, bringing up the extreme rear of the army. The retreat required seven days, as the division returned on the same route they had taken before. Sedgwick led his men through Charles City Court House, Barrett's Ferry, Williamsburg, Yorktown (where their head- quarters was a house built by John Tyler), Big Bethel, and ulti- mately to Newport News. The disheartened mood of the soldiers was reflected in the widespread foraging; they systematically stripped cornfields for a mile on either side of the roads. Leaving the ranks, stragglers stole food from farmhouses, climbed trees for fruit — ripe or green — dug for potatoes, and milked cows. One reporter remarked, "I doubt if there remains a cock to crow tomorrow morn- ing on all the route between here [Yorktown] and Harrison's Landing."[12]

At Newport News, the 2d Division waited three days for transportation. A war correspondent accurately analyzed the situa- tion: "The Army of the Potomac, like the coffin of Mohammed, hangs between heaven and earth. It is for the time being, neither threatening Richmond nor defending Washington."[13]

On August 25, Sumner and Sedgwick boarded their men on the *Atlantic*, *Baltic*, *Vanderbilt*, and other first-class transports. The steamers were crowded with men to the point of suffocation. During the voyage of a day and a half to Aquia Creek, the officers enjoyed good meals. Many of the soldiers, however, became intoxicated from drinking liquor purchased on board, and fights broke out. Despite these problems, many considered the Army of the Potomac to be delivered from a most unhealthy location. Sedgwick was helpless, cooped up on an overloaded vessel on the Chesapeake Bay, realizing that Lee would be able to take advantage of this slow Federal movement.

The Army of the Potomac was losing its effectiveness. McClellan originally planned to disembark his army at Aquia Creek, and then march his troops to the Rappahannock River to support Pope. After seeing the miserable facilities at Aquia Creek, however, McClellan went to nearby Falmouth to confer with Maj. Gen. Ambrose E. Burnside, who had just returned from North Carolina with his 9th Corps to aid Pope. Their conference resolved nothing except to await orders from Halleck. Burnside's private secretary, Daniel Larned, noted, "Both Generals McC & Burnside are here but with no commands. The Army of the Potomac is split up and sent off."[14] Sedgwick and the other division commanders were even more uninformed as they stoically awaited their own orders.

During August 26 and 27, units of Sedgwick's division began arriving at Aquia Creek. The 106th Pennsylvania had endured an especially frustrating voyage. First there was difficulty finding a pilot to navigate the Potomac River. After getting a pilot for the *Baltic*, the ship soon ran aground and was unable to push off the bottom. Finally the *Nellie Baker* came alongside and provided passage for the stranded soldiers. The regiment landed about 4 P.M. on August 26 and immediately marched two miles inland for the night's bivouac.

Sedgwick's men expected to march to Pope's relief, but as they were getting ready to make camp on the evening of August 27, they were suddenly ordered back to Aquia Creek Landing. The news arrived that Pope had been outflanked on his right wing, had had communications broken, and was retreating to Manassas. With this latest report, McClellan ordered all his troops back on board the transports and directed Sumner "to proceed directly to Alexandria."[15]

At the landing, Sedgwick's troops found Brig. Gen. Oliver O. Howard, now sufficiently recovered from the loss of his right arm at the Fair Oaks battle. Howard was assigned to the 2d Corps as a replacement for the wounded Brig. Gen. William W. Burns. Embarking that evening, the steamers made the night voyage to Alexandria in three hours, anchoring for the arrival of dawn.

In the morning of August 28, Sumner's corps landed and assembled at Alexandria. Sedgwick marched his troops through the city, past great camps of convalescent soldiers and huge earthworks. The 2d Corps veterans tramped about four and a half miles to Cloud's Mills on the Little River Turnpike for an overnight encampment. Pope's disorganized army lay about twenty miles to the west. The next morning, Sedgwick received reinforcements; the 75 new recruits were unarmed, however, so he sent them back to Washington for weapons. Receiving his orders late in the afternoon of August 29, Sedgwick headed for Fort Ethan Allen, which protected the Chain Bridge. This strategic point had to be held because the turnpike from Leesburg crossed the Potomac above Washington at this point. After reaching the fort, Sedgwick's division bivouacked for the night.

Anticipating a day's rest, many of the troops went swimming to clean up and to wash their clothes. Sedgwick found the opportunity to write home for the first time in many weeks. Reflecting the tension of the campaign, he wrote,

> Washington people seem to lose their senses at the most unfounded rumors, but there may be some cause for it now. The enemy are not far off, and things here are not in the best state to receive them. . . . I am in camp near the one I occupied last winter. The men are tired and to some degree dispirited, but a few days' rest will bring them up. I know but little of what is going on; no one does but General Halleck and the enemy.[16]

During August 30, the men could no longer relax; they could hear heavy cannonading in the direction of Centreville, some fifteen miles to the west. Before night fell, Sedgwick received urgent orders to push westward at once to join Pope's army. At the Second Battle of Bull Run, or Manassas, Pope had been badly defeated and was in danger of annihilation or capture. His retreat quickly became a rout. That night, Sedgwick drove his men forward to Centreville in a heavy rain. Many of the soldiers did not have shoes. Although there were several long halts, the soldiers were exhausted. The next day, August 31, one of Sedgwick's men, Alfred Gray Gardner of the 1st Rhode Island Light Artillery, Battery B, recorded the agony of the moment:

> An awful battle yesterday. Prisoners of both sides coming in, first about six hundred of our paroled men, then seven hundred Rebel prisoners, dirty, ragged, and bare-footed. A strange Sabbath; men on horseback on the dead run, coming and going. Cavalry, Infantry, Artillery; thousands of soldiers lying on the ground, so common it's not thought of. . . . Saw about thirty wagons loaded with wounded soldiers; they looked sad enough.[17]

Throughout this crisis, Sedgwick acted on pure military instinct. With a disintegrating situation in Washington, Halleck struggled, harried and sleepless in haphazard attempts to coordinate movements. He, McClellan, Stanton, and Lincoln sought to resolve their differences to present a defense of the capital. Thus, during the first two days of September, Sedgwick acted in a virtually independent role within Sumner's corps. During this relative absence of a Union high command, Sedgwick noted, "We made a forced march, one for its length and rapidity has not been equalled in this war; in thirty-six hours we made fifty miles, and after a rest of a few hours twenty-five miles more."[18]

As Pope's army of stragglers was streaming back toward Washington on September 1, Sedgwick made a reconnaissance toward Centreville, passing through Maj. Gen. Irwin McDowell's beaten corps. Near Chantilly, Sedgwick deployed his division almost as a skirmish line and advanced. This ruse worked as the Confederates believed a large force to be in reserve. The Southerners arrested their lines to regroup. Sedgwick's strategy had worked, as Lee's thrust was halted for several hours, and gained valuable time for the Union army.

At 4:30 P.M. fighting broke out, and Sedgwick, having accomplished his objective, fell back, pressed by the enemy. By the early morning of September 2, the 2d Division formed a line of battle near Fairfax Court House and awaited attack. The Confederates were content to hurl a few artillery shells. Continuing his delaying tactics, Sedgwick positioned his forces near Flint Hill. Lee's artillery belched shell, shot, and railroad iron. When the Southerners pushed ahead, they were drawn into an ambush prepared by Col. Alfred Sully of the 1st Minnesota. A Confederate commander inquired, "Who are you?" Sully gave an evasive answer that enticed the enemy to advance another twenty-five yards. Then Sully yelled, "Fire!" The volley practically annihilated the enemy. No further attack was made on the line. Such stop-and-fight tactics by Sedgwick and other Union officers — acting independently and totally uninformed — blunted the Confederate push after the Second Battle of Bull Run. Lee's army was spent, and any attempt to invade Washington at this time would have been foolhardy.

After this engagement, Sedgwick returned to Chain Bridge and continued on to Langley, Virginia, arriving about midnight. During the night's march, a tragic incident occurred. The exhausted men had fallen asleep during a short halt. They were awakened by a crashing noise in the rear and the sound of horses' feet. Many suspected a Confederate cavalry charge and rushed into the woods for cover. All the excitement was caused by a runaway team of horses, but in the confusion someone injudiciously fired a shot that resulted in accidental firing among Sedgwick's own men. There were twenty-eight casualties.

The next morning, September 3, the general's division crossed the bridge and encamped at Tenleytown, near the city of Washington, on the Washington and Frederick Turnpike. There Sumner gathered together his scattered regiments for the next several days to rebuild his corps. Pope's campaign was over. Sedgwick had performed admirably in his relief of the battered Army of Virginia, but his division was unable to reverse the effects of this overwhelming defeat.

To support Pope, Halleck had stripped McClellan of his army, and now there was bitterness throughout the army against Pope. "The cry for 'Little Mac' grows louder every day, not only from his own old army, but from all other troops," wrote Col. Charles S. Wainwright.[19] Realizing the magnitude of Pope's defeat and hearing about the 30,000 stragglers, and despite the opposition of the radical Republicans and members of his own cabinet, the president decided to reinstate McClellan and offer him command of all the forces. When this news reached Union troops in the defenses of Washington, the effect on their morale was electrifying. On September 5, the Army of Virginia was absorbed into the Army of the Potomac, and Pope was relieved. McClellan struggled to reorganize and reequip this consolidated army.

Although happy that McClellan was back in command, many Federal officers still possessed grave doubts about any forthcoming success. Sedgwick was disgusted with the political machinations and with the caliber of the Union troops. He wrote from camp, "The enemy have outgeneralled us. Their hearts are in the cause; our men are perfectly indifferent. . . . The few officers that are disposed to do their duty, from a sense of doing it, are so outnumbered by the vicious that they can do but little. . . . I am in despair of our seeing a termination of the war till some great change is made."[20] Nonetheless, it was the job of McClellan, Sumner, and Sedgwick to restore confidence to this beaten army.

At Tenleytown, Sedgwick labored to prepare his division for any emergency. Gen. Oliver O. Howard, now commanding the 2d Brigade, told his troops to "draw [y]our pay, new clothes, with plenty of rations . . . and respect the property and rights of the citizens."[21] Although no leaves were to be granted, the kind-hearted

Uncle John allowed a few officers to enter Washington on "regimental business." Lt. Oliver Wendell Holmes, Jr., of the 20th Massachusetts, was one of the lucky ones; he obtained "the necessaries of life which I've been without till now."[22] During the encampment at Tenleytown, Capt. Charles A. Whittier was appointed to serve on Sedgwick's staff.

While the Army of the Potomac remained in the environs of Washington, Lee decided to carry the war into the North. An invasion at this time, the Confederate general reasoned, would be most propitious: the war would be drawn away from Virginia, and the state of Maryland might join the Confederacy, thus isolating the Federal capital. The route north into Maryland, and indeed onward to Pennsylvania, was now rich with crops to feed his soldiers and horses. The Lincoln government, according to Lee's logic, would be compelled to watch him and cover Washington, thus reducing the threat to Richmond.

To execute this bold plan with an anticipated force of 70,000, Lee decided to strike while the Federal army was still undermined by defeat. On September 3, the Confederate army disappeared before the Washington defenses; two days later the *New York Times* headlines announced, "STIRRING WAR NEWS. THE REBELS ATTEMPTING TO INVADE THE NORTH."[23]

At Tenleytown, General Sumner commanded the center wing, comprised of both his own 2d Corps and the 12th Corps of Brig. Gen. Alpheus S. Williams. On the afternoon of September 5, Sedgwick left his encampment with Sumner's forces and tramped about ten miles west to Rockville. The next day McClellan quit his Washington headquarters with about 75,000 troops in an attempt to smash the Southern invasion. Aide William F. Biddle wrote on the day of departure, "The Gen'l has at last fixed things his own way, and has his own will in everything he makes a stand for. The Gen'l seems in good spirits, and expects to beat them."[24]

The stakes involved in Lee's Maryland invasion were enormous. The military, political, and diplomatic consequences of the outcome were critical for the survival of the Lincoln administration. The nation's future lay in the hands of McClellan and his corps and division commanders.

The center wing bivouacked several days near Rockville, which Sumner called Camp Defiance. No one knew whether Lee intended to move down the Potomac and attack Washington from the north, to move on Baltimore, or to invade Pennsylvania. Barlow related the latest rumors: "The enemy is reported to have crossed the [Potomac] River with 30,000 men and to be at Poolesville in our front. We are lying here in a strong position in case they advance on us." Additional troops came up to join Sumner's force during this time. A war correspondent accompanying the center wing reported, "If this army finds the enemy, it will beat him. . . . The soldiers are under the immediate command for the most part of fighting Generals, and will fight themselves."[25]

With vague indications that Lee's real purpose was to invade Pennsylvania, Sumner continued west on the Frederick Road. After passing through Middlebrook on September 10, Sedgwick captured Hyattstown the next day and occupied the heights. A brisk skirmish quickly dislodged the Southerners. Three or four loyal citizens of the town joined the 2d Division's advancing columns with offers of information about the roads.

The location of the Confederate advance was still unknown. After an encampment at Urbana, the center wing marched through the city of Frederick on September 13. Both Sumner and Sedgwick with their staffs rode at the head of the columns. For the first time during the campaign, they received a patriotic welcome. Cheering citizens lined the streets and supplied the men with water, pies, cakes, and bread. When McClellan appeared, Sumner's forces and the townspeople greeted Little Mac with enthusiastic cheers.

The good feeling of the day did not remain with Sedgwick, however. He sat down that evening at his bivouac at Farm Willow Grove, a mile west of Frederick, and gloomily wrote to his cousin: "For three years I have not slept absent from my command, for two years I have not lived in a house; my division has been in as many engagements as any other. . . . I hope some day to go home and die at the old place [Cornwall Hollow] and be buried beside my and your father."[26] It was an uncharacteristically pessimistic letter for Sedgwick. He felt his efforts for the Union army had been fruitless and were unappreciated.

That same night, however, McClellan demonstrated his confidence in Sedgwick's abilities. Visiting in McClellan's tent, Brig. Gen. John Gibbon was present as Little Mac struggled to find a suitable replacement for General Williams of the 12th Corps. (The commanding general was still reorganizing his army while it was on the march.) Although he was a capable soldier, Williams lacked a

West Point education and was unfortunately associated with the failures of General Banks. According to Gibbon, one of McClellan's aides read off Sedgwick's name among others. McClellan said, "He will do. Publish an order assigning Sedgwick to command that corps." The aide protested, "I don't think General Sedgwick wants it, General; I think he would rather command his present division." McClellan answered, "I can't help that. He must take it. Issue the order."[27]

At Farm Willow Grove, Sedgwick received special orders assigning him temporarily "to the command of the Second (Banks's) Corps, late, the Army of the Virginia [renumbered as the 12th Corps in the Army of the Potomac], and will immediately enter upon duty accordingly. Brig. Gen. O. O. Howard will relieve . . . Sedgwick in command of the division." It was a most tempting assignment if one desired rapid promotion. But Sedgwick declined the command, as he "felt he could do better service with the troops which he knew and which knew him";[28] he placed this consideration above advancement. To replace Williams, McClellan ultimately chose elderly Maj. Gen. Joseph K. F. Mansfield.

The next morning, September 14, Sumner and his corps left camp early. Cannonading could be heard in the distance. He pushed his soldiers forward over Catoctin Mountain. From the summit, everyone could see westward to the next ridge of South Mountain with its three gaps. The scene was one of shelling and troop movement. After a twenty-two-mile tramp over varied terrain, Sedgwick halted his division for an overnight bivouac at Bolivar, near Turner's Gap, anchoring down the north wing of the Union army. Sumner's main body of troops was in position at Fox's Gap, a few miles south. With his advance troops, McClellan had fought and won the Battle of South Mountain and captured the strategic passes. With the coming of daylight, Sedgwick's division saw about 400 Confederate prisoners under guard. After a two-mile march, Uncle John and his boys rested on the summit ridge of the mountain, overlooking a field dotted with Confederate dead.

With the invasion checked, McClellan ordered a rapid pursuit. During the day of September 15, Sedgwick drove his division without faltering. Continuing over South Mountain, through Boonesboro and Keedysville, he marched for thirteen miles before camping for the night. The next day the 2d Corps remained massed near Pry Farm to the east of Antietam Creek. Throughout this extremely hot day, the Confederate artillery periodically poured shot and shell into the Union lines. Sedgwick's troops lay concealed on the eastern slope of a ridge. Shells flew over the crest and caused a few casualties.

With dusk approaching, Sedgwick's troops packed everything in their knapsacks, which they would leave behind during any advance. Each man received eighty rounds of ammunition. Four men of the 19th Massachusetts volunteered to take the canteens of their regiment and search for water. Apparently they dreaded the approaching battle, though, for they did not return. That evening at McClellan's headquarters at the village of Keedysville, Sumner received an order to support Fighting Joe Hooker, who had crossed Antietam Creek during the afternoon. Sumner was further instructed to hold his own corps in "readiness to march for the same purpose an hour before daylight." Sumner then came to Sedgwick's tent and told him, "General, we are to move tonight or tomorrow morning. I . . . shall attack in columns of five lines and smash the enemy, I hope, and drive them into the river."[29]

Wednesday, September 17, dawned cloudy and cool. The soldiers of the 1st Minnesota remarked, "Thank the Lord, we won't have to fight today under a broiling sun."[30] As the day wore on, the fog burned off but a gentle breeze tempered the burning heat of the sun. After a quick breakfast, many of Sedgwick's men climbed to the high ground where they had a perfect view of Hooker's forces fighting in the distance. At 7:20 A.M., upon receiving his actual orders to march, Sumner went to Hooker's relief. For Sedgwick, the Battle of Antietam, or Sharpsburg, had begun.

Planning to fight a defensive battle, General Lee had formed his lines east of the village of Sharpsburg, with both flanks almost on the Potomac. With two corps led by Lt. Gen. Thomas J. "Stonewall" Jackson and Maj. Gen. James Longstreet, Lee commanded approximately 58,000 effectives at Antietam.

McClellan relied on a force of approximately 70,000 to 75,000 men divided into seven corps led by Hooker, Mansfield, Sumner, Darius N. Couch, FitzJohn Porter, William B. Franklin, and Ambrose E. Burnside. The Federal line extended roughly north and south along Antietam Creek, a tributary of the Potomac, and enjoyed excellent artillery positions.

To reach the hotly contested cornfield and support Hooker,

Sedgwick was hampered by the terrain. From Pry Farm, he led his troops forward in three lines to Antietam Creek. The water was waist-deep and swiftly flowing. Many men locked arms by fours to prevent being swept downstream. Carrying ammunition in their pockets, they struggled to keep it dry. After fording, the men walked a mile through woods, fields, over fences, and through a barnyard; despite these obstacles, though, Sedgwick maintained his lines and closed up the breaks.

Arriving at the East Woods, a grove of oak trees without underbrush, Sumner and Sedgwick discovered that Hooker's corps had been subjected to terrible punishment while fighting in the cornfield. Coming to Hooker's relief, General Mansfield was killed. With these two corps repulsed, Sumner and Sedgwick approached the battlefield, where they saw Fighting Joe Hooker being carried off the field on a stretcher. He had suffered a superficial but painful wound and was in a weakened condition. The two 2d Corps generals sought to question him about where their reinforcements might best be placed and for other specific information about the battle. Hooker fainted and on recovery could offer little advice. Sumner and Sedgwick had to proceed with virtually no current intelligence on the existing situation and practically no reconnaissance.

Sedgwick's troops passed through the East Woods and saw the results of the early morning fighting. Dead and dying Union soldiers lay under the trees. In the cornfield, they saw "a very horrible harvest, a crop of shot men."[31] Sedgwick formed his brigades into three lines, about sixty to seventy paces apart, and faced them toward the southwest and Sharpsburg. Gorman commanded the first line, Dana the second, and Howard the third and rear line. Sedgwick's veterans advanced through the cornfield, watching the ground to avoid stepping on the wounded. Enemy batteries, concealed by woods, began shelling the advancing lines, but to little effect. Union batteries to the rear responded, causing a slight wavering in the third line.

Sumner never questioned McClellan's orders; he was a soldier who obeyed every command literally and without hesitation. And in his haste to assault the Confederate line, Sumner did not wait for his other division commanders, Maj. Gen. Israel B. Richardson and Brig. Gen. William H. French. French was scheduled to follow Sedgwick and cover the ground on his left; Richardson was to move an hour later. "Sumner does not wait," wrote Francis A. Walker. "All his life in the cavalry, he has the instincts of a cavalry commander."[32]

The time was now between 9 and 10 A.M. As Sumner approached the Hagerstown Pike near the Dunker Church, about a mile north of the village, he said to Sedgwick, "General, where are your other two lines?"

"Just behind," replied Sedgwick, and added incredulously, "You don't want them up here?"

Sumner answered, "Yes, bring them close up to this line."[33]

Aide Charles A. Whittier was sent to the rear and brought the lines up to within thirty paces of each other. Massing the troops together was a military blunder, but Sedgwick did not protest his old chief's decision.

Sumner's impulsiveness led to tragedy. French had been slightly diverted and could not keep up with Sedgwick's division, so there was a break of 400 yards in the Union line to the left. Sumner's rash impatience left Sedgwick's command "in the air." Gorman's lead brigade advanced straight into the West Woods and put to flight the ostensibly weak Confederate line. Southern Gen. Jubal A. Early's brigade of 600 men appeared to be no match for Sedgwick's 6,000. Gorman's troops pushed to the edge of the field and captured a Confederate battle flag, but this Union advance proved to be the farthest penetration against Lee's left wing. At this moment, when Sedgwick's thrust was overextended, fresh Southern troops fell on the unprotected left flank and rear. Gorman commented, "My whole brigade became hotly engaged, giving and receiving the most deadly fire it has ever been my lot to witness." In more direct language, Howard stated, "That three-line advance had run Sedgwick's division into a trap well set and baited."[34]

For twenty minutes a holocaust engulfed Sedgwick's command. Protected by the cover of ledges and led by Maj. Gen. Lafayette McLaws and Brig. Gen. John G. Walker, two Confederate divisions poured in fire from three directions. The Union soldiers in the second and third lines were afraid to shoot because they would fire into the ranks of their own men. A colonel of a second-line regiment lost sixty men and came off without firing a musket.

Then, without warning, someone raised the cry, "The enemy is behind us!" Less than thirty-five feet away, the surprised men of the

20th Massachusetts in the rear line saw enemy forces coming at them. The hidden Confederate batteries found the correct range: Northern soldiers fell in groups, knocked over by solid shot. Everything — shell, spherical case, shrapnel, grape, canister, and apparently even railroad iron and nails — tore into Union ranks. The survivors remarked that whole blacksmith shops were discharged against them. A colonel of the 19th Massachusetts was so shaken by the carnage that he halted his men under the withering fire of the enemy. In hopes of restoring a semblance of confidence and order, he then put them through commands in the *Manual of Arms*.

Attempting to repel this attack from the rear, Sumner turned his third line around. This tactic proved futile; the men were unable to hold their position. Lines crumbled and broke. As one regimental historian wrote, "A shot fired at Sedgwick's Division would hit it somewhere and hurt somebody. The Division was as easy to hit as the town of Sharpsburg." Realizing his mistake, Sumner exclaimed, "My God! We must get out of this."[35] He took off his cap and waved it as a signal to retreat.

Sedgwick seemed to be everywhere during this terrible slaughter. Riding to rally his division near the forward line, he saw the shot fall like hail. A bullet pierced his leg, but he ignored it. Another shot struck his wrist. Somehow he clung to his saddle. Almost faint with the loss of blood, he would not relax his efforts. His horse was shot. Surgeon Samuel Foster Haven, Jr., of the 15th Massachusetts, examined the general's wounds and advised him to go to the rear. He refused. Haven then offered the commander his horse. Sedgwick mounted the animal, but discovered he could not ride with a broken wrist. When he received a third wound in his shoulder, the general finally turned the command of his division over to Howard. Uncle John was carried off the field in a faint, slightly over an hour after receiving his first wound.

Utter confusion prevailed in the Union ranks. With all the dust, smoke, and noise, many officers were uncertain whether Sumner had ordered a retreat. Howard saw Sumner without his hat and motioning violently with his arms. At the front line, several of Sedgwick's aides attempted to rally the division in the general's absence. Many officers tried — unsuccessfully — to halt the retreat. Escaping the death trap by retreating to the north — the only safe route out of the West Woods — Sedgwick's survivors finally were rallied near the cornfield. There they formed a defensive line, facing Sharpsburg. Sedgwick's magnificent force had suffered 2,210 casualties, the highest of any Union division at Antietam.

Under the impossible circumstances encountered, Sedgwick had fought as well as he could; he had obeyed orders and was unable to curb Sumner's rashness. General Williams, who had witnessed Sumner's advance across the cornfield, noted, "Hundreds of lives were foolishly sacrificed by generals . . . who would come up with their commands and pitch in at the first point without . . . looking for the effective points of attacks." Sedgwick's aide Charles A. Whittier bluntly stated, "Rarely during the war, in my judgment, has an experienced officer so bungled as Sumner did here."[36]

As the Battle of Antietam continued, Sedgwick was carried to the rear for medical treatment. Seeing a battery coming, the revived Sedgwick inquired which one it was. When told it was Battery A of the 1st Rhode Island Artillery, he disputed the information. The artillerymen told them they belonged to him but had been wrongly placed. Sedgwick commented, "They are lost, and it is the first one I ever lost, and the best one in our corps."[37]

Sedgwick's wounds, although painful and disabling, were not dangerous. He was taken to a little hut alongside a road. The fate of his cousin and chief aide was not as fortunate. William Sedgwick had been struck in the back by a musket ball and lay mortally wounded on the field under fire. Taking out his notebook, he wrote a farewell letter to his wife and children and prayed to God to forgive his sins. Young Sedgwick's message illustrates the strong patriotism of many Union soldiers:

> I wish my friends to know that I have fallen while doing my duty as well as was possible, which I can truly assert, and that I have not uttered a groan as yet, lying alone on the hard ground in the sun with no friend near.[38]

Later he was discovered and carried off to a field hospital at Keedysville. Ten days after the Battle of Antietam, William Sedgwick died.

The battle raged the rest of the day while General Sedgwick remained in his hut. Sumner attacked piecemeal with French's and Richardson's divisions along the center of the Confederate line. Bloody fighting occurred at the Roulette Farm and at the Sunken

Road, directly south of East Woods. While posting his line, Richardson fell mortally wounded. At 1 P.M., Burnside, commanding the left wing of the Union army, made a belated attack across Antietam Creek. His drive toward Sharpsburg was blunted by the timely arrival of Confederate troops from Harpers Ferry. The fighting of "the war's bloodiest day," as it is commonly known, ended at nightfall. The Union army of 75,316 effectives suffered losses of 12,410. The Confederate force of 51,844, present at the battle, endured 13,724 casualties.

Sedgwick's division anticipated the battle to continue the next day, September 18. Lt. William B. Rhodes of Battery G, 1st Rhode Island Light Artillery, wrote, "We were all up early this morning, expecting a fight to begin by daylight. There were some few shots about sunrise, but they did not amount to much." As he was moving his troops toward the Union line, Col. Charles Devens, Jr., of the 15th Massachusetts, was notified by his orderly that Sedgwick was lying in a nearby hut. Devens jumped off his horse and ran in for a moment. Uncle John spoke about his wounds and then remarked, "Your old Fifteenth was magnificent yesterday; no regiment ever fought better."[39]

The day passed without fighting. Alfred Gray Gardner, one of Sedgwick's artillerymen, wrote his wife, "All quiet now. . . . Haven't unhitched our horses for two days. Men and horses killed all around us. . . . The cannonading was terrific and continuing till dark. . . . There is not a spot where you cannot view the dead, and burying going on all the time. I have seen a battlefield. It is what I expected."[40] In view of the enormous casualties Sedgwick's division suffered, his soldiers were most certainly content that they did not attack on September 18.

During the evening, the 2d Corps veterans heard sounds and noises that gave them the impression Lee was retreating. The next morning, Sumner's skirmishers discovered that the Confederate army was gone, leaving the battlefield in Union control and giving McClellan a strategic victory.

Controversy surrounds the Battle of Antietam and the possibility of a Federal attack on the following day. McClellan contended, "The general result was in our favor. . . . It was a success."[41] McClellan was right: Lee's invasion had failed, and the Confederate government did not obtain recognition from the British and French ministers. But the Lincoln administration expected McClellan to follow up his victory. Most students of the battle believe McClellan should have pursued Lee.

In the days immediately following the battle, Sedgwick's troops interpreted the results most positively and hoped that now there would be no delay. First Lt. Henry Ropes of the 20th Massachusetts commented, "We have beaten the enemy badly, and they acknowledge it. I should not wonder if the war was now brought to a speedy end."[42]

Sedgwick remained at a field hospital near Keedysville. His division again witnessed the grisly business of cleaning up a battlefield. Alfred Gray Gardner was repulsed by the scene: "One thing was awful, the scent of the field; had to turn our backs to it to eat, and it was all we could do to keep food down. Hundreds of men had lost all form of men."[43] The Battle of Antietam was an experience Sedgwick and his men never forgot.

Within a few days, Sedgwick was carried into Hagerstown in an ambulance wagon. Cavalryman J. I. Schock with his mounted command was nearby as the ambulance driver stopped. Schock went up to the wagon to offer any kindness to the wounded and spoke with Sedgwick. Learning the identity of the general, Schock "then told our boys who you was and about your fighting on the retreat from Richmond, and when you started, I had our boys to give you three cheers." After the train of ambulances had passed, Schock noticed on the road a pocketbook containing stamps and a draft for $200. Discovering it to be the property of John Sedgwick, Schock mailed the pocketbook to Cornwall Hollow. Including a letter of explanation, Schock offered to serve the general "in any capacity that I would be fit for."[44] The considerate officer never became an aide, but his efforts were appreciated.

After a safe journey to Cornwall Hollow, Sedgwick recuperated for almost three months under the care of his unmarried sister, Emily. Although he found inaction to be unpleasant and tedious, the general did enjoy living in his new home. The original house had burned in 1859, and Sedgwick was seeing the newly constructed buildings for the first time. After inspecting the stables, the grounds, and the garden, Sedgwick told Emily that he was pleased, "but I would gladly give it all up for the dear old home." Howard and Sumner wrote him, expressing their sympathy about his cousin and hoping for the general's quick recovery. The pious Howard included his official report of the battle for approval and added, "I hope you are feeling comfortable. . . . May God bless you." Sumner "regretted very much that I could not see you after you were wounded, but you know how much we have to attend to, after such a battle. . . . Don't come back till you are entirely well."[45]

There may have been a dilemma in Sedgwick's mind about his return to active service. Always a well-informed person who subscribed to several newspapers, the general read about the inactivity of the Army of the Potomac and the location of his old division. Sumner's corps had marched to Harpers Ferry and encamped at Bolivar Heights. The soldiers were physically and emotionally fatigued; so were many high-ranking officers in Washington. An old army friend, U. A. Nichols, wrote to Sedgwick from the adjutant general's office:

> And when is all this to stop! For myself I do not see the beginning of the end — we are not yet in earnest. The North has too many *isms* to settle, whilst the South has put its shoulder to the wheel and all are pushing together. The raid into Penna. seems to have attracted all eyes in that direction, but my opinion is that Lee is withdrawing his forces towards Richmond and will en route strike a blow at Heintzelman and Sigel and use them up.[46]

Sedgwick was upset further by what he read in the newspapers. After crossing the Potomac, McClellan had advanced southward. By early November, the Army of the Potomac was centered around Warrenton, Virginia, with the 2d Corps stationed at Rectortown. On November 7, Lincoln relieved McClellan from his command for the last time and replaced him with Maj. Gen. Ambrose E. Burnside. Many soldiers received this announcement with grief and indignation. In a final farewell ceremony on November 10, the troops of the 2d Corps watched their beloved Little Mac leave them, and "when the chief had passed out of sight, the romance of war was over for the Army of the Potomac."[47]

If Sedgwick ever contemplated retiring from the army, the autumn of 1862 presented the proper opportunity. The public would not have questioned his decision. After almost thirty years in the army, the death of his cousin, severe wounds, and the removal of his friend McClellan, he must have thought of quiet retirement. From his doorway on a high Berkshire hill overlooking the Housatonic landscape, he often remarked to his relatives and friends, "Is there another spot on earth so beautiful as Cornwall Hollow?"[48] Despite this temptation, he left his farm and reported back to Washington during early December. His overwhelming sense of duty had prevailed.

Forcing himself to return before his wounds were completely healed, the general spent about two weeks in the nation's capital before resuming field duty. He kept busy with army correspondence. Recognizing talent and ability in younger officers, Sedgwick vigorously endorsed Lt. Col. Alexander S. Webb for the post of assistant inspector in the army. At the request of Gov. John A. Andrew of Massachusetts, Sedgwick reviewed the entire record of the Massachusetts regiments under his command. The general praised these units and their officers. With regard to the usual system of promotions and appointments, Sedgwick suggested, "It adds to an officer's usefulness to place him in a regiment in which he has no acquaintances, and this holds good to a greater extent in promotions from the ranks."[49]

On December 22, 1862, Sedgwick reported to the Army of the Potomac headquarters at Falmouth, Virginia. When he returned, it was a most depressing time for Burnside's army: the Union forces had suffered an overwhelming defeat on December 13, as they attempted to storm the heights at Fredericksburg. On December 24, Burnside ordered Sedgwick to report to his old commander, General Sumner.

During November, Burnside had reorganized his army and placed Sumner in command of the Right Grand Division, embracing the 2d Corps under Maj. Gen. Darius N. Couch and the 9th Corps led by Brig. Gen. Orlando B. Willcox. As Couch was on a leave of absence, Sumner returned Uncle John to his old corps. Sedgwick notified his troops, "All existing orders will remain in force."[50]

The 2d Corps, which had attacked the impregnable stone wall at Fredericksburg, was in deplorable condition. It had suffered monstrous losses of 3,833 men out of an aggregate of 28,543. The men were despondent.

Sedgwick's aide, Charles A. Whittier, was embittered, complaining in correspondence to a friend,

You are disgusted with the conduct of the War. Who is not? There is no officer down here, whom I have met, who is not of the party which says, "Burnside says he has no confidence in himself as commander of the army — Can the Army then have confidence in him?"[51]

Sedgwick's presence was unable to counteract this demoralization. The problems were beyond his control. Many soldiers feigned sickness. Confidence in Burnside's generalship among the soldiers was practically nonexistent. At a review of the 2d Corps shortly after the Fredericksburg battle, attended by both Burnside and Sumner, the commanding general was greeted with frigid silence. When the men in the ranks were called on for cheers, all they could muster were a few derisive cries. Discontent through the Army of the Potomac was further aggravated by the failure of "Major Cash" to make his appearance at headquarters. As Burnside himself admitted, "The army had not been paid for several months, which caused great dissatisfaction among the soldiers and their friends at home, and increased the number of desertions to a fearful extent."[52]

With the beginning of 1863, the inactivity continued, but the situation was somewhat improved. Reinforcements had arrived, and the general weather conditions were favorable for a movement. The Army of the Potomac was cheered by the news of Maj. Gen. William S. Rosecrans's success at Stone's River. Burnside knew that he needed a victory to win the confidence of his troops and the Lincoln administration. Although the president had prevented Burnside's original plan to move during early January, there were rumors of an advance. During this time of indecision, Sedgwick commanded the Right Grand Division for a few days during Sumner's absence; Howard took the 2d Corps. On the return of both Sumner and Couch, Sedgwick was shifted into another slot. On January 16, Sumner gave him command of the 9th Corps in place of Willcox, who now awaited reassignment.

As Burnside completed his plans, the Confederate soldiers extended their lines. Southern pickets shouted across the Rappahannock, "We know where you are at; we are ready for you." On January 20, the Army of the Potomac finally marched with pleasant weather and good roads. Burnside left Sumner's Right Grand Division (now actually the left wing of the army) in position at Falmouth as a holding force. With the Left and Center Divisions, Burnside hoped to march rapidly up to Banks Ford and United States Ford in a massive turning movement. If successful, this operation would outflank Lee. The plan was basically sound, certainly better than his frontal attacks during the previous December. Sedgwick was assigned the role of remaining behind to pin down Lee's army at Fredericksburg, and perhaps cross the river by pontoons to make a feint below the city. The 9th Corps stayed in full view of the enemy, with artillery posted at Franklin's Crossing.

While strategically well conceived, Burnside's plan turned out to be a disaster. No sooner had the movement up the Rappahannock begun than a furious storm struck. The hurricane blew for over twenty-four hours, and the Union army became mired. Mules and horses dropped dead. Men had to be pulled out of the mud. Burnside canceled the operation, and his troops struggled to return to Falmouth. His last opportunity to redeem his defeat was gone.

Sedgwick's 9th Corps did not move, but the men shared in the frustration of the four-day operation. His soldiers saw the spattered messengers and the bedraggled troops return to Falmouth. One of Sumner's officers, Francis Walker, encountered a party of twenty men and asked their sergeant, "Who are these men?" The sad answer was "Stragglers of the Seventeenth Maine!" Pvt. Theodore Barton reported a situation that had made Burnside the laughingstock of his own troops: the Confederates across the river had offered to help dig the Federal pontoons out of the mud. Sedgwick's troops shared their rations with the returning victims of "Burnside's Mud March," as it soon became known throughout the North.[53]

Changes came quickly. On January 23, Burnside wrote Lincoln a shocking order. Accusing Hooker and several other generals of insubordination and efforts to undermine his postion, Burnside demanded their immediate dismissal from his army. Sedgwick was not named and stayed aloof from this quarrel. When Lincoln did not support Burnside's actions, the harried general offered his resignation. Attempting to avoid an open clash among his disaffected generals, Lincoln refused Burnside's resignation, but relieved him from command at Burnside's own request. The president conferred the command on Maj. Gen. Joseph Hooker. Several generals including Sumner had no faith in Hooker and hence submitted their resignations. On January 26, Sumner bade farewell to his Right Grand Division. The men in the 2d and 9th Corps were told that their commander's retirement from active field duty was necessitated by feebleness and poor health, but everyone knew the real reason. With this shakeup in the Right Grand Division, Couch superseded Sumner. Sedgwick remained with the 9th Corps, but realized that Hooker was bound to reorganize the army to his own satisfaction.

Sedgwick and Hooker had been classmates at West Point. Although he undoubtedly had heard stories about Hooker's alleged excessive drinking, questionable moral behavior, and impetuous personality, Sedgwick could not deny the new commanding general's reputation as a fighting soldier. The overall response in the Northern press to this appointment was positive. The new atmosphere of industry at headquarters impressed correspondents. One exclaimed, " 'Fighting Joe Hooker' has already won the name 'Working Joe Hooker.' "[54]

After selecting his staff, Hooker concentrated his attention on the reorganization of his army. On February 5, 1863, he discarded Burnside's arrangement of the Army of the Potomac into grand divisions and returned to the corps plan. In parceling out his troops, Hooker faced a problem with the 9th Corps, Sedgwick's command of less than a month. Having Burnside, the 9th Corps's original commander, resume his old post would create much friction. Hooker decided instead to transfer the 9th Corps to Fort Monroe under Maj. Gen. William F. Smith. This action at the same time would remove Smith, a strong McClellan supporter, from the scene. (On February 7, Hooker ordered Brig. Gen. Orlando B. Willcox, Sedgwick's predecessor as commander of the 9th Corps, to report for duty at Fort Monroe to serve under Smith.) To fill the vacancy created by Smith's removal as head of the 6th Corps, Hooker selected Sedgwick. Although Sedgwick was privately a great admirer of McClellan, he was not as outspoken as Smith and represented a much less controversial figure. Burnside returned to Washington, where he again formally tendered his resignation as a major general of volunteers to Lincoln. But the president refused it, remarking that he had "other fish for him to fry."[55] Ultimately, in March 1863, after several more consultations, Lincoln placed Burnside in command of the Department of the Ohio.

Smith had been a popular commander and on February 8 spent nearly two hours shaking hands with his officers before leaving by special train for his new field of operations. Sedgwick attended this farewell ceremony. The next morning, Sedgwick and his staff arrived and formally took command of the 6th Corps with its head-quarters located in a grove at White Oak Church. Uncle John had to restore confidence to a badly demoralized corps.

The spring of 1863 was coming, and another campaign would begin. Unlike many Union officers who had resigned in disgust or were forced out of the service, Sedgwick discovered his reputation rising rather than falling. Perhaps "Fighting Joe" Hooker had plans for him.

CHAPTER 3

STORMING OVER
MARYE'S HEIGHTS

DURING THE LATE winter and early spring of 1863, Maj. Gen. Joseph Hooker, commander of the Army of the Potomac, and John Sedgwick of the 6th Corps worked diligently to elevate their troops to fighting trim. Completing his organizational rebuilding, Hooker selected as his corps commanders Major Generals John F. Reynolds and Darius N. Couch for the 1st and 2d corps respectively, and Gen. Daniel E. Sickles for the 3d Corps. Retaining command of the 5th Corps was Maj. Gen. George G. Meade. The 11th Corps was originally led by Maj. Gen. Franz Sigel, who was soon replaced by Maj. Gen. Oliver O. Howard. To command the 12th Corps, Hooker designated Maj. Gen. Henry W. Slocum. Sedgwick was a personal friend of these commanders and had previously campaigned with them.

Sedgwick quickly selected his personal staff for his corps of about 24,000 men. On February 26, Maj. Charles Whittier, the general's aide-de-camp, announced their names. The close subordinates included Lt. Col. Martin T. McMahon, assistant adjutant general and chief of staff; Col. Charles H. Tompkins of the 1st Rhode Island Artillery, chief of artillery; and Maj. Thomas W. Hyde of the 7th Maine Volunteers, provost marshal. The positions of chief quartermaster, chief commissionary of subsistence officer, medical director, and medical inspector were also announced. For each of his three divisions, Sedgwick had reliable West Point graduates: The 1st Division of three brigades was commanded by Brig. Gen. William T. H. Brooks; the 2d Division of two brigades, Brig. Gen. Albion P. Howe; and the 3d Division of three brigades, Maj. Gen. John Newton. With personnel matters settled, Sedgwick could now devote full attention to the pressing physical needs of the corps.[1]

Hooker realized that the first priority was to improve the health of his army. To this end, Surgeon Jonathan Letterman organized an ambulance system and upgraded the medical department. On February 10, Letterman issued a circular stating, "Fresh vegetables and occasional change of diet are indispensable to the health and consequent efficiency of the troops." These simple improvements greatly cheered the soldiers. The men were instructed to notify their regimental superiors if they were not receiving ample beef, bread, potatoes, and other staples. Hooker ordered, "Should your complaints not be attended to by the commissariat or Quartermaster, come to me."[2]

Sedgwick instituted Hooker's reforms with great energy. Through the medical director of the 6th Corps, Dr. Charles O. Leury, Sedgwick urged his men to donate to the hospital fund. "Above all we must remember," Sedgwick advised, "that we have no right to deprive the sick soldier of his due — we are doing so in neglecting to secure it for him." Sedgwick's mess was well known throughout the Army of the Potomac. His staff officers ate well; Hyde wrote, "We breakfast at 8:30 on steak, potatoes, & buckwheat, generally; Lunch at one on soup, meat, etc., dine at 6 on soup, meat, potatoes, vegetables & pastry. Supper at 10, bread, cheese, & cold meat." These improvements helped win the battle of morale.[3]

Other reforms reduced desertions. Hooker worked out a system of granting leaves. Realizing that idle men become demoralized, Hooker and Sedgwick kept their troops busy at drills, reviews, and inspections. They appeared personally to supervise this training. Hooker also saw the value of designating distinctive badges for each corps. Sedgwick's men proudly wore the insignia of the Greek Cross for the rest of the war.

At his headquarters near White Oak Church, a few miles east of Falmouth, Sedgwick began to notice the results of these efforts. Many of his men had been sick and often hospitalized; improved medical facilities and diet had restored them to health. Still suffering from the pain of his wounds endured at Antietam, Uncle John set an example for his men. Once he laughingly said, "If I am ever hit again, I hope it will settle me at once. I want no more wounds." His men also appreciated his attention in another matter: the troops' being cheated by sutlers and by peddlers who did not have proper passes. Sedgwick discovered two Yankee "hawkers" in Howe's division. Uncle John notified Hooker, who ejected them and confiscated their "traps" of several hundred dollars. Hooker and Sedgwick proved themselves excellent administrators who slowly infused fresh vigor into the army. One correspondent wrote, "The name of McClellan has vanished from the minds of the soldiers, and the army today . . . is about as much Hookerized as it was at one time McClellanized."[4]

As old veterans, both Hooker and Sedgwick realized that their commands were entitled to fun and relaxation when the occasion warranted it. On February 22, the anniversary of Washington's birthday, the Army of the Potomac fired salutes from several batteries. No celebration was heard from the Confederate batteries on the south side of the Rappahannock. During late February, many of Sedgwick's regiments engaged in snowball fights. The Vermonters were generally victorious. In his diary for March 6, Sgt. Thomas Parish Murphy of the 6th Vermont noted, "Playing football on the parade ground." With the coming of spring, the 6th Corps played baseball, with Sedgwick an enthusiastic observer at the games. On rainy days and at free moments, Murphy observed, "All reading Western adventures."[5]

On March 17, Hooker allowed his army to celebrate St. Patrick's Day, an occasion appreciated especially by Brig. Gen. Thomas Meagher's Irish Brigade. Sedgwick walked through the grounds and saw horse racing, footraces, leaping, vaulting, wheelbarrow races, and a chase for a greased pig. Orators delivered speeches from stands while the ladies watched. Uncle John and his men enjoyed a day of rest. As the afternoon wore on, heavy firing was heard to the west, believed to be at United States Ford. Meagher immediately announced the end of the festivities, and the soldiers took up arms. No fighting broke out, however.

During March, Sedgwick received the news of the death of his old commander, Maj. Gen. Edwin V. Sumner, who died in New York State from natural causes. On March 25, Sedgwick participated in some of the ceremonies held throughout the Army of the

Potomac in Sumner's memory. Throughout their long association, Sedgwick had always respected Sumner's posture as a professional soldier.

On April 2, Hooker reviewed the entire 6th Corps. Accompanied by his entire staff and a cavalry escort, Hooker "was dressed in full military suit, and mounted upon a magnificent white charger."[6] A lady rode by his side. Sedgwick presented his corps and watched Hooker pass; then several brigades filed in review before the commanding general. Afterwards, Sedgwick invited Hooker to one of his division headquarters for refreshments.

The object of these reviews was to prepare for the upcoming visit of President and Mrs. Lincoln. Sedgwick was invited to dine with the presidential party on April 7, but unfortunately could not attend "on account of my eyes, which have troubled me and not a little alarmed me for the last four weeks." On April 8, Sedgwick was unable to ride out with his advance troops and receive the president. But as the cavalcade approached the grounds, announced by a salute of twenty-two guns, Sedgwick then rode out to meet Lincoln and Hooker. It was a proud moment for Uncle John. On an elevated spot, the president, with his head uncovered, sat on a beautiful black steed; Mrs. Lincoln was in a carriage. As the 6th Corps passed in review, the soldiers glanced at the president's face. Pvt. Wilbur Fisk of the 2d Vermont thought "the President looked very thin and careworn." The army bands played patriotic music while the soldiers marched on the parade field — a plateau two miles back from the Rappahannock River and directly opposite Fredericksburg, in full view of the Confederate forces. Everyone agreed the whole display was a splendid affair. Sedgwick wrote simply, "The large review went off very handsomely; troops looked and marched well." Mrs. Lincoln visited the hospitals and gently offered comforts to the sick. Lincoln gave straightforward advice to Hooker and Couch: "Gentlemen, in your next battle, put in all of your men." On April 11, the president's party returned to Washington. The general and his troops had greatly appreciated the president's visit. Now the Army of the Potomac hoped to give the tired chief executive a victory; he had waited long enough.[7]

High spirits pervaded the Army of the Potomac, especially the 6th Corps. The New York Times war correspondent reported, "For the past few months it has steadily increased in size the number of returning convalescents more than balancing the number discharged from sickness." The troops "feel that they are invincible." To add to the rising optimism, several paymasters arrived on April 11. Armed with greenbacks, they paid the men, many of whom had not seen money for a long time. The Union soldiers also sensed a lowering of Confederate morale. Southern pickets on the river said they had a new general who treated the soldiers with great severity. When asked about his name by the Union pickets, Lee's men replied, "General Starvation, by God." Union soldiers saw a Confederate deserter attempt to enter their lines by swimming across the river. Exhausted by the swift current, the man was swept back to the Southern lines, where he was seized. Sedgwick's men anticipated a victorious campaign.[8]

As an old professional, Sedgwick was not carried away by the general optimism. He was practical in his outlook. On April 20, he wrote, "We are still stuck in the mud. . . . All the streams are up, and no move can take place for a few days. . . . Many of our oldest and best regiments are soon to be discharged, as well as the nine months' troops. I am afraid the measures taken to secure their re-enlistment will not prove effective. No troops with but a few days to leave are going to risk much in a fight." By the first of May, over 20,000 effective soldiers would be eligible for discharge; to utilize these troops Hooker would have to begin his offensive before that day arrived.[9]

Hooker had already won the statistical battle, with about 130,000 soldiers present for duty at the beginning of the campaign. General Lee's forces comprised approximately 60,000 men. Thus Hooker possessed a two-to-one advantage in manpower. But statistics alone do not determine the outcome of battles; strategy and tactics are more important, and the corps commanders were in the dark as to Hooker's plans.

Hooker had indeed formulated a plan, but was attempting to keep his proposed movements secret, owing to Lee's military intelligence forces. The plan was to swing the greater part of his army rapidly up the Rappahannock about twenty miles to turn Lee's left flank. This main force would cross the river at Kelley's Ford, then ford a tributary, the Rapidan, and concentrate near Chancellorsville, at a road junction in a tangled area of second-growth forest called the Wilderness. If this move succeeded, Lee would undoubtedly — as Hooker saw the situation — be forced to evacuate his strongly fortified Fredericksburg position and fight in the open to save his communications with Richmond, or else fall back on the defenses of the Confederate capital. Federal cavalry would sever Lee's links to the west. A holding force, commanded by Sedgwick, would make demonstrations at Fredericksburg and attempt to pin Lee to his original position along the lower Rappahannock, while Hooker's main wing swung eastward and caught the outnumbered Confederates in a gigantic vise. In this coordinated battle plan (which required a most demanding timetable and the assumption that Lee would be caught napping), Sedgwick was either to pin down the Confederates, or, if they retreated, to cross the river and attack.

On paper and on a map, this well-concerted plan seemed to possess great merit. But to General Couch — apparently one of the few in whom Hooker confided — Sedgwick's assignment seemed excessively difficult. As Couch remembered it, "While riding back to camp, and revolving over what had been imparted to me, I said to myself, that Sedgwick could never carry out such impracticable conditions as were imposed upon him, and I pitied him from the bottom of my heart." Sensing the complexity of his mission, Sedgwick soberly wrote on April 28, "I have been given a large and important command, and I feel a great responsibility. . . . I hope for the success of our arms and am confident."[10]

Tension affected Sedgwick's troops. Pvt. Edwin Wentworth analyzed the situation, writing, "We can bring larger armies into the field than the rebels can, but we have to make the attacks, and storm their works. They fight behind stone walls and from rifle pits. One man behind a wall with a gun is equal to three in the open field. We have to take things as they come — good or bad." Pvt. Wilbur Fisk of the 2d Vermont recorded in his diary, "Part of the officers' tents were taken down and sent off. Things in general began to assume a warlike appearance." Less than a week before the movement, he noted, "No drill. Nothing to read; dull times; ho hum, well, this is camp life." The waiting grated on everyone's nerves. Sedgwick's corps both anticipated and dreaded the campaign. No one really knew what to expect.[11]

After cavalry reconnaissance in the upper Rappahannock region, Hooker felt ready. Monday, April 27, 1863, marked the beginning of his plan of execution for the Army of the Potomac. Hooker accompanied his main striking force — 5th, 11th, and 12th corps — on its turning movement; Sedgwick remained behind at

Stafford Heights. He was in charge of the entire left wing of the army, a holding force of about 56,000 — his own 6th Corps, together with Reynolds's and Sickles's troops, which were soon to be detached for a movement up the Rappahannock. Couch's 2d Corps occupied Falmouth.

From the very beginning of the campaign, Sedgwick was in an awkward position. Unlike Hooker's striking forces, which enjoyed a degree of maneuverability in unfortified country, Sedgwick inherited Burnside's situation of the previous December. The opportunity to maneuver was limited by topographical features — a river, canals, stone walls, and heights — and by the dictates and whims of his superior officer. The Confederates had had months to fortify and improve their defenses on Marye's Heights above Fredericksburg. Sedgwick's men were also restricted to a holding action, while Hooker's forces would attack and receive all the glory. The assigned role of the left wing was crucial but not overly exciting.

On Tuesday, April 28, Sedgwick, in compliance with orders, began an advance. Marching down from their encampment, they approached the vicinity of Franklin's Crossing, on the Stafford Heights bank of the river about three miles below Fredericksburg. Reynolds occupied the ground about a mile downstream from the 6th Corps, as Sickles took a position in the rear. Taking precautions, Sedgwick had all the troops camped that night without fires behind the heights, and concealed from the enemy's observation. Despite his conscientious effort to keep his operation a secret from the Confederate pickets, Sedgwick undoubtedly knew that it was impossible to conceal the movement. Moreover, it was difficult to maintain effective communications with a superior who was miles away.

During the night, Sedgwick worried about the next step in the operation — laying pontoon bridges across the Rappahannock so that his force could cross and threaten the Confederate lines. His men were already exhausted from carrying 60-pound packs with rations for eight days. (This heavy load corresponded to standard army practice. Although a burden, the men needed to carry sufficient rations as they had no idea how long a battle might last.) In the darkness, the troops began to move heavy equipment through thickets and bogs. To reduce noise and to preserve the element of surprise, Brig. Gen. Henry W. Benham of the Engineers Brigade insisted that human muscle, not wagons and mules, be used. Benham, who retained independent authority in this phase of the operation, contended that if done otherwise, the rumble of wagons would be heard across the river. One of Sedgwick's aides, Capt. Richard F. Halsted, had already had an unpleasant row with Benham, and it would have been unwise for Sedgwick further to aggravate Benham. Sedgwick knew he was only as effective as the degree of cooperation he received from his associates: he had to go along with Benham's plan.[12]

One of Reynolds's officers, Brig. Gen. James S. Wadsworth, was directed to begin the work for this pontoon bridge operation. He ordered seventy-two men to carry each of the forty-four boats, which weighed 1,500 pounds apiece. It proved to be an impossible assignment. The officers had to take hold with the men, and man after man dropped to the ground with exhaustion. Finally Wadsworth became convinced of the futility of this method. Sheer manpower alone could not move the boats to the shore before dawn. Taking the matter into his own hands, he ordered wagons to transport the boats. At daybreak, Wadsworth was ready to cross. This incident demonstrated to Sedgwick that the left wing would also be forced to improvise as the campaign continued. When Hooker's plan and schedule began to break down, Sedgwick wisely resorted to common sense.[13]

Uncle John's painstaking patience to save lives was not entirely without reward. Four companies of the 15th New York did succeed in quietly launching their boats and crossing the river; they began laying a pontoon bridge in a remote sector. Brig. Gen. David Russell's brigade crossed without detection and surprised the Confederate pickets behind their earthworks. So sudden was the appearance of these men that Lee's pickets delivered but one volley, and "immediately skedaddled over the fields and into some neighboring houses."[14] There the Union advance forces found the officer of the picket detail asleep in bed. Some half-dozen prisoners were taken.

Along the length of the Union lines, however, the majority of Sedgwick's force was detected. Confederate pickets, aware that something was amiss, hailed the Union soldiers with, "Hallo there, Yank, what's going on over there?" Sedgwick's men answered, "Johnnie, we're coming over after you." Forty boatloads left from shore in the early morning and were lost in ground fog before they went twenty feet. Suddenly the single cry, "Fire," rang out, and the blaze of Confederate musketry along the whole river bank for 200 yards resembled one great mouth of flame. Encountering his first great problem of the campaign, Sedgwick sought to cross the river with a minimum of casualties. The situation was tense. It was "a night of anxiety and suspense, the whole affair appeared to be badly managed & everyone anticipated a signal failure."[15]

A major problem throughout this operation was the strange behavior of General Benham. Usually reliable and dependable, Benham performed poorly on this occasion. He poured two glasses of sherry into a canteen, filled it with water, and drank this to relieve his thirst. He constantly argued with Sedgwick's aides and ordered them put under arrest. He then fell from his horse, cutting his face badly. At daylight, he rode to Reynolds's headquarters and, rushing up to the general, exclaimed, "Hurrah Josh! [a nickname of General Reynolds] Hurrah for here and Buena Vista!"[16]

Benham's drunkenness delayed the laying of the bridges for four hours. Despite this problem, Sedgwick managed to carry out his assignment. Fortunately for the cramped men in the boats, the Confederates aimed their fire too high; only one soldier was killed in the first volley against the 6th Corps. After securing the opposite side, the business of constructing the bridges began. Farther downstream, Reynolds's force had encountered more determined resistance. With enemy bullets whizzing overhead, his troops stepped into the boats and called out, "Here's for Libby [Prison]," "Farewell, Mother," and "Good-by, my lover, good-by." By noon engineers completed the bridges for Reynolds's corps, and the soldiers crossed.[17]

During the day of Wednesday, April 29, Sedgwick transported his force across the Rappahannock to a wide plain where Franklin's Left Grand Division had fought during the previous December. After his initial success, Sedgwick now experienced serious problems in conducting proper reconnaissance. Hooker was using the cavalry for raids on Lee's communications, so the 6th Corps commander was dependent on the "Chief of Aeronauts," Professor Thaddeus S. C. Lowe, for observations. During the afternoon, Hyde, acting as Sedgwick's chief aide for the day, went up with Lowe in a balloon. Aerial intelligence of troop movements, rifle pits, and the sighting of smoke, however, proved to be of limited value for the Army of the Potomac during this campaign. Mist and fog reduced its effectiveness, and there were windy days during which ascension was impossible. As the campaign progressed, Lowe provided occasional but insufficient information to Sedgwick.[18]

By early evening, the general had his men deployed on the plain below the heights to the west. With the approach of darkness, the artillery barrages ceased. Pvt. Peter M. Abbott of the 3d Vermont believed, "If nothing hapens, we will have a Dress Parade in Fredericksburg Hights before saturday night." Hooker's involved plan seemed to be working.[19]

The next morning, April 30, Maj. Gen. Daniel Butterfield, Hooker's chief of staff, who served as the coordinator between the left and right wings of the Army of the Potomac from the old Falmouth headquarters, sent Sedgwick a message via the military telegraph line. Hooker and Sedgwick were now separated by a great distance: in a straight line, fifteen miles broken by Confederate-held ground; via the roads skirting the meandering Rappahannock, which marked Union exterior lines, perhaps twice that. This factor hampered adequate communications between the two wings. (Whether by accident, mechanical failure, or human error, the communications from Hooker and Butterfield to Sedgwick were usually late, garbled, or misleading throughout this campaign.) When Hooker heard about Sedgwick's successful crossing and the failure of the Confederates to attack him, he had decided to reinforce his own striking wing. Sedgwick was informed that the 3d Corps was being detached. "Dan" Sickles and his 16,000 troops left immediately to join Hooker at Chancellorsville. Sedgwick still retained Reynolds's corps under his command, which now numbered about 40,000 men. To strengthen his position, Sedgwick had his troops dig a line of trenches to connect his bridgeheads.

The day progressed — strangely quiet. Union soldiers demolished some old homes to get materials for their defenses. Rats escaped in scores, and the men chased them in wild whoops of delight. The Northern pickets a couple of hundred yards ahead stood around together, while indifferent Confederate battery gunners and sharpshooters sat on the grass. A deer, trapped between the lines, was chased by the men of both armies and was finally captured on the Union side without the firing of a single shot. One Federal regiment took advantage of the lull and was mustered for pay. The hurry and the tension of the previous two days was replaced by a relaxation and boredom resembling regular camp life.

The strange calm continued, as Sedgwick and Reynolds waited patiently for Hooker's orders for a demonstration. But for some unknown reason Fighting Joe had become defense-minded. He believed that perhaps Lee might be enticed to attack him. After outgeneraling Lee with his swift advance to Chancellorsville, Hooker pushed his forces eastward toward Fredericksburg during April 30 and May 1. Losing his confidence when he learned that Lee intended to fight him, Hooker decided to pull back to his original position in the Wilderness. With this strategy in mind, Hooker did not want Sedgwick to upset his plan by starting a demonstration to bring on a general engagement.

Finally, at 1 P.M. on April 30, Reynolds received orders to initiate a probe against the Confederate lines, but Hooker counter-manded his order before the scheduled time for attack. When Sedgwick reported to his commander that Reynolds had spotted troop movements — possibly fresh Confederate troops arriving from Richmond — Butterfield answered, "General Hooker hopes they are from Richmond, as the greater will be our success." The peculiar response must have alarmed Sedgwick, for the arrival of more Confederate soldiers made his assignment more difficult and risky. He had already lost Sickles's corps, and his remaining forces would be compelled to fight an enemy waiting behind superb defenses. Throughout the late afternoon until darkness the action increased. Lee's artillery of ten-pounders and British Whitworth guns on the western ridges and hills shelled Sedgwick's line. Hooker's flippant remarks displayed cockiness and bravado, not common sense.[20]

Hooker appeared to be losing his aggressiveness, and Lee decided to take advantage of it. Investigating the feeble Union demonstrations in front of his lines, Lee and his chief subordinate, Lt. Gen. Thomas J. "Stonewall" Jackson, had personally ridden along the top of the heights to reconnoiter Sedgwick's lines. Jackson wanted to attack. But Lee, aided by the valuable reconnaissance reports of Maj. Gen. James E. B. "Jeb" Stuart that large Union forces were converging on Chancellorsville, rejected this suggestion. Deciding to send the bulk of his forces (Jackson's corps and Maj. Gen. Lafayette McLaws's division) westward toward Chancellorsville the night of April 30, Lee achieved a brilliant redistribution of his forces.

The next day, May 1, was also wasted by the Federals: Hooker's offensive had become a waiting game. At 5:30 A.M., Butterfield, apparently relying on rumors and dubious informers, telegraphed Hooker that a deserter had revealed that "Jackson's whole corps is opposite Franklin's Crossing." The same message was probably sent to Sedgwick. During the day, an informal truce between the two sides was again observed. Some Union soldiers demonstrated their strength, marching with as much show as possible to deceive the enemy. Others continued their games of ball or quoits, cut hair, or slept. Many officers stayed in their little shelter tents to read novels. A chaplain harangued the unlistening soldiers gathered together for religious services.[21]

As the day wore on, communication between the two wing commanders became poor, with unaccountable difficulties and delays. It was finally discovered that the telegraph line between Chancellorsville and Falmouth had broken down. At 5 P.M., after it was repaired, Sedgwick received Hooker's order to conduct a demonstration "as severe as possible without being an attack." There was only one problem — the designated time for this action was 1 P.M., four hours earlier. Interpreting a sense of urgency in the order, Sedgwick decided to go ahead. He executed Hooker's instructions with a display in force of Reynolds's corps and one other division. As the *New York Tribune* correspondent, Thomas M. Newbould, observed, "Mr. Secesh was not affected by this. He too made a 'demonstration.' " Within a short time after the limited attack began, Hooker telegraphed again to countermand it. Sedgwick called his men back. After nightfall, Sedgwick and his troops saw many fires lighting up the sky along the ridge; many believed that the Confederates were still there in force. With no orders to attack and with few resources to conduct proper reconnaissance, Sedgwick was unable to determine Lee's actual strength.[22]

During the last two days, Lee had correctly analyzed these many halfhearted demonstrations as a mask for Union troop build-ups elsewhere. He decided to leave a holding force of his own at Fredericksburg. Interior lines aided Confederate strategy. To hold Sedgwick in check, Lee called on his grizzled veteran, Maj. Gen. Jubal A. Early, a West Point classmate of Sedgwick. After deciding that Early's corps and a brigade commanded by Brig. Gen. William Barksdale — some 10,000 troops — would suffice to defend his Fredericksburg line, Lee left during the afternoon of May 1, to assume personal command of his main force near Chancellorsville. It was a shrewd gamble on Lee's part; the initiative, as well, had passed to him, as Hooker had immobilized both his left and right wings.

Saturday, May 2, was destined to be a crucial day for the Union forces. Sedgwick saw his forces further stripped. Col. Charles S.

Wainwright, one of Reynolds's artillery officers, graphically jotted down the event, "About seven o'clock this morning an aide of General Sedgwick's came to us, with his horse all in a foam, with orders for the [1st] corps to proceed at once to United States Ford, and join General Hooker."[23] Some mismanagement was clearly evident; although the telegraph line supposedly had been repaired, the message had taken twenty-four hours to reach Sedgwick.

Hooker's delayed order urged that the 1st Corps make a forced march to Chancellorsville to join him by daylight on the same day. Sedgwick simply obeyed orders; if they were delayed, he could do little about it. Included also in this dispatch, dated 1:55 A.M., was an additional order: Hooker wanted the bridges at Franklin's Crossing taken up before daylight. To carry out this order now, in daylight and in full view of the enemy, Sedgwick reasoned, would be poor military strategy. The enemy would realize that they were free to proceed against Hooker. Sedgwick instead sent one division to cover Reynolds's withdrawal across the river and left the bridges intact. Seeing a heavy troop concentration at the bridges, the Confederate batteries shelled Reynolds's departing troops. Sedgwick immediately telegraphed headquarters to report his handling of the situation. No reply came back. With this latest redistribution, Sedgwick's wing was pared down to about 24,000 men — his own 6th Corps plus Brig. Gen. John Gibbon's 2d Division of the 2d Corps. Gibbon still occupied Falmouth.

The relative calm of the last two days was broken by increased activity on the part of skirmishers. During the late afternoon, Sedgwick and his troops heard the din of battle far to their right; all knew that they too would soon be involved in heavy fighting. Two more dispatches came. Sedgwick struggled to understand exactly what Hooker meant. Just before darkness, at 6:30 P.M., Sedgwick received orders, dated 4:10 P.M., to "capture Fredericksburg with everything in it, and vigorously pursue the enemy. We know the enemy is flying." Hooker's second dispatch read, "The major-general commanding directs you to pursue the enemy by the Bowling Green Road."[24]

Something did not add up, Sedgwick thought. For three days, the 6th Corps had had pickets stationed on the Bowling Green Road, which extended south following the river to Bowling Green and Richmond. (The Bowling Green Road, also known as Old Richmond Road or River Road, generally paralleled the Richmond,

Fredericksburg, and Potomac Railroad, where the Confederates were supposedly defending their trains.) Contrary to Hooker's assumption, the enemy was not retreating by Bowling Green Road; Sedgwick's pickets, in fact, saw troops opposing them, and on the previous day, Jackson's troops were marching *up* that road. If Sedgwick were to chase these nonexistent troops down that road, he would be leading his army south and away from Hooker's force. As Sedgwick analyzed the situation, he and his troops again saw the ridge line bright with many fires burning in the darkness. They thought the Confederates were kindling their stores and trains to prevent them from falling into Union hands; the Southerners, however, were setting the torch to their old winter camps. It was difficult for Sedgwick to determine whether the many fires indicated the presence of a large enemy force, or whether they were a ruse of war.

Interpreting Hooker's dispatches in the most practical way, Sedgwick advanced on the right, driving the enemy from the Bowling Green Road and into the woods. The general reestablished his line on this road. A pursuit was pressed. Sedgwick's troops found knapsacks, canteens, haversacks, one or two Bibles, and other equipment abandoned by Early's men in their hasty flight. They also discovered seven "dummys," or stone men, posted on the sides of the road. With all going well, another dispatch, dated 10:10 P.M., was received by Sedgwick about an hour after it was sent. This important (and later controversial) order considerably altered Sedgwick's previous instructions:

> The major-general commanding directs that you cross the Rappahannock at Fredericksburg on the receipt of this order, and at once take up your line of march on the Chancellorsville road until you connect with him. You will attack and destroy any force you may fall in with on the road. You will leave all your trains behind except the pack-mule train of small ammunition, and march to be in the vicinity of the general at daylight. You will probably fall upon the rear of the force commanded by General Lee, and between you and the major-general commanding he expects to use him up.[25]

Hooker did not mention in his dispatch that his military situation was critical during that evening of May 2. Jackson with 32,000

Confederate troops had completely surprised and routed Howard's 11th Corps and was pushing eastward toward Hooker's own head-quarters at Chancellorsville. The desperate order to Sedgwick was an attempt to relieve his own precarious position. Yet this rash dis-patch did not realistically apprise the conditions affecting his left wing. Sedgwick's position was four miles below Fredericksburg and roughly fifteen miles from Chancellorsville. The problems of taking up the bridges, marching up the Stafford Heights side of the river, and relaying the bridges at Fredericksburg would require much time and energy; the Union forces would then have to cross the river at night, capture the town, and assault and carry Marye's Heights before marching west to Chancellorsville. Using sensible judgment, he analyzed the problem: "To recross for the purpose of crossing again at Fredericksburg, where no bridges had been laid, would have occupied until long after daylight. I commenced, therefore, to move by the flank in the direction of Fredericksburg, on the Bowling Green Road."[26] By adjusting Hooker's orders to apply to the actual situation, Sedgwick's decision was militarily sound.

At about 1 A.M., on Sunday, May 3, Sedgwick's column advanced northward with General Newton in the lead. Although bright moonlight aided the march on Bowling Green Road, their advance was slow. The soldiers had to ford Deep Run and Hazel Run, two unbridged streams on the way. At Hazel Run, the enemy made a determined stand with well-placed pickets. Early's men gradually fell back toward Fredericksburg, as four Union brigades struggled to dislodge the Confederates from rifle pits in the town. A delay occurred when a slave came into the Union lines and reported that the enemy was cutting the canals to flood the roads. Sedgwick took time to check out this false rumor.

To combine his forces, Sedgwick authorized Gibbon to lay bridges over the Rappahannock, and Gibbon's unit crossed over to join the 6th Corps in Fredericksburg. Despite minor problems, the general successfully completed the first phase of Hooker's instruc-tions. Sedgwick then directed the placing of batteries to shell Marye's Heights and the deploying of troops, with Howe on the left near Hazel Run and Gibbon on the right. Trying to place his troops more advantageously, Gibbon found his efforts blocked by a canal across his front. Several bridges across the canal had been destroyed by the Confederates. Enemy fire prevented the laying of a new bridge, thus thwarting Gibbon's advance. The dilemma was painfully clear to Sedgwick: the same heights, sunken road, stone wall, and canals that had formed an impregnable defense against Burnside's hammerings were still there. He tersely commented, "Nothing remained but to carry the works by direct assault." With characteristic disregard for his own personal safety, and ignoring the protests of Col. Martin McMahon, Sedgwick rode out from his line for a quick assessment. With bullets whizzing about them, Sedgwick pulled down his old slouch hat and exclaimed to McMahon, "By Heaven, sir, this must not delay us."[27]

On his return, Sedgwick and General Newton and their staffs held a council in an open space at a street intersection. The Union and Confederate artillery were exchanging rounds. An elderly matron, whose brick mansion was in range of the Confederate fire, came out and accosted Sedgwick, saying, "General, I wish you would remove that gun; you are drawing fire right on my house." To this request Sedgwick replied, "Well, madam, if you are afraid, you had better go down cellar."[28] Other regiments were behind churches and houses; the men lay nibbling hardtack as they awaited orders to move.

Guides were needed to lead the Union troops over the heights and on to the Plank Road toward Chancellorsville. Butterfield had already offered his own grisly advice, telegraphing, "Seize the mayor, or any citizen. Put them ahead as guides on pain of death for false information." But Sedgwick did not resort to such inhumane tactics. Calling his personal staff together, he said solemnly, "Now, young gentlemen, here is a chance for you to distinguish yourselves by leading the storming columns."[29] Maj. Thomas Hyde, who understood Sedgwick's sense of humor, realized this suggestion was a joke and hurriedly called back young Capt. Henry Farrar, who had taken the general's words seriously.

Resigned to the grim task at hand, Uncle John looked over the men of the 7th Massachusetts. His expression, according to one soldier, seemed to say, "There will be a thinning out in your ranks very soon." Without uttering a word, the general walked away with a solemn countenance. The order came to pile up knapsacks; soldiers began to form in line as the head of storming columns. No one dreaded this moment more than Sedgwick.[30]

Realizing that the heights would have to be taken by direct assault, Sedgwick was unable to devise intricate military strategy. Lack of time and the nature of the topography prevented such an opportunity. Sedgwick called his chief subordinates over for a conference and told them their assignments. The left assault column, under Col. George C. Spear, contained the 61st Pennsylvania and 43d New York regiments. On the right, Col. Thomas D. Johns commanded the men of the 7th Massachusetts and the 36th Massachusetts. The task of securing the line of battle was the responsibility of Col. Hiram Burnham of the 6th Maine.

After leaving the general, Burnham rode down to his command, lying in the ditches, and said, "Boys, I have got a government contract."

The men shouted, "What is it, Colonel?"

"One thousand rebels, potted and salted, and got to have 'em in less than five minutes," answered Burnham. "Forward! Guide centre!"[31]

Before leading his column, Spear called together all the sergeants of the 61st Pennsylvania and explained their proposed movement. "You are dismissed and God bless you," Spear said.[32]

Sedgwick could do no more; all that remained was to give the command and hope the assault would be successful.

The time was 11 A.M. The day was very warm. Everything was ready. The Union line of battle was 300 yards below the stone wall. From the garden of a brick residence on the outskirts, with a full view, Sedgwick and Newton waited. Then Sedgwick cried, "Forward!" The storming columns moved up double-quick without firing a shot. The Union artillery trained its fire on the Confederate positions. When the two attacking columns approached, the covering fire ceased. From their defenses, the Confederates — comprised mostly of Mississippi regiments — returned the fire. When the Union troops came within range, they used their muskets. The right column was almost swept away, and Spear was killed. The head of Johns's left column was checked, broken for a moment "as bullet and canister cut up the ground." There were cries of retreat, but some yelled, "Forward! Don't go back! We shan't get so close again." Rallying his men, Johns fell shortly thereafter, but was not disabled. Johns later commented, "I got my men up the third time, and we went right ahead and did not stop at all. We pushed right ahead." Near the stone wall, Johns fell, severely wounded, and was carried off the field. Burnham fell wounded from his horse. Sedgwick and Newton watched this terrible scene in silence.[33]

Some soldiers of the 7th Massachusetts, taking a breathing spell behind a high board fence, caught a glimpse of the Confederate right flank. It lay unprotected. One of the Massachusetts officers requested a brief truce to remove his dead and wounded in front of the 18th Mississippi line. Without consulting his brigade commander Col. Thomas M. Griffin of the Mississippi regiment granted this request. Griffin's men allowed themselves to be seen as the wounded Northerners were being carried away. Studying carefully the vulnerability of the defense, the concealed Union soldiers notified the attackers. On the next charge in this sector, troops cried out, "Massachusetts colors to the front," as they slammed into the enemy's flank and turned it.

Sedgwick's staff performed remarkably during the assault, rallying their disorganized units. Col. Thomas S. Allen, Burnham's replacement, inspired his men, saying, "When the signal, 'Forward,' is given, you will start at double-quick, you will not fire a gun, and you will not stop until you get the order to halt. You will never get that order."[34]

Capt. Richard Halsted, standing with Sedgwick to observe the attack, described the terrible scene:

> The whole force moved on steadily, magnificently, without firing a shot, the men dropping like leaves in autumn. Their approach to the works seemed, from where we stood watching, terribly slow. Every second that the dreadful fire continued diminished the strength of the attacking party by scores. One portion of the force almost seemed to come to a halt just on the edge of the sunken road. . . . It was a very anxious moment; but it was only a moment, directly in front of the batteries. One single color (that of the 6th Maine) never for one second faltered until the very crest of the heights was gained, and it became a sign of victory and a rallying-point for the men who had met more obstacles in their way. There were only a few of us gathered about the General at this moment, but a cheer, weak as it was, could not be refused.[35]

Many lay dead in this charge, but few faltered. Reaching the top, the victorious Union attackers used the bayonet and the butt of the musket. As the stone wall was overrun, many Confederates became panic-stricken. In their flight they threw away all their equipment; nevertheless, many were not fast enough and were captured. Seventeen pieces of artillery were also taken. At the crest, the 6th Maine captured the famous Washington Artillery of the Confederate Army. The commander of the battery remarked, "Boys, you have captured the best battery in the Confederate service." As the 5th Wisconsin overwhelmed the Confederate fortifications, a few fanatical Southerners refused to lay down their arms, even after seeing that they were completely outnumbered. One Confederate challenged the Yankees to shoot him, saying he would never surrender. Within moments, a dozen Union riflemen took the defiant soldier for his word and shot him.

The charge was over in only ten or fifteen minutes. Sedgwick's desperate assault had succeeded. The capture of Marye's Heights was the crowning point of his Civil War career.

The work of the 6th Corps was not yet done, however, as the Confederates still controlled a second crest, which was covered by enfilading fire from the batteries on Lee's Hill. Newton, with the 2d Vermont and the 26th New York regiments, advanced on the crest. After resting a few moments in old Confederate rifle pits, the men of the 2d Vermont heard their brigade commander, Col. Lewis Grant, tell them, "Up now, my brave boys, and give it to them." Several charges were halted at great cost before the two regiments received reinforcements and finally overran the second crest. Other Vermont troops captured Lee's Hill on the Confederate right. The whole plateau was a scene of fleeing soldiers, riderless horses, and runaway artillery and wagon trains. Sedgwick had won a magnificent victory, but only a portion of Hooker's instructions had been completed.[36]

The victory had cost the 6th Corps an estimated 1,500 men, or about 7 percent of its total strength. Hyde recalled, "The green slope was dotted all over with still forms in blue, and the prisoners were streaming down the hill in hundreds." The Confederate losses in dead and wounded are not recorded, but Early lost 1,500 in prisoners alone. Hyde collected these men and marched them into Fredericksburg. Many Union soldiers carried their wounded comrades to the churches and private homes in the town, and surgeons began immediately to administer medical treatment. Before nightfall, over 3,000 wounded had been brought into Fredericksburg. The successful attacking columns, exhausted by the night march and the assaults, were allowed to halt for a short time. Many soldiers fell asleep, while others made coffee and ate their first meal that day.

To avoid complete disorder and excessive straggling, Sedgwick wisely allowed his scattered men to regroup before continuing.[37]

Sedgwick prepared to march westward on the Orange Plank Road toward Chancellorsville, now ten miles away. He faced a dilemma. According to orthodox military tactics, Sedgwick, having broken a portion of the enemy's line, should now turn on the separate fractions and disperse them before safely pursuing the retreating force. He could turn on the scattered remnants of Early's force in the environs of Fredericksburg and perhaps destroy the enemy depot at Hamilton's Crossing to the south. But the objective was to march westward toward Chancellorsville, and not to run down the enemy to the south and north. In carrying out Hooker's orders, Sedgwick knowingly allowed Early's and Barksdale's scattered and disorganized troops to retreat and reform to the west of Fredericksburg. As Col. Selden Connor assessed the problem, "We had not the force to hold the heights and *advance too*. So we had to obey orders and advance, leaving the heights unoccupied."[38]

At 1 P.M., Brig. Gen. Gouverneur K. Warren, accompanying the Union left wing, reported the victory at Marye's Heights to Butterfield and added, "The Sixth Corps is in splendid spirits." Butterfield transmitted this message on to Hooker at 2:30 P.M. A short time later, a dispatch from Chancellorsville notified Butterfield that his commanding general had been slightly wounded earlier that morning at his Chancellor House headquarters. Unbeknown to Sedgwick, Hooker's injuries about the side and head had temporarily (perhaps permanently) disabled him to the extent that he could not command his army. For the next two days, Sedgwick would receive either belated or confusing messages from Hooker, for the wounded general would not relinquish his command.[39]

After a two-hour rest, the men received Sedgwick's command to march west to join Hooker's troops. Slow in getting started, Sedgwick could have begun his advance earlier. Without a rest, however, his men might have melted away on the road from fatigue and heat. Advancing on the Orange Plank Road, the general met with his division officers near the Guest House about 2 P.M. As Brooks's division seemed to be the freshest, Sedgwick placed these troops at the head of the column, with Howe's and Newton's soldiers in the rear.

The general was compelled to move ahead cautiously with his

skirmishers well in advance; the Confederates had carried off a few pieces of artillery and were taking advantage of every good defensive position in the rolling countryside. Sedgwick halted his corps periodically to dodge shelling and finally had to call up his artillery to silence the enemy batteries. "All this took time, valuable time," explained Halsted. "The ground was undulating, and here and there slightly wooded. We went on slowly but carefully, so as not be drawn into any trap."[40] The Confederates simply fell back with their advantage of interior lines, while Sedgwick was forced to pursue over unfamiliar territory. He attempted to heed Hooker's timetable and yet avoid heavy losses, as he had no replacements.

Four miles west of Fredericksburg, the Federal troops approached Salem Church, a small red-brick building situated on a ridge covered with dense woods and undergrowth. It was a perfect place for Early's men to make a stand. At 3:25 P.M., the 6th Corps clashed with dismounted Confederate cavalry. After fighting a rear-guard action, these advance Southern troops fell back to the main defensive line along the Salem Heights ridge. Sensing that Hooker's wing of the Union army would not advance again, Lee had sent four available brigades (one from Banks's Ford and the others from the Chancellorsville front) to halt the Union advance at Salem Church. Early and the leader of the relief forces, Maj. Gen. Lafayette McLaws, commanded about 10,000 men with twenty-two pieces of artillery. Against this heavily reinforced line, Sedgwick was facing a situation similar to the one he had already encountered at Marye's Heights, but he now had fewer men to form assaulting columns. Two major battles in less than half a day was even more than Fighting Joe Hooker would attempt; however, he expected Sedgwick to fight on indefinitely.

Realizing his vulnerability, Sedgwick made provisions to save his command. Despite roving bands of Confederate cavalry, he succeeded in maintaining the ground northward to Banks's Ford to enable communication with Butterfield. Aides contacted General Benham, now sober, who built a pontoon bridge across the Rappahannock. Sedgwick concentrated his troop strength at Salem Church and decided he could not waste men defending Fredericksburg. Butterfield had prohibited signaling because he believed the messages would be intercepted by the enemy. To solve this serious communication problem, Sedgwick sent Warren during the afternoon to report to Hooker's headquarters. These actions, intelligently ordered when there was still time, provided Sedgwick an escape route in an emergency.

Sedgwick's advance beyond Fredericksburg halted after four miles. For the rest of the afternoon, the 6th Corps was unable to penetrate the Southern defenses at Salem Church. After the Union artillery had shelled the Confederate battle line, Brooks's division made an assault. Shooting at a range of eighty yards, some Alabama regiments almost broke the column. Brooks's second brigade momentarily gained the heights and captured a schoolhouse, but another Alabama regiment, held in reserve, was thrown in at the cirtical moment and repulsed the Union drive. Powder smoke filled the air. As they were falling back, Brooks's men saw Salem Church through a clearing of the smoke. From the windows in the building, Confederate riflemen were shooting with a destructive fire. To prevent a sustained enemy counterattack, Sedgwick himself supervised the placing of batteries to anchor his line. By nightfall, the fighting ended. The Union forces lost about 1,500 men during this battle; Confederate casualties are unknown. Despite the general's determined efforts to break through and advance toward Chancellorsville, his decimated corps was too weakened to achieve a success.

Although the fighting was over for the day, Sedgwick and his men sensed no relief. The wounded were sent back to Fredericksburg. Sedgwick's men could hear the shrieks and cries of the wounded men who could not be reached by relief parties. During the warm night, the woods caught fire, and many wounded perished in the flames. The 6th Corps men lay down with their arms and tried to sleep. Many Federal soldiers were without food or coffee. One wrote:

> We slept in line that night with the dead of the day's battle lying near us. The stretcher bearers with their lamps wandered here and there over the field, picking up the wounded, and loaded ambulances rattled dismally over the broken plank road. . . . Sedgwick scarcely slept that night. From time to time he dictated a dispatch to General Hooker. He would walk for a few paces apart and listen; then returning would lie down again in the damp grass, with his saddle for a pillow and try to sleep. The night was inexpressibly gloomy.

Fires were not allowed to be lighted, and there was not even the excitement of a picket alarm to relieve the singular stillness.[41]

Sedgwick remained all night by the roadside just behind Williston's battery. He knew from the rumbling of wheels that Lee was diligently reinforcing his Salem Heights line. With his corps facing in three directions, forward, to the left, and back toward Fredericksburg, Sedgwick sensed that he was being surrounded.

At 6:30 in the morning, on Monday, May 4, the general received a startling dispatch from Warren. On arrival at Hooker's headquarters at about 11 o'clock that night, Warren had awakened his injured commanding officer and reported Sedgwick's situation. Warren asked him if he had any instructions for his 6th Corps commander, and Hooker answered, "None." Assuming responsibility himself, the tired Warren had telegraphed this key dispatch at midnight:

> I find everything snug here. We contracted the lines a little and repulsed the last assault with ease. General Hooker wishes them to attack him tomorrow; if they will, he does not desire you to attack again in force unless he attacks him at the same time. He says you are too far away for him to direct. Look well to the safety of your corps, and keep up communication with General Benham at Banks's Ford or Fredericksburg. You can go to either place you think best; but Banks's Ford would bring you in supporting distance of the main body, and would be better than falling back to Fredericksburg.[42]

The communications were again faulty and inefficient, and this dispatch reached Sedgwick six hours after it was sent. No further news or orders were received from Hooker during most of the day. It was obvious to Sedgwick, and to his men, that Hooker could not be counted on for relief. Faced with this indifference, the 6th Corps had to fend for itself. Banks's Ford was the most obvious route in case of retreat.

With brilliant strategy, Lee gambled that his Chancellorsville front would remain stationary, and he left with the bulk of his army on a march to Salem Heights. Only one Southern corps, now commanded by Stuart replacing the mortally wounded Jackson, was left

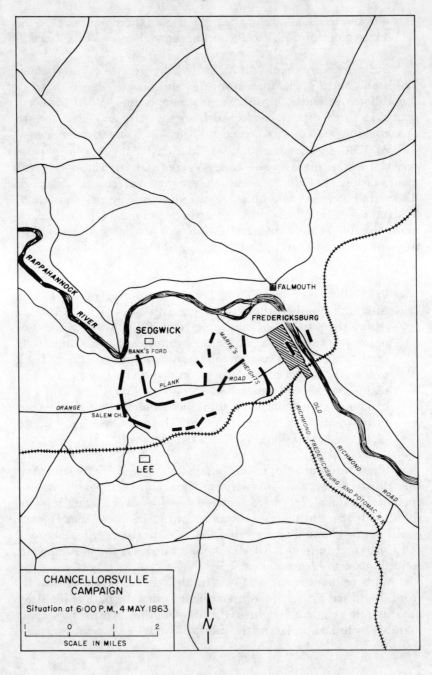

CHANCELLORSVILLE
CAMPAIGN

Situation at 6:00 P.M., 4 MAY 1863

SCALE IN MILES

behind to face Hooker. During the morning, Sedgwick saw this numerically superior Confederate force enclose him on three sides with only the ground toward Banks's Ford secured as an escape route. The necessary abandonment of Fredericksburg and Marye's Heights, which had cost so many Union lives, sickened Sedgwick's staff officers. Sedgwick was confronted with the distinct possibility that his entire corps might be annihilated.

The morning became increasingly hot. Cannonading from Confederate artillery struck Sedgwick's rear line; the enemy had recaptured Marye's Heights and was pushing westward with a strong force. The general sent Hyde to Banks's Ford with a message and reopened contact with Butterfield. On his return to Salem Church, Hyde learned the Southern army was tightening its noose to surround Sedgwick's troops. It would be necessary for the 6th Corps to cut its way through to escape at the ford. Confederate prisoners openly boasted to their captors that the Federal troops would be driven into the river. The situation looked increasingly ominous.

A young staff officer, who enjoyed a frank and open relationship with Sedgwick, remarked, "General, it looks as if the Sixth Corps was going to close its career today."

"It has somewhat that appearance," said Uncle John.

"Then," continued the aide, "if the Sixth Corps goes out of existence today, I hope it will be with a blaze of glory that will light the history of this war for all time."

Sedgwick smiled and said, "I will tell you a secret; there will be no surrendering."[43]

Sedgwick's ten-mile battle line, defended with a force of about 18,000 men, was formed in the shape of a horseshoe, with both flanks resting on the Rappahannock River above and below Banks's Ford. Brooks and Newton faced their men toward Chancellorsville; Howe extended his division from the Plank Road on which they had marched from Fredericksburg to the river. From Confederate deserters, Sedgwick learned that Lee had 40,000 troops to throw in against him. In spite of Lee's numerical superiority, Sedgwick was blessed with unexpected luck. Lee overestimated his opponent's strength, as he believed that Sedgwick still retained Reynolds's corps. Hesitant to attack, the Confederate leader spent most of the day getting his troops into position. This reconnoitering gave Sedgwick valuable time; he announced to his troops that "the emergency of the case is such, that a regiment must do the work of a brigade."[44]

The waiting frayed the nerves of the Federal soldiers. Col. Moses Tyler remembered, "All the afternoon we watched the Rebels moving through the woods on our front, and every now and then uttering the Rebel yell, at times apparently forming into lines of battle and preparing for attack. It was one of the most anxious six or seven hours that I ever spent."[45] Sedgwick, however, was patiently waiting for Hooker's permission to withdraw and for the coming of darkness to facilitate escape.

In late afternoon, Lee finally attacked what he considered to be Sedgwick's weakest point — Howe's division facing Fredericksburg. Hyde, who was delivering a message in this area heard the Rebel yell from the woods, and suddenly the whole hillside was alive with charging troops. The Confederate batteries aimed ahead of the advance. General Lee was seen personally directing the charge. Sedgwick was facing his third major battle within two days.

Sympathy and concern for Sedgwick and his men prevailed among the other Union troops secure in their trenches on the Chancellorsville line. Pvt. Josiah D. Hicks of the 125th Pennsylvania recalled, "Whilst we lay in the woods hiding, we could hear the report of the firing of Sedgwick's men . . . as the sound grew further away, we knew this battle was going against our men. By evening the sounds became quite distant." Col. Charles S. Wainwright was baffled by Hooker's failure to come to Sedgwick's aid: "We did nothing all day, though the noise of the attack on Sedgwick was plainly heard along our whole line for several hours before dark. Why we did not move I cannot say."[46] Sedgwick's haunting doubts were realized; he was left to extricate himself from this trap without help from Hooker. Fighting Joe, paralyzed in mind and deed, belied his famous nickname.

Lee's attack on Sedgwick's line was fierce: three divisions charged out of a ravine against Howe's defenses. Most Union regiments withstood the shock, but a German unit buckled in retreat. Seeing this massive attack, Hyde immediately rode "hatless and breathless" on his fast horse to inform Sedgwick. Standing in the road with General Newton, Sedgwick asked Hyde, "What force is attacking us?"

"About as many as corps showed on the last review [20,000 men]," he answered.[47] Carrying out orders, Hyde then led Brig. Gen. Frank Wheaton's brigade to reinforce Howe.

The Union soldiers gallantly resisted and repulsed the Southern attack. The coming darkness, a concealed second battle line, and broken-up terrain worked to the advantage of the 6th Corps. With a rising full moon, the Union artillerymen could see the advancing enemy almost as well as in the daytime. Pvt. Wilbur Fisk, watching the artillery firing, observed, "At every discharge the grape could be heard rattling against the trees like throwing a handful of pebbles against the side of a building. No enemy could stand such a fire, and they were soon driven back."[48] Exact Confederate casualties are unknown, but they suffered fearful losses. Several hundred prisoners were captured by the 6th Corps. Nevertheless, 1,000 Union soldiers were killed defending this crest.

Sedgwick wisely decided to retract his line preparatory for a general retreat. About 6:45 P.M., he issued orders for a withdrawal. All noncombatants, except surgeons and wounded, were sent toward Banks's Ford. His men were able to carry off many wounded soldiers, but Uncle John was forced to leave the dead unburied on the field.

The arrangements for defense were entrusted to Newton, a skilled engineering officer. Newton prepared defenses on the high ground in front of Banks's Ford, and coordinated his plans with General Benham. Benham realized the need for another bridge and completed one at the ford by 10 P.M. A friendly fog settled on the ground in the vicinity of the river and helped hide the Union activities.

Time was running out. After exchanging many messages with Hooker's staff officers and receiving no satisfactory answer, Sedgwick bluntly explained at 11:50 P.M.: "My army is hemmed in upon the slope. . . . If I had only this army to care for, I would withdraw it tonight. Do your operations require that I should jeopardize it by retaining it here? An immediate reply is indispensable, or I may feel obliged to withdraw."[49]

While these exchanges were going on, the entire 6th Corps, closely pursued by the enemy, fell back successfully to a perimeter around Banks's Ford. Withdrawing the picket line in front and on the left of Salem Heights ridge, Brig. Gen. David A. Russell of Brooks's division dismounted and warned his troops, "Quietly, men, quietly; don't make any noise." The jingle of canteens and other unavoidable sounds had revealed the withdrawal to the enemy. The Union soldiers on this rear-guard action ran on the double-quick to join the main troop concentration near the ford. After a run of two

miles in the heat of the unseasonably warm evening, many men collapsed on reaching the rifle pits near the Rappahannock. Two or
three dropped dead of exhaustion. Confederate batteries were firing
from several directions, but these shells missed both the men and the
bridges.[50]

Sedgwick was momentarily expecting Hooker's authorization to
cross the river, and he finally did receive a message. Hooker ordered
Sedgwick to remain where he was. In the early morning of Tuesday,
May 5, Sedgwick replied, "I shall hold my position as ordered on the
south of Rappahannock." At 2 A.M., however, Butterfield notified
the 6th Corps commander, "Withdraw, cover the river, and prevent
any force crossing." At long last, the general sent his battered command across the pontoon bridges. The 5th Maine was the last regiment to walk across to safety. At 3:20 A.M., Sedgwick received still
another message from Hooker, dated 1:20 A.M., which stated,
"Order to withdraw countermanded." Realizing this order was
wholly impracticable, Sedgwick telegraphed that fact to his commander. The bridges at the ford were immediately taken up.[51]

The harrowing ordeal was not yet over for Sedgwick's
exhausted troops. Still hearing the screech of artillery shells, the
tired men had to move many times during the night to escape the
areas of bombardment. They ducked barrages throughout the night.
Toward daybreak, there was a pouring rainstorm. The men could
rejoice that they were alive, but not much beyond that.

Since the original movement to Franklin's Crossing, the forty-
nine-year-old Sedgwick had been on his feet for practically a week.
Speaking for Sedgwick and indeed for the entire 6th Corps, Halsted
commented on the psychological effects of the fighting: "In such
times one lives on excitement. Eating and drinking is too insignifi-
cant a matter to think about. As for sleep, a few minutes thrown in
here and there seem to be quite sufficient for the needs of nature."[52]
Three months of training and preparations had been expended in
seven days of hard fighting; considering his losses, Sedgwick must
have wondered if it were worth the staggering price.

Hooker and his main striking force recrossed the Rappahannock during the night of May 5, and the Army of the Potomac took
up its old position at Falmouth. The battle of the Chancellorsville
campaign was over. The Army of the Potomac, with 133,868 men
present for duty, lost a total of 17,278 in casualties, or 13 percent of
its strength. The 6th Corps alone lost 4,610, or 19 percent of its

original force. Lee's Army of Northern Virginia of 60,892 men was reduced by 12,821 men — 22 percent. Although Chancellorsville was not a repetition of the easy 1862 Fredericksburg battle, Lee had won a great victory. Confidence and morale in the North were greatly shaken.

Sedgwick submitted his official battle report on May 7. In direct prose he defended his corps' operation in the campaign, praised his officers and men, and cast no blame on anyone. Privately, however, the general believed that he and his corps would be criticized. To his sister, two days later, he confided, "I have received nothing but congratulations for the splendid conduct of my corps — except the General, and he dare not come out boldly and accuse me or my corps of any want of skill in handling or bad behavior on the part of the men. I will not attempt to say where the fault lay. It will some day be exposed."[53]

Almost a year later, before the Joint Congressional Committee on the Conduct of the War, which was dominated by Radical Republicans favorable to Hooker, Sedgwick defended his conduct in the Chancellorsville operation. Shrewdly interspersing his testimony with the actual dispatches he had sent and received, Sedgwick groused about Hooker's complete inactivity while the 6th Corps was at Salem Heights. He explained, "I believed that if he [Hooker] had ordered an advance they could have gone right through. I can offer no explanation why he did not attack, and I cannot tell why he withdrew."[54]

To the day of his death, Hooker was convinced that Sedgwick had deliberately failed him in carrying out orders and should be branded for the Union defeat. On May 11, Captain Halsted saw Hooker personally and mentioned Sedgwick's hard fight. Hooker remarked in a very disagreeable way that he had heard of it, and said, "There were very few troops in front of you, however." Halsted quickly left. Less than a month after the battle, Colonel Wainwright and other high-ranking Union officers heard Hooker's version. Wainwright recorded, in disgust, "He [Hooker] was very bitter against 'Uncle John,' accusing him of being slow and afraid to fight; also of disobeying orders directly."[55]

Hooker repeated his story before the Joint Congressional Committee on the Conduct of the War. The Radical Republicans pampered Hooker, their pet general, and did everything possible to bolster his reputation. On Sedgwick's performance, Hooker contended, "He was a perfectly brave man, and a good one; but when it came to maneuvering troops, or judging of positions for them, in my judgment, he was not able or expert." After listening to the testimony of many army officers, the committee exonerated Hooker and cast Sedgwick in the role of scapegoat. His movement toward Chancellorsville, the Radicals insisted, was "made without promptness and energy, was executed but partially, and proved entirely ineffective for the purpose for which it was ordered."[56] Despite their harsh judgment, Sedgwick still retained command of the 6th Corps and was vindicated by the vast majority of military and civilian leaders. Hooker was unable to undermine his reputation.

Sedgwick clearly had been put in a cruel position during the night of May 2, when he received Hooker's order to advance. Fighting Joe had asked for an impossible military feat. This thought was obviously on Sedgwick's mind when he encountered Hooker at Falmouth shortly after the battle. A stormy scene occurred between the two men. Sedgwick told Hooker that the commanding general's reports were a pack of lies. The Army of the Potomac was tragically reduced to petty bickering and personality clashes. The battle retains its controversial flavor to this day.

Most writers are strangely mute on Sedgwick's role in the Chancellorsville campaign. To them, Sedgwick's marches and battles were merely a sideshow. In two rare comments on this phase, William Swinton, a perceptive war correspondent, and Walter Hebert, Hooker's biographer, agree that Sedgwick's storming of the heights represented a brilliant exploit. In his analysis, Martin T. McMahon strongly defends his old commander, declaring, "Any man who says that the failure could in any degree whatever be attributed to Sedgwick, insults every soldier of his command and dishonors the memory of the dead."[57]

Perhaps the best compliment to Sedgwick and his men came from the Confederate pickets who called across the Rappahannock that none of the Union army could ever cross the river again except "the fellows who took those heights."[58] But this past glory offered Sedgwick and his 6th Corps little consolation as they marched back nine miles in rain and mud to their White Oak Church headquarters. They had to begin their work all over again.

CHAPTER 4

A NIGHT MARCH
TO GETTYSBURG

AT THEIR WHITE Oak Church headquarters, Sedgwick and the 6th Corps began the herculean task of reorganization. Problems of every kind had to be solved. The Chancellorsville defeat had caused dissension to spread within the Union forces; units blamed one another for not doing their job. "The good feeling between the different corps was sensibly weakened," wrote one officer. The attitude toward General Hooker was "We have no further use for you." Many considered him a failure.[1]

On the morning of May 7, 1863, President Lincoln and General Halleck arrived at Falmouth to discuss matters with Hooker and his officers. With characteristic patience and tact, Lincoln refused to single out anybody to blame for the defeat and did not relieve Hooker. Over lunch, the president and his general in chief talked with the corps commanders. Sedgwick attended and heard the president explain "that the disaster was one that could not be helped."[2] In spite of its losses, the Army of the Potomac still totaled about 100,000 men. But the question remained: Who was the best qualified general to lead these men?

Speculation that Hooker would be replaced was common talk within the army and appeared openly in the Northern press. There were rumors that McClellan might be coming back. Returning to their old camps after the recent campaign, Maj. Gen. Darius N. Couch and Sedgwick mutually agreed that "Hooker's removal was but a question of time; the next thing was, who would be his successor." Couch named Maj. Gen. George G. Meade as the best fitted of the corps commanders to be elevated to commander of the Army of the Potomac. Sedgwick made no reply, and from his subsequent remarks Couch concluded that Uncle John "was not averse to having the place himself."[3]

Many stories, evoking the romance of a campfire rumor, state that Sedgwick was at this time offered the command of the Army of the Potomac. Other variations suggest a later date. No reliable evidence supports these assertions. It is, nevertheless, a personal and professional tribute to Sedgwick by his contemporaries to hold him in such high esteem as a potential candidate for this post.

Sedgwick himself dismissed such loose talk. "I know my name has been mentioned," he confided to his sister late in 1863, "and I think I could have had it if I had said the word, but nothing could induce me to take it."[4]

During his brief visit to Falmouth, it is clear that President Lincoln had no immediate plans to replace Hooker. Lincoln met with the corps commanders in a group and did not hold personal talks with any of them. When asked about his opinion of this matter, Sedgwick exclaimed, "Why, Meade is the proper one to command this army."[5]

Shortly after the president's visit, Sedgwick, along with Couch and Maj. Gen. Henry W. Slocum, indicated their lack of faith in Hooker's leadership and sent word to Meade that they were willing to serve under him. With admirable personal sacrifice, these senior officers placed the interests of the Union above their own professional careers. Meade himself did not seek the position and was reluctant to undermine Hooker. Yet Sedgwick still felt, "There must be some change. I hope it may be such a one as will satisfy the army."[6]

The troops of the 6th Corps had more pressing things on their minds than worry about idle rumors concerning the problem of the high command. On May 10, several 6th Corps officers made arrangements with Confederate authorities to transport 1,500–1,600 wounded Union soldiers at Lacy House (now serving as a hospital) across the Rappahannock under a flag of truce. As the Confederates had taxed their own ambulance system to the breaking point in conveying their own casualties, they permitted a large number of Union ambulances to pick up the Federal wounded for the trip across the

river. Always a humanitarian, Sedgwick sent his injured men immediately to various Union field hospitals.

Sedgwick struggled to maintain the numerical strength of his
corps. The Army of the Potomac was discharging one thousand men
a day, which would accrue at this rate to thirty thousand men by
June 15. Reinforcements were not coming in. To his regret,
Sedgwick lost his Light Brigade on May 11. This famous unit was
split up and reassigned to other divisions because those soldiers who
had enlisted for thirty-three months were discharged from service.
This action caused general depression throughout the corps, but
Sedgwick could do nothing about it. The strength of his 24,000-man
corps dipped to about 18,000.

Another problem involved the chronic poor health of his 1st
Division commander, Maj. Gen. William T. H. Brooks. He left the
6th Corps for a desk job as commander of the Department of the
Monongahela. The War Department replaced him with Brig. Gen.
Horatio G. Wright. A native of Connecticut and second in his class
of 1841 at West Point, Wright had commanded the Department of
the Ohio on his previous assignment. He made a favorable impression on Sedgwick when he arrived at White Oak Church during late
May.

The hygenic conditions of the 6th Corps, and indeed the whole
army, became intolerable. After the troops had lived in the same
area for months, the garbage, the dead mules and horses, the half-
buried entrails of cattle slaughtered for food, and the polluted
drinking water compelled moves to new sites to prevent epidemics.
The 6th Corps moved a mile in back of its old encampment to a better site. Located in a grove about five miles from Aquia Creek, the
new area had a good water supply and plenty of wood for fires. This
move also gave the men a chance to burn off excess energy.

During this lull, with plenty of work still to be done, Hooker
went to Washington for consultation, leaving Sedgwick in command
by reason of his seniority. His main problem was to combat the
growing boredom among his soldiers. He held a division review on
May 20, showing the men his personal interest in their welfare and
problems. The hot weather affected many soldiers and sapped their
energies. Pickets came in almost melted. Lt. James W. Latta
observed: "Stayed around camp all day, weather almost intolerable,
nothing of interest transpiring, the dull monotony of camp life
continues; the occasional distant shouts of troops whose terms of

enlistment have expired may be heard day after day."[7] Both Sedgwick and Lee suspended campaigning during this heat wave.

Another problem stemmed from the practice of the Confederate pickets fishing from the south bank of the Rappahannock. Regular squads from Lee's army were detailed to this duty to supplement the generally meager diet. Soon some inhabitants from the Falmouth side began to cross the river for the avowed purpose of buying fish. Sedgwick viewed this apparently innocent practice as a stratagem. Although these civilians were closely watched, he believed they were passing on information to the Confederates. Sedgwick sent a note to General Lee to stop this fishing business and to thus cut off communications between the two armies.

As camp life continued in this relaxed atmosphere, Sedgwick encouraged his corps to keep active with games and sports. Capt. E. B. Beaumont built a riding course, and the general's staff enjoyed cutting dummy heads with the saber at full speed. With indulgence, Uncle John watched many cockfights. The pace became so leisurely that the Vermonters of Maj. Gen. Albion Howe's division built a special hall for a dance that was attended by ten wives on a temporary visit to their husbands. Ice cream from Washington was brought in for the occasion.

In a letter home, Sedgwick explained the reason for this inactivity:

> We cannot move at present, unless Lee forces us by some demonstration towards Maryland. Our troops are in fine condition, and all we want is to have our regiments filled up. There is no earnestness at the North. Governors only think about sending new regiments, and the number of appointments it will give them.[8]

But General Lee ended the month-long lull. Shortly after the Chancellorsville battle, Lt. Gen. James Longstreet had joined Lee at his Fredericksburg headquarters. Together, they worked out plans to invade the North for a second time. Lee hoped this campaign into Maryland and Pennsylvania, if successful, would draw many Federal troops from Maj. Gen. Ulysses S. Grant's army, now surrounding Vicksburg, Mississippi, and the besieged city might be saved.

By May 27, Hooker had learned from deserters that Longstreet had joined Lee; he sensed a surprise attack might be in the making. Hooker did not want to resume the offensive; he wanted Lee to show his hand. It was not a long wait. On June 3, Lee began to withdraw his army from Fredericksburg for a concentration at Culpeper Court House to the northwest.

The following day, June 4, Hooker, who was aware of the Confederate moves, decided the proper strategy was to attack Lee's rear columns. This action, he thought, would stop any Confederate invasion by threatening Lee's line of communications to Richmond. To check out his intelligence, Hooker decided to probe the enemy's strength across the river. At 7 A.M. on June 5, Butterfield ordered Sedgwick to "hold your command in readiness to march at short notice; that you furnish any assistance required by General Benham in throwing a bridge across the Rappahannock."[9] For the third time within six months, the Army of the Potomac prepared to lay bridges at Franklin's Crossing to secure the opposite bank just below the mouth of Deep Run. By 5 P.M., all the batteries of the 6th Corps except one were moved to the brow of Falmouth Heights and had begun a brisk shelling of the Confederate breastworks.

The next morning, June 6, Sedgwick selected Howe's 2d Division to make a reconnaissance in force. The 26th New Jersey and the 5th Vermont infantry regiments led the attack. Wives of the Vermont officers, who had been dancing just a few nights ago, now had the novel sensation of watching from the relative safety of the opposite bluffs as their husbands went into action. As he viewed the preliminary proceedings, Howe realized that the bridges could not be laid without serious loss; he therefore directed Col. Lewis Grant of the Vermonters to cross the river in pontoon boats. Grant's men soon crossed, drove out the Florida troops from their rifle pits, and secured the south bank for the construction of bridges.

At 10:30 A.M., from his temporary headquarters at Upper Bernard House on the south bank, Sedgwick reported to Butterfield, "Our pickets are on the Bowling Green road. . . . I cannot move 200 yards without bringing a general fight. Before bringing over the rest of my corps, I await orders. . . . A contraband reports that Generals Lee and Longstreet were at this place last night. All the prisoners confirm this information."[10] Visiting the front himself, Hooker did not want to precipitate a general engagement, so Sedgwick did not advance farther. With all available intelligence, Sedgwick judged that Lee was still holding his Fredericksburg lines in force. It was a difficult decision to make — one on which Hooker had to devise his entire strategy.

It was obvious to the reconnaissance force that the Confederates were still there. In this action, Sedgwick lost fifty-seven men, including nine killed. Howe's division took about thirty-five prisoners. Lively cannonading continued across the river, with both sides firing away. The Confederates fired a powerful Whitworth gun from such a distance that neither the smoke nor the sound of its explosion could be perceived. The only announcement of its presence was the scream of the steel projectile. A member of Sedgwick's staff asked him, "General, I would like to know if there is anything you are afraid of." Uncle John replied, "I don't like these Whitworth bolts."[11]

This probe energized the men again. "It was an exciting and brilliant affair. . . . Officers and men behaved as becomes Vermonters during the entire time," wrote Col. Lewis Grant. After the fighting died down, the Union reconnaissance force saw many Southern troops on its front. Soon an informal truce began, and Howe's men exchanged sugar and coffee for tobacco. The Confederates also received a bonus — religious tracts to convince them "of the error of their ways, and desist from further fighting."[12] Howe's order stopped these exchanges.

On June 7, Sedgwick undoubtedly began to question his original estimate of the enemy forces. During the day the constant marching and countermarching of the Confederates appeared to indicate the presence of a strong force. But this activity was discovered to be a ruse, as balloonists and deserters indicated that the main Confederate force was slipping away.

The mystery surrounding Lee's exact movements extended throughout the Army of the Potomac. General Hooker kept telegraphing Washington, attempting to convince Lincoln of the validity of his plans to strike against Richmond. On June 8, Meade wrote, "Both Lee and Hooker appear to be playing at cross-purposes." A lieutenant colonel of the Army of the Potomac graphically depicted the "hurry-up-and-wait" atmosphere during early June:

> We were sold again. After turning out at midnight and packing our traps, and preparing for a battle which somebody

seemed to think impending, our orders were countermanded. So we have rebuilt our canvas cities and settled down again. The fact is, somebody is very much exercised lest the terrible Lee may do something dangerous. Three times now of late this army has been turned out of house and home to lie sweltering in the sun, only to have its marching orders countermanded. The boys have long ago learned to take such things philosophically. They tear down and build up cheerfully, with the shrewd observation that "it is only Johnny Reb fooling the balloon again."[13]

General Hooker did not receive Lincoln's permission to advance toward Richmond, and he was skeptical about Sedgwick's reconnaissance report. So he assigned his cavalry, commanded by Maj. Gen. Alfred Pleasonton, to flush out the Confederate forces. This Union probe resulted in the great but indecisive Battle of Brandy Station on June 9. As Hooker gradually became convinced of Pleasonton's claim that Lee's main forces were massing in the Culpeper area, he shifted more and more troops to the northwest. The commanders of both armies were trying to outguess one another. Lee correctly judged Sedgwick's demonstration to be merely a reconnaissance in force, not a prelude to a general movement toward the Confederate capital.

Sedgwick still occupied the south bank of the Rappahannock with Howe's division, holding down the extreme right wing of the Army of the Potomac. He awaited Hooker's orders. During the lull, some men swam in the river. Pickets talked to one another, suggesting a fistfight to settle the war. During the evenings, the Confederates serenaded the daytime enemy with singing and instrumental music. This informal truce was occasionally broken at night by false alarms that triggered sporadic firing. Sleeplessness grated on men's nerves.

Soon the persistent rumors about Confederate movements could no longer be ignored. On June 13, loyal citizens of Culpeper gave positive information to Hooker that two Confederate corps were continuing northward in the Shenandoah Valley. Some advance units were already at Winchester. At Hooker's headquarters, Butterfield ordered Sedgwick to move all his men back to the north bank: "The withdrawal is not to commence until after dark. The general suggests that you cover the bridges with hay or boughs to conceal any noise of artillery or troops in crossing."[14] That night, Howe's division recrossed the Rappahannock to rejoin Sedgwick's main force.

The next morning, June 14, Hooker broke up his headquarters at Falmouth and marched north to Fairfax Court House. Sedgwick stayed behind to guard the rear and to destroy the army's supplies, lest they fall into the hands of the enemy. Observing the terrible waste of war, Sedgwick's men threw bedding, glass, earthenware, instruments, medicine, and cooking utensils into a fire. The destruction of supplies was enormous but necessary. Sedgwick was now free to begin his pursuit of Lee.

The great race northward between the two armies had begun. Lee's movements were not an attempt to outflank Hooker's right wing, but a full-scale invasion of the North. With the advantage of a day's march, the Confederate troops poured through gaps in the Blue Ridge Mountains and entered the Shenandoah Valley, moving northward to the Cumberland Valley of Pennsylvania. The mountains effectively screened their operations. By June 16, the Northern press announced the news of Lee's offensive. The *New York Tribune* placed on its front page a large map of this theater of war and headlined its alarming lead story, "ADVANCE OF THE REBELS. INVASION OF PENNSYLVANIA."[15]

The mood of the citizens of Pennsylvania had changed drastically within one year. During the Antietam campaign of 1862, they had rushed to arms and crossed the Potomac to fight. Now they were strangely indifferent, concerned more with saving their property than defending their homes. War correspondent Charles C. Coffin noted bitterly, "In '62, the cry was 'Drive the enemy from our soil!' In '63, 'Where shall we hide our goods?'" This general apathy continued during Lee's invasion northward, and one newspaper editor pleaded, "Let us hear no more of what we will do on the Connecticut or Penobscot [rivers], but crush the Rebels in Pennsylvania and that right soon!"[16]

Hooker pressed his army northward to intercept the Southern drive. With the advantage of interior lines and the chance to pick up reinforcements along the way, he used his forces to shield the major eastern cities. Because the 6th Corps had been operating on the extreme left of the Army of the Potomac, Sedgwick was required to travel the longest distance. He and his staff worked out the complicated logistics of moving the 6th Corps — the largest in Hooker's command. During June the corps comprised about 18,000 men at full strength, including thirty-six infantry regiments, eight batteries of artillery, and a cavalry complement. When on the march without their trains, the infantry units stretched about ten miles on the roadway and required three hours to pass a given point.

The men of the 6th Corps started marching northward on June 14, and their tramp lasted until July. The heat was most intense in Virginia, where the soldiers walked on dirt roads with loose sand and dust. All extra garments — underclothing, overcoats, and suits — were quickly thrown away. One good-natured soldier, big Joe Walker of the 139th Pennsylvania Regiment, had worn out his special size-twelve boots, and the corps quartermaster did not have another pair for him. As this veteran briefly rested his bare feet, he replied to one of his army comrades, "Oh, I'm all right. If the Johnny Rebs are going up to Pennsylvania, they will find me there too, if I have to wear these feet up to the stumps." The heat and dust of the day frequently changed to heavy rainfall at night. These terrible storms created muddy roads, and the batteries were frequently stuck in mire. During night marches on these slippery roads, many soldiers fell down steep embankments. Someone would invariably call out, "Have you a pass to go down there?"[17]

Long tramps and brief halts continued every day and sometimes half the night as Sedgwick marched northward through the villages of northern Virginia. Overnight encampments were of short duration, as rumors now circulated that Lee was rapidly making his way through Maryland and into Pennsylvania.

At 5 A.M. on June 27, the general broke camp at Dranesville and marched three miles to Edwards Ferry to cross the Potomac River into Maryland. Later that day, "Jeb" Stuart's cavalry reached Dranesville to find the campfires of the 6th Corps still burning; the Confederates captured several stragglers. Passing through Poolesville, Maryland, Sedgwick's corps continued its grueling pace. On Sunday, June 28, the men rested briefly at Barnesville and ate lunch. Some attended a worship service at a Catholic church.

Approaching Hyattstown for the evening encampment (after a day's march of eighteen miles), the 6th Corps learned that General Meade had replaced Hooker as the commander of the Army of the Potomac. Hearing this news, Sedgwick "struck his spurs into his gigantic and phlegmatic steed" and led his men at a quick gallop for some time. The general vented his emotions in this way and did not say anything. Although he did not actively seek the command, Sedgwick was disturbed that a general, junior to his grade, had obtained this nod from the administration. Uncle John also sensed that members of his staff would be disappointed, as they were ambitious to serve under a commanding general. He knew, however, that Meade was a capable soldier.[18]

Many in the Union army reacted to Hooker's sudden dismissal with astonishment, if not indignation. It was soon learned that an argument had developed between Halleck and Hooker over the disposition of a Union garrison at Harpers Ferry. Hooker wanted to detach these troops to build up his own force to maximum strength. Yet Halleck insisted on holding Harpers Ferry. Whether or not Hooker believed his resignation would be taken as a bluff by the Lincoln administration, the president and his advisors took Hooker at his word. Lincoln did not wish to have Fighting Joe engage in another general battle — especially on Union soil — so he used this incident as a pretext and relieved him in favor of Meade. Highly regarded by Lincoln, Meade took command and was given the Harpers Ferry contingent without question.

Sedgwick's personal relations with Meade were much smoother than they had been with the tempestuous Fighting Joe. Yet, with an impending battle, it would take time for a new commander to coordinate troop movements and plan his strategy. Meade, a West Point graduate of 1835, had compiled a solid record throughout his military career. Although he specialized in military engineering and often had trouble controlling his temper, Meade commanded respect. He wasted no time. Retaining Butterfield as his chief of staff, Meade moved his headquarters to Middleburg on June 29. He urged his corps commanders to summon an extra effort from their men. When Meade ordered Sedgwick onward to New Windsor, Sedgwick said that he could not make it. Meade's mild rebuke so incensed Sedgwick that he pushed his exhausted men for a tramp of twenty-two miles for the day to reach his prescribed destination.

These days of constant marches showed Sedgwick's indomitable will to lead his command. The 6th Corps infantrymen called themselves "Sedgwick's Cavalry" and declared "they were kept on the gallop." The general halted only when his horse, Cornwall, gave out. When he stopped briefly to encourage his passing columns, his men shouted out in good humor, "Get another horse and come on;

we'll wait for you, Uncle John; we're in no hurry, Uncle John."
Amused by these remarks, Sedgwick responded with a kind smile,
whereupon the shouts turned into laughter.[19]

During the corps's journey through Maryland, the blazing heat
of the day often turned to rain at night. Too tired to put up their
tents, the soldiers slept beneath the open sky. Showers fell. In the
morning, the men would fold up their wet blankets. The next night,
they were forced to wrap themselves in the soggy folds. There were
more than a few cases of insomnia.

On Tuesday, June 30, General Meade issued his orders of
march for the various corps, which were designed to put his army
in good position to defend either Harrisburg, Baltimore, or Washington. Establishing his new headquarters at Taneytown, Meade
wanted Sedgwick's corps placed at Manchester to anchor down the
eastern, or right, wing of the Army of the Potomac. With his usual
4 A.M. start, Uncle John headed for Manchester — some twenty-three
miles to the east. As the 6th Corps passed through Westminster, the
residents of the town welcomed the troops with joy, which was all the
more earnest as the Confederate cavalry had left the town only two
hours before. By evening the exhausted soldiers halted two miles
from Manchester. In four days they had marched about a hundred
miles, in hot weather, with each soldier carrying his rifle, knapsack,
haversack (containing five days' provisions), and forty rounds of
ammunition.

June 30, 1863, was a crucial day for the Army of the Potomac.
As reports and rumors came into his Taneytown headquarters,
Meade devised a flexible strategy. Since most of Lee's army had
pushed into the Cumberland Valley and was threatening Harrisburg, Meade struggled with the dilemma of both relieving pressure
on this city and, at the same time, preventing the Confederate forces
from turning abruptly on his flanks to advance toward Washington
or Baltimore. About noon, Meade ordered Maj. Gen. John F. Reynolds of the 1st Corps to test the strength of Lee's forces converging on
the village of Gettysburg, and to fall back if attacked in force. Meade
wanted to fight a defensive battle, and that evening he sent out a circular to his corps commanders offering a tentative plan and recom-
mending a suitable line along Pipe Creek on which the various corps
could fall back to resist attack. The Pipe Creek Circular reached the
hands of the corps commanders the morning of Wednesday, July 1.
Meade was awaiting Reynolds's report. During the early afternoon,

a messenger notified the harried commander of the Army of the Potomac that Reynolds, an excellent corps commander, had been killed in a developing battle on the western outskirts of Gettysburg.

Sedgwick was always the last to know about significant developments because his corps was the most distant from Meade's headquarters — some twenty miles to the east. Yet when he received the Pipe Creek Circular, Sedgwick must have felt a sense of relaxation after these long marches. The circular showed him that his men were already in position, for the balance of the Union army, as it fell back according to this plan, would align itself on the 6th Corps. His present position would constitute the extreme right wing, if the plans presented in the circular were carried out.

Among the citizens of Manchester and the neighboring farms, news spread quickly that a Union force had arrived. One soldier of the 119th Pennsylvania remembered that the hospitality accorded the 6th Corps "was a novel one; we had no such experiences before or after. . . . The people in apparent sympathy with the Union cause crowded the camps, mingling freely with the troops. The scene much resembled a county fair." People thronged into the camps and offered free food. Some hawkers appeared. With a chance to relax after the strain of many hard marches, some soldiers lost all sense of military discipline. Finding large supplies of rye whiskey and brandy available in Manchester, they soon became drunk. Sedgwick was forced to issue orders for the arrest of anyone bringing liquor into camp.[20]

At noon on July 1, Sedgwick greeted one of Meade's staff officers, Maj. James Biddle, who had arrived from Taneytown. Meade's instructions were to move "in such direction as may be required at a moment's notice." Sedgwick invited Biddle to stay for lunch and asked him if Meade had retained Butterfield. When Biddle confirmed this belief, the general's reaction was that Meade would live to regret it. He was correct.[21]

But the exigency of the Union army's military situation demanded harmony; communications must be maintained. During the afternoon, Sedgwick sent Colonel Hyde to Meade's headquarters for instructions. At 8 P.M., Sedgwick received the first of three messages sent from Butterfield that night: "Move your command to Taneytown to-night. . . . I regret to inform you that Major-General Reynolds was killed at Gettysburg this morning."[22] As informing his troops about Reynolds's death would only weaken morale, Uncle

John confided this painful news only to a few aides. With great energy, the general managed to accomplish the awesome task of getting 18,000 men moving within the hour, on a hot summer's night. The few soldiers who could not shake off their drunkenness were thrown into the bushes by the road and left to be gathered up by cavalry squads that were scouring the countryside for stragglers. It was a long twenty-mile tramp to be undertaken in darkness with poor maps.

At army headquarters, Meade was again analyzing the overall situation. As various reports indicated that Lee was concentrating his army at Gettysburg, Meade made his decision to fight there. Changing Sedgwick's original set of orders, Meade now wanted the 6th Corps on the way to Gettysburg to join the rest of the army. Butterfield wrote out a second message and Lt. Paul A. Oliver was sent to contact Sedgwick. At 11 P.M., Oliver reached Sedgwick, having ridden down two steeds in his efforts to deliver this urgent message. He exclaimed, "General, you must be at Gettysburg by afternoon of tomorrow." The general answered, "Say to General Meade, I will be at Gettysburg with my corps at 4:00 tomorrow afternoon." Then Sedgwick read Butterfield's message:

> A general battle seems to be impending to-morrow at Gettysburg; that it is of the utmost importance that your command should be up. He [Meade] directs that you stop all trains that impede your progress, or turn them out of the road. Your march will have to be a forced one to reach the scene of the action, where we shall probably be largely outnumbered without your presence.
>
> If any shorter road presents itself, without difficulty in getting up, you will use your discretion in taking it. . . .
>
> The general desires you to report here in person without delay, the moment you receive this. He is waiting to see you before going to the front.[23]

Sedgwick pondered what to do. After marching seven or eight miles already, he was now ordered to change his route. To leave his men and proceed with a small escort to Taneytown, in the midst of guerrilla-infested country, would have demoralized his troops and would have taken the rest of the night. Oliver's exhausted horses had demonstrated to the general that reaching Meade within a reasonable time was plainly impossible. Judging the order in its larger, more practical application, Sedgwick decided to remain with his command. Meade had probably left for the Gettysburg front anyway.

After losing both time and mileage, the 6th Corps was finally headed in the right direction on its march to Gettysburg, the most famous march on either side during the Civil War. In spite of the heat, dust, distance, and the aftereffects of whiskey and brandy, the 6th Corps pushed ahead through the night. By this time, Hyde had returned and saw Sedgwick's straw hat appear through the trees at the head of his corps. He delivered Butterfield's third message of the night, which suggested a better and faster route. Sedgwick managed to find a crossroad and located the Baltimore Pike, the road Meade and Butterfield had recommended, and continued his march. Each hour, Uncle John stopped for a few moments to breathe the men.

Finally at daybreak, Thursday, July 2, Sedgwick called a short halt. Many soldiers kindled fires to prepare a rude breakfast. Sedgwick ate nothing, but passed constantly among his troops. After thirty minutes he gave the order to resume the march. Some Billy Yanks of the 93d Pennsylvania Regiment lingered around their fires, trying to boil coffee, and ignored momentarily the order to "fall in." Officers approached and kicked over the coffeepots. Throughout the march, when any of the general's officers suggested more halts or when the corps straggled, Uncle John repeated, "Have you seen Meade's order?" The 6th Corps trudged away again in the heat. The broken white limestone with which the Baltimore Pike had been originally paved had been ground by long use into a powder, which created choking dust. As the tramp continued, one soldier yelled out, "Boys, it's rough, but I tell you it's regular."[24]

Many men fainted in their tracks, and within a short time the ambulances were full. By 9 A.M., everyone could hear the booming of cannon in the distance, which confirmed the persistent rumors that a great battle was being fought. Although they tried to maintain their pace, the men suffered terribly from thirst. Each farmhouse along the road had a spring or well, but the corps could not stop long enough to be supplied and there was never enough water. A soldier of the 61st Pennsylvania saw a chain pump in the front yard of a house, went to it, and began vigorously turning the crank. No water came. The owner of the place, a woman, stood nearby, with her arms akimbo. The soldier asked, "Can't you tell me where to get some water?" The woman began to cry, saying, "No, I can't even give you a cup of cold water."[25]

Filled with the wounded, a long line of ambulances enroute to the rear caused a temporary delay in the march. The walking wounded offered no encouragement. Rushing to the rear, a brawny fugitive with bleeding arm and bandaged head exclaimed, "You fellows will catch it; the whole army is smashed to pieces!"[26] In the early forenoon, a farmer told some of the soldiers that General Reynolds had been killed the day before in a fight at Gettysburg. The average soldier had never heard of Gettysburg.

At 10 A.M., the 6th Corps crossed the Pennsylvania state line. The 93d Pennsylvania Infantry Regiment unfurled its colors, beat its drums, increased its pace, and sang "Home, Sweet Home." As Sedgwick and his men marched over the ridges crossed by the Baltimore Pike, they could see a valley some miles ahead filled with smoke. Some soldiers insisted it was burning straw, but before long everyone saw "the white cotton balls in the air, the this smoke of bursting shells."[27] Beyond question a terrific battle was in progress.

The strain became almost unbearable. At about 4 P.M., Sedgwick stopped his corps to get his forces together. The halt was made at Rock Creek, a short distance east of Little Round Top, about two miles from the battlefield. The members of the 37th Massachusetts stopped at a spot where the creek had been dammed up for a mill. Within minutes, many soldiers had stripped off their clothes and jumped into the water for a refreshing bath. It was full of blood-suckers. Every soldier picked them off as he emerged from the water. New York troops fried pork and boiled coffee "in the most unconcerned manner, paying no attention to the fact that there, but a little distance in front, hundreds of cannon were thundering."[28] Other troops were too exhausted to eat and threw themselves wearily to the ground. The 6th Corps had arrived reasonably intact after an eighteen-hour march variously estimated at from thirty-two to thirty-five miles.

At Meade's headquarters, staff officers were anxiously awaiting the 6th Corps. They finally saw a cloud of dust on the Baltimore Pike. Amidst speculation that Jeb Stuart's cavalry might be threatening the Union rear, officers gazed with their field glasses. One said, "It is not cavalry, but infantry. There is the flag. It is the Sixth Corps."[29] It was a most inspiring sight for them.

The achievement of this march was considerable. As one of

Sedgwick's staff officers explained, "It does now and then occur that well-ordered marches as effectually beat an enemy as the most decisive battle could do."[30] Sedgwick and his men brought a formidable concentration of Union troops along a line that the Confederates could not penetrate. For the first time since the battle had begun, the Union army enjoyed a preponderance of military strength. Earlier in the day, Meade was outnumbered by the Confederates, with 68,000 men to Lee's 75,000. When Sedgwick arrived, the Union side totaled 85,500 men.

Sedgwick and his chief of staff, McMahon, reported immediately to Meade's headquarters, a little white farmhouse belonging to a widow, Mrs. Leister, which was located on the west side of Taneytown Road. Hoping to consult with Meade, both to pick up his orders and to find out what had happened thus far during the battle, Sedgwick found that his commanding general was absent temporarily on a reconnoitering visit. As he waited for Meade, the general had a chance to look over the terrain of the battlefield. The Baltimore Pike, over which he had traveled, was one of ten roads leading into Gettysburg, a village about a mile north of the Leister House. The Union position was concentrated on Cemetery Ridge, anchored on its right flank by Cemetery Hill and Culp's Hill. To the south, the Union forces were fighting to control Little Round Top, a strategic point that commanded a view of Devil's Den, the wheatfield, and the peach orchard. The Union line, resembling a fishhook, was about four miles long. The attacking Confederate army, holding a five-mile line, occupied Seminary Ridge across a valley to the west and was attempting to overrun both Union flanks.

When Meade returned from the front, he told Sedgwick about an altercation with Maj. Gen. Daniel E. Sickles. Against orders, Sickles had advanced approximately a half mile to take up an exposed position. Sedgwick asked why Meade had not ordered him back. Meade replied that it was then too late, as the Confederates had attacked Sickles's corps near the peach orchard. As a result of Sickles's blunder, Longstreet's Southern troops had forced an opening in the line, which was only partially closed by two Union corps. In this moment of urgency, Meade ordered Sedgwick to blunt Longstreet's attack.

As they awaited the return of their general, the men of the Greek Cross rested in the shade of trees near Rock Creek and listened to the tremendous noise of fire over the hills. Riding down over a hill and swinging his hat, McMahon shouted, "The general directs the corps toward the heavy firing." The half-sleeping soldiers immediately sprang to their feet, pushed down fences, and headed for Little Round Top, nearly a mile away. While they were moving toward the battle, members of the 119th Pennsylvania Infantry Regiment saw a wagon loaded down with household goods, with an attractive young girl walking alongside as her father handled the horses. She exclaimed, "I wish I were a man; I should promptly return and lend my feeble support to the cause of my country." This so impressed one young officer's sense of patriotism that he told his men he would marry her on the spot if she would consent. But there was a battle to fight.[31]

Immediately after McMahon appeared, Sedgwick followed and, without waiting for the brigade or regimental officers, sang out to the soldiers of the 139th Pennsylvania Regiment, "Fall in, boys, move quickly." The nearby 93d Pennsylvania Infantry followed their commander, Col. David J. Nevin, into action to the west. Two brigades of the 6th Corps joined in the fighting, and two were held in reserve. Sedgwick personally led one brigade and formed a line on the brow of a low, rocky knoll covered with scattered trees, just to the right of Little Round Top. When his men ducked their heads at the sound of bullets, Uncle John told them, "No dodging, my boys." Other units arrived just in time to help repulse Longstreet's last attack from behind a stone wall. To Hyde, this Confederate charge was like "the last wave on the beach, stopping and being pushed up a little more and a little more from behind." The 6th Corps brigades advanced beyond the stone wall to take prisoner the Confederates hiding behind rocks.[32]

As evening approached, the general found himself without any soldiers. Meade had decided to use Sedgwick's corps as a manpower pool, and he detached two brigades for the 12th Corps in the Culp's Hill sector. Another brigade, led by Brig. Gen. Alexander Shaler, was sent to the left center of the line. The entire artillery of the corps was placed under the direct orders of Brig. Gen. Henry J. Hunt, the chief of artillery. For a general who had been in charge of 50,000 troops during the Chancellorsville campaign, Sedgwick now "had not a man or a gun under his command except for a few orderlies." The general told his staff "he thought he might as well go home." In such a critical time, it was a waste of managerial talent for Meade to ignore Sedgwick's experience. With the single exception of Slocum,

Sedgwick outranked by seniority all the commanders to whom he was supplying his men.[33] But he remained a good soldier and did not harp publicly over the circumstances that had left him powerless.

As darkness fell and the Confederate assaults ceased, a feeling prevailed throughout the Union army that the fighting was over for the day. Many 6th Corps troops lay down "with muskets and swords in hand, upon a thick mat of moss." Sedgwick's close aide, Maj. Charles A. Whittier, mentioned confidentially to a few staff officers that the corps was going to march twenty miles back to Westminster. While his men were sleeping, Sedgwick left his headquarters at the foot of Little Round Top and headed north to report to his commanding officer. Meade had called a council of war.

About 9 P.M., twelve Union generals assembled at the Leister farmhouse to plan strategy for the next day. In a small, stuffy bedroom, Meade and Butterfield met with the chief engineer, Brig. Gouverneur K. Warren; two wing commanders, Maj. Gen. Henry W. Slocum and Maj. Gen. Winfield S. Hancock; and seven corps commanders. After a few informal comments about the day's fighting, the problem was presented: "Here we are; now what is the best thing to do?" Everyone agreed to hold the present line and to give battle there. After suggesting that the questions be formulated in writing, Butterfield jotted down three in his minutes of the meeting. Meade wanted to know: (1) Should the army remain or retreat? (2) Should the army attack or await the attack of the Confederates? (3) How long should they wait? Sedgwick's responses agreed in substance with the other opinions; he wanted (1) to remain, (2) to await attack, and (3) to wait at least one day. Just as the council was breaking up near midnight, Meade mentioned to Gibbon what he believed Lee's objective would be: "He has made attacks on both our flanks and failed, and if he tries it again it will be on our center."[34]

Controversy developed later about Meade's intentions during the evening war council of July 2. When the Joint Committee on the Conduct of the War conducted its inquiry during early 1864, Butterfield and Maj. Gen. David B. Birney accused Meade of wanting to retreat. Testifying under oath before the committee, Sedgwick asserted, "I never heard of any such order. . . . I was second in command there, and reported to General Meade at a critical time; and if he contemplated so important a move, he would have informed me." Sedgwick's comments agree completely with his actions on his return to headquarters the night of July 2. Before retiring for a meager night's rest, he assured his staff that they would not be retreating to Westminster.[35]

Sedgwick awoke on Friday, July 3, to a bright dawn and clear sky. By early afternoon, the heat was oppressive. The temperature had reached 87°F in the shade, and in the open meadows the humidity must have seemed like 100 percent. During the day the general had little to do, as his troops were distributed temporarily to other units. Maj. Gen. George Sykes commanded the largest number of 6th Corps brigades in the vicinity of Little Round Top. Meade, who possessed an uncanny ability to shuffle troops in and out of sectors for maximum military effectiveness during this battle, sent two of Sedgwick's brigades to Newton in the center. One brigade, led by Brig. Gen. David A. Russell, was shifted three times in two days. The 1st New York Light Battery, led by Capt. Andrew Cowan, after being sent originally to General Newton's 1st Corps, found itself at the call of any superior officer who needed an extra battery. As one of his artillery units was crippled and out of ammunition, Brig. Gen. Alexander S. Webb of the 2d Corps plucked Cowan's battery and directed it into position to the left of a clump of trees. To the right of these trees was the 4th U.S. Artillery, commanded by Lt. Alonzo H. Cushing.

At 1 P.M., 138 artillery pieces began to hurl projectiles toward the Union lines at the rate of six per second. This deafening barrage was the most intensive Confederate shelling of the entire war, but fortunately for the Union troops on the front lines on Cemetery Ridge, many missiles were overshot. The eighty Union guns responded, and a terrific exchange of cannonading continued for nearly two hours. By 2:30 P.M., it was evident that Lee's gunners were concentrating on the center, and in particular the ground covered by General Webb's men in the area of the clump of trees. The Union artillery stopped its barrage to conserve ammunition, to cool the guns, and to prevent the accumulation of smoke, which would offer a screen for a charging enemy infantry attack.

Sedgwick stayed at his headquarters in a heavily wooded area just north of Little Round Top, considerably distant from the fierce firing. His trusted aide, Capt. Richard F. Halsted, was probably with the general; he spoke for both of them, writing, "I cannot tell you anything of any consequence about the fight. . . . I saw so little of it that I cannot describe it."[36]

Lee lifted the bombardment at 3 P.M., and sent 15,000 infan-

try, consisting of Maj. Gen. George E. Pickett's division and Brig.
Gen. James J. Pettigrew's division, across a mile of open field to
assault the Union center. Pickett's charge moved eastward. To the
Union troops reviewing the Confederate advance from a safe distance, it was an awesome sight. Watching from the summit of Little
Round Top, Hyde observed, "On they came: it looked to me like
three lines about a mile long each, in perfect order."[37]

Sedgwick's troops were widely scattered and, in his words,
"were more or less exposed to the fire of the enemy's artillery, but
. . . they were at no time seriously exposed."[38] The 6th Corps' most
notable performance during Pickett's charge was the stand of Capt.
Andrew Cowan's battery. After the Confederate columns had
crossed Emmitsburg Road, Union batteries opened fire to break up
the enemy's lines, 300 yards away. With only a low stone wall for
natural defense, and with limited infantry support, Cowan and
Cushing faced overwhelming odds. Pickett's soldiers charged the
wall as Cowan's battery, Cushing's three guns, and thousands of volleys from muskets tore into their ranks and opened holes in the
Southern lines.

Cushing was mortally wounded; partly cut in two, he held his
body together with one hand and fired his last canister. His death
left Cowan with Webb's infantry regiments to defend the line along
the clump of trees. Some of Pickett's soldiers, led by a young officer
waving his sword and shouting, "Take the guns," scrambled over the
wall. Cowan fired canister, which "literally swept the enemy from
my front, being fired at less than twenty yards."[39]

The Confederates rallied for one final charge. Cowan wrote,
"It was then I fired my last charge of canister, many of the rebels
being over the defenses and within less than ten yards of my pieces.
They broke and fled in confusion."[40] The high-water mark of the
Confederacy crested and fell back.

From his vantage point, Hyde thought the Union center was
pierced. He rode down to Sedgwick's headquarters for orders, as he
knew Sedgwick would want to attack at once in full force with all the
6th Corps troops he could muster. But the Confederate assault had
been blunted, and Sedgwick received no orders to attack or pursue
the enemy.

About 4 P.M., Sedgwick watched Sykes send out a strong reconnoitering party to find out if the Confederates were retreating. He
later observed a sharp skirmish in front of Little Round Top and
saw this reconnaissance force return about evening.

The Union survivors slept in peace that evening. Wainwright jotted in his diary, "A great relief seemed to rest on the minds of everyone; a sense, as it were, that the worst was over."[41] Enormous losses on both sides prevented quick renewal of fighting. The Army of the Potomac lost an aggregate of 23,049 men. Sedgwick and his staff counted total losses for the corps at 242, including 27 killed. Confederate losses for the three-day period were determined at 20,451.

Sedgwick's role in the Battle of Gettysburg was minor. The attention centered on Reynolds, Meade, Sickles, Webb, and Hancock. The 6th Corps historian, George Stevens, stated simply, "It is true we did not do much fighting . . . but we did all that was necessary or possible to do."[42]

The next day, Saturday, July 4, was spent burying the thousands of dead and attending to the tens of thousands of wounded, with "no thought of celebrating the anniversary of the Nation's birth."[43]

The 37th Massachusetts was assigned to picket duty and could occasionally see the glimmer of muskets as the Southerners rested under trees across the meadows. No one expected Lee to attack again. Sedgwick attended to the many details that demand immediate attention after a battle. His men buried ninety-five Confederates. He sent Hyde and Lt. John Andrews to visit the field hospitals to estimate the number of Confederate wounded. In the afternoon, he ordered his pickets back to the main line and set the men to digging rifle pits. Some 6th Corps soldiers were posted on a ledge of rock that formed a hollow; after afternoon and evening showers, the defenders were standing in a pond.

That evening, Meade summoned his corps commanders for another conference. Consulting with Sedgwick, Meade worked out a plan of pursuit to capture Lee's army. Since the 6th Corps was relatively fresh, Meade picked Sedgwick's troops as the logical force. "Be ready at four and a half o'clock A.M. tomorrow," were Meade's orders. Later instructions emphasized that Sedgwick was to lead a reconnaissance to ascertain the position and movement of the Confederate army, but not to bring on a battle. Once the "desired information has been obtained," Meade wrote, "you will return to your original position, ready for the general movement."[44]

As Sedgwick prepared to begin his direct pursuit on the morning of July 5, Meade added two more corps — the 1st, led by Newton, and the 3d, commanded by Maj. Gen. David B. Birney (replacing

the wounded Sickles) — to form the right wing of the Army of the
Potomac. Wright's division began the probe, followed by the other
divisions of the corps and the supporting troops. After crossing the
valley and occupying Seminary Ridge, which had been held by the
Confederates the day before, Wright spotted some Confederate sol-
diers on his right and directed artillery to open up on the enemy.
The Southerners did not return the fire, but continued their retreat.
This was the last shot fired by either side in the Battle of Gettysburg.

At 12:30 P.M., Meade urged Sedgwick to "push forward your
columns in a westerly direction. . . . Time is of great importance as I
cannot give orders for a movement without explicit information
from you."[45] The recent heavy rains had ruined the roads for a
quick pursuit. Sedgwick was following the Confederate rear guard
westward to Fairfield, and this traffic mired the roads even more.
Fog also hindered the Union advance. At 5 P.M., Wright's division
caught up with Lee's fleeing rear detachment about two miles east
of Fairfield. A sharp engagement resulted, with slight losses on both
sides. Taking 250 prisoners of war, Sedgwick halted his force on the
outskirts of town.

The people of the Union, after hearing rumors for several days,
finally learned from their newspapers about Meade's victory at Gettysburg. The *New York Tribune* announced on July 6 in large headlines, "THE GREAT VICTORY. THE REBEL ARMY TOTALLY
DEFEATED. ITS REMAINS DRIVEN INTO THE MOUNTAINS.
IT IS THERE SURROUNDED AND HEMMED IN. ITS RE-
TREAT ACROSS THE POTOMAC CUT OFF." The glorious news
of Maj. Gen. Ulysses S. Grant's successful siege and capture of Vicksburg became known at about the same time. During the next few
days President Lincoln expressed the hope of the Union for a total
destruction of Lee's army. Everyone expected Meade to duplicate
Grant's success. Lee must not be permitted to slip away.

For the Army of the Potomac in the field, the situation was not
that simple. Sedgwick was apprehensive when he sent a message to
Meade on the morning of July 6. He reported, "I have sent forward
General [Thomas H.] Neill's brigade to move cautiously toward the
gap. I am afraid to move my whole command on account of the
character of the country and density of the fog. . . . I believe from
the immense number of camp-fires seen last evening, that the enemy
have a very strong rear guard, and will hold the gaps strongly."[46]
The wild Catoctin mountain range prevented rapid pursuit as Lee

controlled the passes. Sedgwick decided to remain where he was and await orders.

After receiving Meade's order to continue his advance according to his own judgment, Sedgwick moved by the flank to avoid Fairfield Pass. During the day Meade ordered his whole army in a general advance toward Middletown. Sedgwick pushed on and reached Emmitsburg shortly before daybreak. Neill's soldiers remained at Fairfield with orders to harass the enemy from the rear and to advance westward through the gorge when possible.

The 6th Corps suffered many hardships during July 7 and 8. Everything went wrong. They had to cross the Catoctin range to continue their pursuit. A fifteen-mile march in a heavy storm brought them to the steep mountain as darkness closed in. The infantry struggled to climb a road that degenerated into little more than a footpath, scarcely wide enough for two. The jagged rocks and high boulders, the mud, and the blackness of the night compelled the infantry to make a rude overnight encampment. The men nicknamed the steep mountain "Mount Misery," and the narrow passageway through the rocks became known as "Sedgwick's Pass."[47]

The artillerymen suffered even more. Col. Charles Tompkins told the general that it was impossible to move his artillery over this steep, narrow, rocky road. When Colonel Wainwright, attached to a different corps, passed Tompkins with his guns and gained the summit, Uncle John was angry. But, to save the horses's ebbing strength, he ordered his artillery and ammunition trains to take another, much longer road around the mountain. The wagon masters mistook their orders, however, and were driving their exhausted animals up the mountain road. The horses finally could no longer draw their loads. Hyde and another orderly finally got the trains on the right roads, and at 3 A.M. they found a barn where they rested until daybreak.

Early the next morning the infantry crossed the crest of the Catoctin range near Hamburg, Maryland. Someone discovered a stream, and many men plunged into the water, clothes and all, to wash away the night's accumulation of mud. With the dirt off their faces, the soldiers could again recognize one another.

Lee continued falling back toward the Potomac River. The recent heavy rains had raised the level of the river to such a height that it would be a few days before they could attempt to ford it. The Union army received news generating additional hopes that Lee might be trapped: Maj. Gen. William H. French, on a raid to Lee's rear, had cut loose some boats and pontoons, and also burned a bridge at Williamsport. It was a golden opportunity for Meade, and the North felt that Lee's whole army could be bagged.

As Sedgwick's chase after Lee continued, Meade advanced in full force and, supported by militia regiments, reached Middletown on July 8. Neill's brigade, which Sedgwick had left at Fairfield, passed through the now undefended gorge and arrived at Waynesboro for an evening's encampment. The pro-Union citizens formed on the sidewalks and handed the soldiers "bread, sliced and buttered, cooked meats, pies, and almost everything in the eatable line."[48]

The next two days, the 6th Corps marched through Turner's Gap over South Mountain, past the village of Boonesboro, and forded waist-deep Antietam Creek. This advance was slow and cautious. Finally on July 10, at Beaver Creek to the east of Funkstown, they caught up with Lee's rear columns. Sedgwick directed McMahon to "put the Vermonters ahead and keep everything well closed up."[49] Col. Lewis A. Grant's Vermont brigade, attached to General Howe's division, forded the creek and spread out as skirmishers on a two-mile front. Uncle John held the rest of his corps in reserve on the opposite bank and, according to Howe, did not want to bring on a general engagement.

To ensure an orderly retreat, Lee desired a stiff resistance; he ordered his rear column to attack. The Vermonters repulsed three Confederate attacks during the afternoon of July 10, at the cost of nine killed and fifty-nine wounded. When the cartridges had been exhausted at the front, the 6th Corps commander sent up a fresh supply on stretchers. After the Confederate retreat, the 6th Corps and the people of Funkstown discovered over thirty bodies and over a hundred wounded Southern soldiers.

But time was running out for the Union army. A week had already passed since the Battle of Gettysburg, and Meade had to act quickly if he was going to capture Lee's army. Lee had been inspecting the terrain around Williamsport for several days. His engineers had constructed a strong defensive position in a semicircle around this town and had thrown up earthworks. The Confederate fortifications overlooked a swamp and open fields to the front. With a flatboat and a wire rope, Lee had managed to bring in supplies from Virginia. He did not fear encirclement.

During the advance westward, Meade met with his corps commanders almost every evening to discuss strategy. At Meade's headquarters was his new chief of staff. As Butterfield had been severely wounded during the last day of the Gettysburg fighting, Meade sought out and eagerly appointed his hand-picked choice, Brig. Gen. Alexander A. Humphreys, promoted to major general when he filled this post on July 12. Unlike Butterfield, who had generated so much friction during his tenure, Humphrey's succession to the position of chief of staff inaugurated a far more harmonious relationship with other Union officers. Sedgwick admired and worked well with the popular Humphreys.

At 8 P.M. on July 12, Meade called his third important council to discuss the advisability of attacking Lee's entrenched position. From their experiences in the South Mountain and Antietam campaign, many of these generals were familiar with the ruggedness of the terrain and were wary of the military situation. Sedgwick proposed taking the 6th and 11th corps from the Union right and, marching through and beyond Hagerstown during the night, occupying by daybreak a new position on the Confederate flank and rear. This force would then begin determined attack to cut Lee off from the river, and the rest of the army could launch a direct attack on Lee's front. The council rejected Sedgwick's plan.

Meade then asked the seven generals for a vote, saying he would acquiesce in the council's decision. Sedgwick voted against an attack, doubtlessly thinking of his experience at Marye's Heights and the inadvisability of sending troops across exposed ground to attack fortified heights. During these crucial days of 1863, when the outcome of the struggle was still in doubt, the Lincoln administration and the Northern citizenry would have been severely shaken by the failure of a massive front assault by Meade on Lee's position. To throw away the Gettysburg victory on such a dubious gamble at Williamsport was senseless.

The votes were counted. A five-to-two decision against the direct assault ended the conference. Only Maj. Gen. Oliver O. Howard and Brig. Gen. James S. Wadsworth supported the plan of frontal attack. Although Meade did not vote, Sedgwick later said, "I believe General Meade expressed himself in favor of an attack. . . . Whether General Meade expressed himself so at the council or not I am not positive, but I am sure he did in conversation with me."[50]

Sedgwick viewed the situation with the detachment of a professional soldier. There was no doubt in his mind that Lee was receiving ammunition across the Potomac. He was also bluntly skeptical of the caliber of his reinforcements: "All the troops sent us are thirty days' militia and nine months' volunteers, and are perfectly useless. I am tired of risking my corps in such unequal contests."[51] To his mind, a direct assault at Williamsport would result in a costly battle of attrition.

On July 13, there was limited action. Sedgwick's corps was placed in the line of battle near Hagerstown and connected with the 11th Corps on the right and the 5th Corps on the left. In this sector, Meade observed occasional sharp skirmishing. Behind Lee's lines, a Federal sympathizer saw that any assaulting forces would be heading into a trap. He had overheard a Confederate officer remark, "If he [Meade] attacks us here, we will pay him back for Gettysburg."[52] Lee himself was hopeful that the Army of the Potomac would attack. Just before nightfall, the Confederates fired several shots from howitzers, to show that they were still there. With the completion of a pontoon bridge and an ebbing of the Potomac, Lee's army crossed the river during the night of July 13 to the relative safety of Virginia.

Gen. Horatio G. Wright was one of the first to realize that Lee had crossed the Potomac; he immediately notified Sedgwick. At 11:30 A.M., at his right wing headquarters, Sedgwick noted, "Appearances indicate that the enemy has crossed the river into Virginia." Sedgwick and others passed over the recently evacuated Confederate position and examined its works. He was convinced that the Federal forces could not have carried these defenses. Wainwright considered the works "by far the strongest I have yet seen . . . and built as if they meant to stand a month's siege." With a parapet and well-placed guns, Lee's position had a perfect crossfire to sweep the whole front.[53]

During the afternoon, the Union cavalry returned from a quick raid and turned about 1,000 Confederate prisoners of war over to Sedgwick. As provost marshal, Hyde corralled them, under guard, in a beautiful field near the bank of the Potomac River. Within a short time, Sedgwick told Hyde to move these captured men without delay, as they were within hail of the Confederate pickets across the river. To prevent their escape, Hyde quickly moved the prisoners to a more secure area.

To the people of the North, the news of Lee's escape into Virginia produced a feeling of frustration. The failure of Lee's invasion and the Union victory at Gettysburg would not satisfy them. Lincoln repeatedly showed his distress and grief, and said, "Our Army held the war in the hollow of their hand and they would not close it." General Wadsworth, who had voted for an attack at Williamsport, offered his views at the White House on July 16, 1863. When a Washington friend asked how Lee escaped, Wadsworth answered gruffly, "Because nobody stopped him."[54]

Sedgwick avoided making a severe judgment on the campaign. The fault lay not with military, he concluded, but with governmental policy. In a letter written July 26, he stated that the Army of the Potomac, with seasoned reinforcements, "could have made it a rout." But the people of Pennsylvania did not offer sufficient assistance to the Union: "not ten thousand men turned out and then refused to follow into Maryland." Sedgwick felt, "We have done an incredible amount of labour, if we have accomplished but little." On a personal note, he added, "I am worn out. I have not had any clothes off since leaving the Rappahannock, and the army and animals are exhausted."[55]

The Gettysburg campaign was over. Meade summed up his feelings, "I start to-morrow to run another race with Lee."[56]

CHAPTER 5

STALEMATE AT
MINE RUN

MEADE AND HIS generals were now determined to begin an offensive to crush the Confederacy. To maintain momentum with depleted forces in hot weather tested both endurance and determination. Sedgwick and his corps were exhausted as they prepared to cross the Potomac at Berlin, Maryland. Lt. Col. Selden Connor of the 7th Maine explained, "We have been on the 'rampage' for more than a month, sleeping whenever we could get a chance in the saddle or anywhere, and eating whenever we could find anything to eat — one day a *feast,* the next often a famine. I don't grumble — none of us do, for we've labored to some purpose." Again the veterans continued the chase.[1]

During July 17 and 18, 1863, Meade sent his army across the Potomac on pontoon bridges. The 6th Corps crossed as the bands played, "O Carry Me Back to Old Virginny." At the far side of the bridge, Sedgwick prevented confusion by hurrying up teams that might have obstructed the way. After directing his men up a rocky hill, the general continued the march for ten miles. They encamped for the night near a clear stream, which was soon filled with bathers.

After a week of grueling marches over rough roads on hot days and in rain, the 6th Corps halted. On July 25, Sedgwick established camp in the hills just west of Warrenton. Here the men enjoyed the first days of rest since they had left the Rappahannock. Many went into the fields to pick wild blackberries that grew in profusion. Sedgwick, however, could not relax. Hearing about the draft riots in

New York City, he felt "their effect must have been more disastrous than the loss of a great battle."[2]

Draft riots had indeed become a serious problem for President Lincoln. The administration's initial steps toward a compulsory draft were resisted by Gov. Horatio Seymour of New York, a leading Democrat. Many residents of New York City were Irish immigrants hostile to blacks and opposed to the war, believing it to be an abolitionist movement. The poor also felt discriminated against because they could not pay for substitutes. On July 13, when Lincoln ordered enforcement of the draft, a riot broke out. Mobs killed blacks and set fire to their homes. To halt further violence, Lincoln temporarily suspended the draft. During this crisis, he ordered Meade to halt north of the Rapidan River and to send four regiments to New York City.

Meade received the order on July 30 and picked two of Sedgwick's regiments, the 37th Massachusetts and the 5th Wisconsin. Col. Oliver Edwards, commander of the former unit, was designated the leader of the demi-brigade of some 1,643 men. Receiving his instructions, Sedgwick notified the two regiments at midnight on July 30. Awakened with this startling announcement, the men packed immediately, marched ten miles to Warrenton Junction, and were loaded on freight cars for the trip north. Edwards's detachment arrived at New York City on August 2.

The matter did not end here. On deciding to renew the draft in August, Lincoln needed 10,000 additional men to patrol New York City. Sedgwick's efforts to maintain his troop strength in spite of this crisis and expiring enlistments were further frustrated. On August 10, he lost his favorite Vermont brigade, about 1,600 men, under the command of Col. Lewis A. Grant. The Vermonters were sent to Tompkins Square, near "Mackerelville," one of the most destitute sections of New York. To maintain control, Grant supplied his troops with live ammunition. One of the soldiers, Sgt. Thomas Murphy, noted in his diary, "The draft has been going on for three days. Seems to be no indication of a row."[3] Order was firmly established by mid-August.

The riots altered the strategy of the Army of the Potomac. Now short of manpower, the Union generals could do little but occupy the fords of the Rappahannock and send out patrols. Regarding the chance of a troop movement, one correspondent reported, "The heat is so great that soldiers are not required to drill, much less to march. Sunstroke and prostration would ensue."[4] Both sides seemed to welcome this summer lull to recoup from the Gettysburg campaign. Pickets talked across the Rappahannock and sometimes got together for a sociable game of cards.

Occasionally officers of the Greek Cross slept at the Warren Green Hotel. Many rode over to the nearby resort village of Sulphur Springs and drank the waters. There were horse races, reviews, and evening serenades. In this relaxed atmosphere, the residents of Warrenton received many of the 6th Corps officers in their homes. Some Southern ladies even went to Sedgwick's headquarters to be entertained by Yankee band music. When these ladies were later asked by their friends about their hospitality, General Lee defended their near-treasonous act, explaining, "I know General Sedgwick very well. It is just like him to be so kindly and considerate, and to have his band there to entertain them. So, young ladies, if the music is good, go and hear it as often as you can, and enjoy yourselves. You will find that General Sedgwick will have none but agreeable gentlemen about him."[5]

Sedgwick himself hoped for a few days' leave to visit Cornwall Hollow, but this wish was not realized. While many general Union officers had enjoyed desk jobs, Sedgwick felt he had done more than his share of field duty in the last few years with the Army of the Potomac.

Now the long-awaited presentation occurred of the 2d Division, 2d Army Corps, to Sedgwick as its old commander — which had been so rudely canceled by Lee's offensive in June. A thousand guests, headed by General Meade, appeared on August 27 at the grounds of a plantation. "Handsome Joe," a thoroughbred black stallion, was brought forward and broke from his groom, nearly kicking over the collation table. In the presentation speech, Capt. George B. Corphill of the 2d Corps remarked that "one-fourth of the officers who formerly knew him [Sedgwick] as their commander had been either killed or permanently disabled within the last two months alone."[6] After the presentation of the horse (whose restlessness caused him to be speedily withdrawn), along with an expensive sword and trappings, the general replied with great emotion, praising the record of Sumner's corps. Champagne and punch flowed freely. Meade and some of the others returned to their quarters for the evening, but a number of colonels lay on the grass and decided to leave the following day.

A few days later, General Meade received a sword in a similar ceremony, during which Gov. Andrew G. Curtin of Pennsylvania delivered a speech. Sedgwick attended and was disgusted, as he felt the event "was made the occasion of a great political meeting." He wrote home, "There is no military news; both sides seem to be waiting for reinforcements."[7]

One day blended into the next. During early September, the pickets of both sides bathed together in the Rappahannock. Officers and privates slept away their hours or read newspapers. Sutlers in the area were selling soda water at fifty cents a glass, and one enterprising individual set up an ice cream business, selling his product at exorbitant prices.

It was Lee who inadvertently broke the peacefulness of the summer. Deciding to reinforce Maj. Gen. Braxton Bragg's army in Tennessee, Lee sent Longstreet's corps of 12,000 men by rail during September 9–10. Evaluating the intelligence brought in by scouts, Meade concluded that some Confederate troops had left their position in front. Meade pushed forward and occupied Culpeper Court House as his new headquarters on September 13; Lee fell back without a fight. Sedgwick wondered, "What the plans are I do not know."[8]

A few days later, Lincoln and his advisors ordered 16,300 soldiers from the Army of the Potomac to travel by rail to Tennessee to strengthen the forces of Maj. Gen. William S. Rosecrans and to counteract Bragg's added strength. Rosecrans was on the verge of being besieged at Chattanooga, and the Federal administration switched its attention to Tennessee. Virginia became the forgotten theater of the war. Dismayed by Meade's lack of aggressiveness, a *New York Times* correspondent reported from the Rappahannock-Rapidan front, "What is to be done with the army?"[9]

With the return of his Vermont troops on September 22, Sedgwick was able to rebuild his reduced corps at Stone House Mountain, three miles west of Culpeper. At the same time he gained some 600 recruits, chiefly substitutes. During the first week of October, the general moved his men forward to relieve the 2d Corps on the line between Cedar Run Mountain and Robertson's River, a tributary of the Rapidan. Across the stream, the 6th Corps could observe Lee's works, long lines of fresh red earth winding with the river. The course of the Rapidan could be followed for twenty miles by the smoke of his camps. To an observant private, Peter M. Abbott of the 3d Vermont, "The Rebs have got as good a position here as they had at Fredericksburg." During the evening of October 5, the 6th Corps band played "Yankee Doodle"; the Confederate band, "Dixie." Then showing the temporary camaraderie of the two armies, the Union musicians struck up "Dixie," while the Southerners followed with "Yankee Doodle."[10]

At a summit outpost on Pony Mountain during the afternoon of October 7, Union officers intercepted a Confederate signal that led them to believe the enemy might be about to make a formidable movement. The signal flag message read, "I am at James City. J. E. B. S. [Maj. Gen. James E. B. 'Jeb' Stuart]. Another intercepted message from Stuart to Maj. Gen. Fitzhugh Lee directed the latter to draw three days' "hard bread and bacon." The next day, Sedgwick spotted indications of a movement of Confederate troops on the Union right. Observations were difficult because of the dense woods and mountains, and the enemy took full advantage of the natural surroundings. Federal cavalry probed at Germanna Ford to gather more information.[11]

Sedgwick was still cautious about making a hasty judgment on this activity. He reported to Maj. Gen. Andrew A. Humphreys, Meade's chief of staff, at 4:20 P.M. on October 9: "Is it not possible that the enemy have discovered our camp at James City and their move is to counteract that? A message from F. Lee to Stuart would indicate that."[12] Meade decided to look for himself. He and his staff passed Sedgwick's headquarters on the way to Cedar Run Mountain, the location of another Union observatory. A short time later, Meade learned from personal investigation and from Sedgwick's pickets that there was no question about a Confederate movement: Lee's infantry and cavalry could be seen crossing the upper Rapidan.

Throughout the afternoon and early evening, Meade consulted with cavalry scouts, while the enemy movement continued. At 7:45 P.M., Humphreys notified Sedgwick, "You will hold your corps in readiness to move."[13] By the next day, it was clear that Lee was attempting to march north to outflank the Union right and to interpose his forces between Meade's army and Washington. At 4:30 P.M., Sedgwick was instructed to fall back in front of Culpeper as soon as it was dark. The summer lull for the Army of the Potomac was over. Determined not to be outflanked, and remembering the hard march to Gettysburg, the Federal troops made the most of every moment as they started their northward tramp.

Meade retreated across the Rappahannock in good order and

directed Sedgwick to recross near Brandy Station and attack Lee. For this reconnaissance in force, Sedgwick commanded his own troops as well as those of the 5th Corps and a division of cavalry. The general carried out his orders with skill but Lee was not intercepted, for the Confederate leader was crossing farther upstream at Sulphur Springs. Undoubtedly realizing the similarity of the situation to that at Franklin's Crossing the previous June, Sedgwick believed the proper strategy would be to strike immediately at Lee's rear at Sulphur Springs. Such an attack would probably have prevented another race to the north as had occurred in the weeks before the Battle of Gettysburg. Meade disagreed with Sedgwick's suggestion. The Union retreat to the north continued.

After its vain attempt to catch Lee, the 6th Corps had an "hour for sleep and breakfast" while engineers blew up the railroad bridge. Sergeant Murphy noted there had been "little loss on either side. Saw a few wounded men, a broken caisson and some dead horses." During the day, Sedgwick pushed forward past Warrenton Junction and Bealeton and halted at 8 P.M., having marched more than thirty miles within twenty-four hours. On October 14 at 3 P.M., the corps arrived at Centreville and formed a line of battle. Sedgwick's men said, "Here is the third Bull Run, but this time the run will be on the other side."[14] Meade had won the race.

Centreville was only twenty-two miles from Washington, but Meade's seizure of the heights successfully blocked Lee's advance toward the capital. Lee sent Lt. Gen. Ambrose P. Hill to Bristoe Station to attack Warren's 2d Corps, which was bringing up the rear of the Army of the Potomac. Warren quickly sent his men to the shelter of an embankment and handily defeated Hill. Sedgwick's troops were not involved in this battle, but there was excitement enough at Centreville. With the rain coming down in sheets, a hatless officer burst into the 6th Corps headquarters tent and exclaimed that he had just escaped from Confederate Col. John Mosby's Rangers. This Southern guerrilla had been operating behind Union lines for some time. Hyde and a squadron of Vermont cavalry began an immediate pursuit in an attempt to cut off Mosby. They failed, but Hyde found out later from an exchanged Union officer that Mosby had escaped only by darting into a ravine at the last moment.

Lee's new offensive was blunted by his defeat at Bristoe, and he retreated. On October 17, Sedgwick led his men in pursuit through the rain and mud, reaching Warrenton in two days. On the way, the corps passed the bodies of many Union cavalrymen who had been killed in the recent skirmishes. Nearly all had been stripped of their clothing by the Confederate troops. On arrival in Warrenton, the corps occupied a ridge near the village for a two-week encampment.

The often pessimistic Meade felt that Lee had succeeded in this campaign by destroying "the railroad on which I depend for my supplies" and preventing a Union advance. For Sedgwick, however, the fighting "has been decidedly in our favour," and he anticipated that "we shall move forward again and offer battle." Although the fighting had been limited, the entire campaign had been an overall failure for Lee, as he had not been able to maintain an offensive drive. The defeat at Bristoe greatly undermined the Confederate morale. Lee told A. P. Hill, "Let us say no more about it."[15]

During late October, in Warrenton, the Army of the Potomac shivered through cold weather and wind. All was quiet except for the operations of Mosby's men in the rear; during one afternoon, Sedgwick lost thirteen officers as they strolled in the woods near headquarters. During this inactive period, General Meade received a telegram summoning him to Washington for several days' consultation. On October 22, Meade and his new personal aide, Lt. Col. Theodore Lyman, stopped by Sedgwick's tent to hand over the command to him during their absence. Lyman noted, "Uncle John received the heavy honors in a smiling and broad-shouldered style, and wished us all a good journey, for he is a cheery soul."[16]

Many of the soldiers began to erect comfortable huts with the hope that the present camp might become their winter quarters. They also started rebuilding the Orange and Alexandria Railroad, which Lee had torn up during his retreat. The corps commanders also conducted grand reviews. On November 4, Sedgwick reviewed his corps; it was a splendid affair to watch. But the privates had a different opinion of these occasions. Private Abbott wrote home, "It would have been quite a sight for you to see the performance, but we have been out on so many that we care nothing about it, after we had passed in review they could not let us cum [*sic*] into camp but keep us out and drilled us a while."[17]

The weather became mild again during early November. Meade was under pressure from the administration to fight battles. Explaining that the railroad was not completely repaired, Meade proposed to move his army to the Fredericksburg area to use the Richmond, Fredericksburg, and Potomac Railroad on a closer and more direct route to the Confederate capital. Lincoln and Halleck disagreed; the latter "could see no advantages in it." Meade was thus pinned to his old position, so he planned on an offensive to occupy the ground between the Rappahannock and the Rapidan. With the arrival of pontoons, the Federal soldiers knew they would soon be leaving their comfortable quarters.[18]

On November 6, Sedgwick was placed in command of the right wing, comprising the 5th and 6th corps, and was ordered to advance the next day to Rappahannock Station, defended by Lt. Gen. Jubal Early. Meade elected to accompany the left wing toward Kelly's Ford. According to Maj. Charles A. Whittier, "Rappahannock Station is a vile place to approach for attack — a plain long and wide with a small hill only for a mile or more till you come to the river bank, which is quite high, naturally a strong position made more so by two redoubts . . . with rifle pits extending a great distance above & below. These works have been constructed with great care & great labor."[19] The Confederate line extended a thousand yards along the river bank.

At daybreak on November 7, Sedgwick headed out on the road to capture this objective (Rappahannock Station was originally a Federal fortification, but was later abandoned during the retreat and improved by Confederate forces). At noon he halted and deployed his men into a line of battle. The men rested for several hours. Union batteries then opened fire, but they made little impression. At 3 P.M., Brig. Gen. Horatio G. Wright, who commanded the 6th Corps for this operation, successfully advanced to drive the Southern skirmishers back to their works.

It was almost dusk. Riding slowly forward with McMahon, Sedgwick saw Wright, and asked him, "Wright, what do you think are the chances of an assault with infantry on that position?"

"Just as you say, General," Wright replied rather hesitantly.

"What does Russell think about it?"

"Here comes Russell; he can speak for himself."

When Russell joined the group, Sedgwick asked, "Russell, do you think you can carry those works with your division?"

"I think I can, sir."

"Go ahead and do it."[20]

The approaching darkness was favorable to this attack, as the remaining daylight enabled the Union troops to see what they had to do before reaching the works, while the oncoming darkness hindered the Confederate defenders, who could not distinguish friend from foe. Many Southerners held their fire.

Within five minutes, Russell had assembled a double skirmish line and commanded, "Forward, double-quick." His objective was to drive to the river, about 1,500 yards away. Although wounded slightly as he advanced, Russell personally led his men against the Confederate works. The 6th Maine and 5th Wisconsin began the attack; they stormed over a formidable ditch filled with mud and water, ran across a field broken with stumps and underbrush, and leaped over a dry moat before breaking over the parapet. The soldiers charged with a terrible yelling that sounded to the Confederate defenders as if the whole Army of the Potomac was coming. A sergeant of the 6th Maine was the first man inside the works, and he discovered himself surrounded. He surrendered, but then, seeing men of his command tumbling over the parapet, he yelled, "I take it back."[21]

After seizing the works briefly, the original storming party was driven out, as the Confederates rallied. The Union regiments regrouped and charged again. At a critical moment, Sedgwick ordered Col. Emory Upton's brigade into the fight. Just before the charge, Upton told his 121st New York Regiment, "Your friends at home and your country expect every man to do his duty on this occasion. Some of us have got to die, but remember you are going to heaven."[22] Upton's brilliant charge carried everything before it. Upton seized the enemy's pontoon bridge to cut off his retreat. Hundreds of Early's troops leaped into the rapid stream in an attempt to escape; many drowned.

Sedgwick notified Humphreys almost hourly of the latest developments. At 9 P.M., he reported, "All the works on this side of the river are in our possession. We hold the bridge."[23] The next morning Sedgwick collected his dead and buried fifteen bodies in the works. He also stopped the enemy from burning the bridge.

The Union loss at Rappahannock Station amounted to 419, while the Confederates suffered 1,674 casualties, most of them prisoners. To the captured Confederate officers, the success of the Union operation was most embarrassing. One told Col. Martin T. McMahon, Sedgwick's chief of staff, that "less than half an hour before our attack he made reply to a question from General Lee, who had ridden over to the works with General Early, that he wanted no more men, and that he could hold the position against the whole Yankee army."[24]

The Rappahannock Station fight, one of the most clear-cut victories of the war, brought tremendous pride to the Army of the Potomac. Maj. Charles A. Whittier, not given to exaggerated statements, wrote, "I am going to 'blow' a little . . . for it was, I believe, the most, if not the only, decided success in which I have participated in the War." When Col. Charles Wainwright went to Meade's headquarters, he noted, "They were all feeling very jolly . . . over this success. . . . 'Uncle John,' Russell, and Upton all deserve great credit."[25]

The Confederates were completely chagrined in losing what they believed to be an impregnable position. One of Lee's closest subordinates, Maj. Walter Taylor, called it "the saddest chapter in the history of this army."[26] In the vicinity of Brandy Station, the Confederates had to abandon nearly completed winter huts, and in their haste to escape many officers left behind their trunks and valises. Some of Sedgwick's men strutted around in the gray uniforms of colonels and brigadiers. To publicize this victory, Meade sent the slightly wounded Russell to Washington. There he presented seven captured battle flags and one staff to Secretary of War Edwin M. Stanton. The secretary acknowledged his satisfaction in a public letter to Meade.

With the coming of colder weather, Sedgwick selected the Welford mansion as his headquarters, nearly opposite the ford on the Rappahannock River. The Welford House, over a hundred years old and framed in England, had been used previously as a Confederate hospital. On their arrival, Sedgwick and his staff found amputated arms on the floors and bloodstains on the floor and the tables. The land on which the house was located was owned by John Minor Botts, a strong Unionist, who had been twice arrested and released by the Richmond government. Botts suffered at the hands of both sides, as soldiers stripped his crops and ripped down his fences for firewood. In their zeal to improve abandoned Confederate huts or build elaborate houses, Union soldiers helped themselves. Within a week, miles of Botts's fences and forests had disappeared. The Federal quartermaster, however, paid him for all the wood. During the winter, Sedgwick, along with Meade and others, frequently dined at

Auburn, Botts's home. The shrewd old man wanted to ingratiate himself with the Union army and receive its protection.

As the days passed during mid-November, Meade and Sedgwick found themselves in a dilemma. On the one hand, conventional military strategy suggested that they keep the Army of the Potomac in position without any more campaigning. The railroad was not completely repaired to assure an adequate supply line. With cold weather and icy roads, a movement would be hazardous. Whittier explained, "I wish that we could have followed, but the route is unpractical, foolish, a waste of material, men, courage."[27] Yet the abolitionist press was crying for action, and this attitude was reflected by the Lincoln administration. The inactivity of the troops promoted drunkenness and declining morale. Meade left for Washington on November 14 for another consultation, and Sedgwick again became temporary commander of the army, with all its problems.

Sedgwick did not demand the rigid discipline that the crusty Meade maintained. Lyman, who remained behind during his commander's brief absence, attended a punch party that was quickly arranged after Meade had gone. Many staff officers and generals sought relaxation that evening; Lyman commented, "But mice play when the cat is too good natured." While Uncle John enjoyed a cigar, a Meade staff officer became decidedly boozy. To Lyman's thinking, "Active operations would highly benefit the army; for whiskey drinking is taken to as a defense against nothing to do." The army was being diminished by death, desertion, and sickness (feigned and real). A *New York Tribune* correspondent mentioned, "A novel mode of *getting sick* was narrated to one of our officers which is to swallow tobacco in such quantities as to keep up constant nausea and vomiting. The *epidemic* is said to have raged to a fearful extent."[28]

The inactivity grated on everyone's nerves, and Meade was often the target of criticism. Maj. Gen. Marsena R. Patrick, the provost marshal, complained, "Meade does not yet move and I don't know much of his plans, but he seems to know little about his Army. He disgusts by his apathy and indifference as regards his troops." The monotony was broken on November 20, when a group of English officers arrived and attended a 6th Corps review. All the Union generals, dignitaries, and their guests enjoyed "a most sumptuous lunch (for which General Sedgwick is noted)" along with champagne and punch at the Welford House.[29]

Camp life along the Rappahannock continued with its usual events while the railroad was being repaired. The 6th Corps regiments played baseball. One division witnessed the punishment of two deserters by branding. During this quiet period, the news of Maj. Gen. Ulysses S. Grant's victory at Chattanooga resulted in enthusiastic rejoicing.

Finally, on November 25, the railroad was completed as far as Brandy Station, the bridge across the Rappahannock was rebuilt, and supplies were brought up. Then two days of stormy weather prohibited any chance for a movement. After considering all factors, Meade had decided to advance, writing, "My army is in excellent condition, and confident of success."[30] His objective was to cross the Rapidan River to the south, and then march westward on the Orange Turnpike. With about 69,000 troops, he hoped to turn Lee's right flank, which was closest to the Federal line. The Confederate commander had about 48,000 troops, but offsetting this numerical disadvantage was Lee's thorough familiarity with the wooded country south of the Rapidan.

On November 26, Thanksgiving day, Sedgwick received his marching orders and awakened his men at 4 A.M. Contradicting Meade's optimism, Captain Halsted remembered, "When we received the order to move, I do not believe there was a single officer at our headquarters but felt apprehensive in regard to the result. It seemed as though we were just going to butt our heads against a very thick stone wall."[31] Sedgwick began his march at 6 A.M. and was scheduled to follow Maj. Gen. William H. French's 3d Corps. But when Sedgwick arrived at French's encampment, the 3d Corps was still asleep. Not a tent was struck or a wagon loaded. Sedgwick had to halt his march until 11 A.M. to wait for French to get underway. Thanksgiving dinner for the 6th Corps, bolted down along the way, consisted of the usual hardtack and pork. After a rugged tramp, the troops finally reached Jacob's Ford long after dark. Crossing the Rapidan was then impossible; the engineers had failed to bring up enough boats to build a pontoon bridge.

The night was very cold and windy as the corps prepared for a midnight bivouac on the wet ground. Since the wagons had not arrived, Sedgwick and his troops were without blankets. Building fires and using their horses' saddle blankets, the general and his staff "managed to get through the night without freezing to death." Hyde and another aide crawled into a bearskin bag.[32]

Forced to improvise, the engineers completed a bridge with poles. At dawn, Friday, November 27, the army crossed the Rapidan, with Sedgwick following the 3d Corps. Again French had his problems, for as he attempted to lead the Union forces to Robertson's Tavern, he took the wrong road. In the thickets of the wilderness, one road or track could not be distinguished from another, and soon French stumbled into Confederate Maj. Gen. Edward Johnson's division. The firing of the enemy troops was very heavy, and French's hard-pressed corps began to yield. The hapless general sent immediately to Sedgwick for support. Sedgwick was so close behind the line of battle that Confederate artillery shells, aimed at the 3d Corps line, often overshot and crashed into the area of the 6th Corps. One cannon ball shrieked by within twenty feet of the general and his staff as they stood under a tree watching two stretcher-bearers carry off a wounded man. The shot struck both of the bearers, killing one instantly and fatally wounding the other; the man upon the stretcher leaped up and, with a maniacal yell, ran for his life into the woods. As shocking as the incident was, Sedgwick and his staff could not suppress a laugh when they saw this speedy recovery.[33]

The firing was so intense in the woods to the east of Robertson's Tavern that Sedgwick's staff compared the artillery barrage to Fair Oaks and Antietam. Both sides charged back and forth, fighting for possession of a wood road. Col. J. Ford Kent, the general's aide near the front, came back to report. With face flushed and eyes sparkling, he said, "General, they charged, then we charged, and we got more ground than they did." All the Confederate charges were repulsed during the rest of the day. Cpl. Edwin Horton of the 4th Vermont wrote home to his wife,

> If I ever lay clost to the ground, it was at this time. This was one of the most heartrending seens [scenes] I ever witnessed although I was not near enough to fire myself. We lay where we was in fair range of the rebs big guns which threw canaister and shells around us like the devil. Here is where I see men piled up in all shapes, you can never have any idea of the horror of a battle until you witness one, although they dont call this but a skirmish."[34]

The Union timetable began to break down as Meade lost the advantage of surprise. By stalling the Federal advance and preventing the turning of their flank, the Confederates were able to fall back in good order to the west. At 11 P.M., Sedgwick received orders to continue in the direction of the Orange Turnpike. He marched during the night to Robertson's Tavern, the destination the Army of the Potomac should have reached twenty-four hours before.

On Saturday morning, Sedgwick made a juncture with Maj. Gen. Gouverneur K. Warren and went into position to form the right wing. During the night the Confederates had retreated and crossed the stream of Mine Run, where they began throwing up defensive works on the west bank. This little river, with high banks on both sides, flows northward, perpendicular to the old Orange Turnpike, and joins the Rapidan a few miles downstream. The Union forces pushed forward to Mine Run without opposition. As he was placing his troops along the high ground above the river, Sedgwick found a bare hill. This lookout commanded a perfect view of the enemy's position from his center to his left.

The opposing lines were quickly drawn. On the right bank of Mine Run, Sedgwick held down the right flank of the Union army, with French in the center and Warren on the left. Across the stream, Lee deployed his forces to form a solid frontal line. So skillful was his defense that Meade halted his movement to reconnoiter the ground and revamp his strategy. Sedgwick spent all day Saturday and most of Sunday looking around as he awaited Meade's orders. About 200 yards in front, around a farmhouse and out-buildings, Confederate sharpshooters had taken cover; now and then, Sedgwick and his staff heard balls whistling about their ears.

From Sedgwick's lookout, the view of the Confederate line was so spectacular that it took the efforts of several staff members to keep back the men, who were no less curious than officers to see "the position." During the cold and rainy Saturday, Meade arrived at the hill for a personal assessment. Meade and Sedgwick, with two other 6th Corps generals, went on a twenty-minute reconnaissance to the bottom of the hill in advance of the Union line of battle. Surveying the Confederate works, Meade remarked, "We have got another Gettysburg in front of us."[35]

Night approached. Sedgwick insisted his headquarters be placed on the hill in a Sibley tent partly concealed by pine boughs.

Halsted recalled, "Some of us tried to coax the General to go to a safer and equally eligible place, but without success."[36]

Sunday, November 29, was frittered away as Meade waited to complete his arrangements. The rain stopped, but the weather became cold and icy. Soldiers who had thrown away their overcoats and blankets during the march suffered intensely. From the Union lines, the men observed that the Confederates had dug a series of strong lines of rifle pits. Sedgwick reported to headquarters, "The enemy were at work last night slashing timber."[37]

Southern pickets fired periodically through the camp. As Sedgwick stood on the crest of the hill with some visiting English officers, a shot "cut the tree off as if with a knife, a foot higher than the general's head." Looking at the Confederate position at that moment, Sedgwick did not even lower his spyglass. The English officers also barely escaped being killed.[38]

That evening Meade called his corps commanders together at Robertson's Tavern. General Warren suggested that his corps attempt a flank movement on his left, cutting Lee off from his communications. On the advice of General Wright, Sedgwick proposed initiating a flank march of his own on the right. Meade approved of both plans and placed Sedgwick in charge of both the 5th and 6th corps, some 30,000 men.

At 2 A.M., November 30, Sedgwick moved his command about two miles to the right, leaving some brigades and batteries to hold the old position. A bright moon helped the troops move through the woods. By 4 A.M., the general's men arrived at their new place. Corporal Edwin Horton, who was posted on the skirmish line, wrote, "It was a frosty night, and I never suffered so much from the cold in my life." Water froze in the soldiers' canteens. No fires or loud talking were allowed. Although the pickets were changed every half hour, a few froze to death. As morning approached, "the men trotted about in their little circles and went through all sorts of gymnastics to keep themselves warm." Yet everything was in readiness; Sedgwick's movement was undetected as he opened fire with his batteries at 8 A.M. The time of the assault was fixed for 9 A.M. [39]

Sedgwick's plan was basically sound, for the Confederate left was not yet fully protected. "Everything was in prime order," Halsted wrote. "We were all very sanguine as to the result." Even the men felt this optimism and bantered with each other as to who

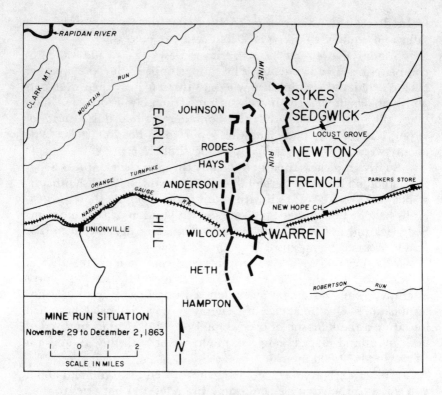

Would be the first in the enemy's works. Bets were taken. Yet these same men "knew that success was to be gained only with immense losses." Many pinned little white patches on their breasts. On these pieces of paper, the men had written their names so that their bodies might be identified if they fell during the assault. Others threw away the slips of paper that were being passed around; they said they did not expect to get killed. Many of the soldiers asked the chaplains to take farewell messages. Others filled their pockets with hardtack so they would "have something to eat while going to Libby." To the chaplains, quartermasters, and other noncombatants, the soldiers handed over money, watches, and other valuables for safekeeping. One distrustful individual buried his watch and money near a tree.[40]

As his artillery pounded away, Sedgwick awaited the scheduled assault. Suddenly, at 8:45 A.M., one of the general's officers came rushing up to Sedgwick, closely followed by Capt. George Meade, son of the general. Young Meade, his face cut in a bad fall from his horse, gasped out, "The order to attack is countermanded." The announcement to cease all operations came as a shock: Sedgwick's staff had firmly believed that an attack would carry the unfinished Confederate fortifications. From Meade's communication, Sedgwick learned that Warren, circling to the left, had encountered strong lines of works that rendered a successful assault impossible. "Useless and hopeless," were Warren's exact words. The suspension of the assault soon reached the ears of the soldiers, who began kidding each other about their prayers and solemn farewell messages.[41]

The delay was a godsend to the Southern troops, who promptly began protecting their heavily threatened extreme left. Halsted noted, "Trees were felled, rifle pits made, batteries moved into position." By the end of the day, the Confederates had constructed a formidable defense line. Sedgwick reported to Humphreys, "I do not believe the enemy's works can be carried in my front by an assault without numerous sacrifices. I regard the chances as three to one against the success of such an attack."[42] This blunt evaluation reflected sound military judgment. The opportunity was lost.

Under the cover of darkness, Sedgwick withdrew to his old position on Mine Run. The next day, Tuesday, December 1, was bitterly cold. More pickets were discovered frozen to death at their posts. Food and supplies ran low; one 6th Corps division drew rations of very hard bread. When Brig. Gen. Thomas H. Neill broke open a cracker, he said to his servant, "Jim, give us one that hasn't so many worms in it." Realizing that further offensive movements were impracticable, Sedgwick made necessary preparations for a night movement. Receiving such an order, he withdrew with his command at 9 P.M. To deceive the enemy about his retreat, he had the pickets build fires and keep up a show of force.[43]

The army retreated across the Rapidan at Germanna Ford on a pontoon bridge. Sedgwick halted his men near Stevensburg on the morning of December 2. Thousands of exhausted soldiers cooked coffee or slept around their fires. Corporal Horton drank coffee, to ward off "an awful cold," and managed to catch a little sleep. "I needed it," he wrote, "for I hadent [*sic*] slept any for the four previous days."[44] His unit was out of rations, and he left for picket duty on an empty stomach. The next day, December 3, Sedgwick resumed his march and reoccupied his old headquarters at Welford's Ford. Arriving at 4 P.M., having had only one meal in the last two days, the men enjoyed a dram of whiskey. Sedgwick had en-

dured the hardships of a common soldier: he had not washed his
face or taken off his boots, even his spurs, for a week.

The Mine Run campaign was over. Both sides suffered relatively light casualties — 1,653 Union men compared to the Confederate loss of 745 soldiers. But in terms of human suffering, the Mine
Run affair was, in the words of Col. Moses Tyler, "the most vexa-
tious we had experienced up to this time."[45]

To the Northern press and to many politicians in Washington,
the campaign was a failure. Compared to Grant's sweeping victory
at Chattanooga, Meade's efforts seemed a fiasco. The *Washington
Star* headlined its story, "The Army of the Potomac and Its Hesi-
tating Generals," and stated, "So long as our army in this quarter
continues to be guided by its present counsels in the field, it is now
clear that it will fail to command public confidence." Rumors circulated that Meade would be relieved. Gen. Marsena Patrick recorded
in his diary entry for December 6, "There is quite an exciting discussion going on among the newspapers about Gen. Meade's successor, the radical papers taking for granted that Meade is to be removed." The old stories that Warren and Sedgwick had previously
been tendered the command, but had declined the appointment,
were again printed. The latest "credited but unconfirmed" rumor
had Maj. Gen. Alfred Pleasonton as the new commander. Within a
week, however, the stories died away.[46]

The soldiers who actually observed the situation at Mine Run
had a different viewpoint of the campaign and their commander.
Lyman respected "the extraordinary moral courage of General
Meade, which enabled him to order a retreat, when his knowledge,
as an engineer and soldier, showed that an attack would be a blunder."[47] Although Sedgwick might have attacked successfully in his
limited sector, it would have been almost impossible to follow up
such a brief triumph; supplies were lacking, and the weather was
extremely cold. The wounded would have perished in such tem-
peratures.

Going into winter quarters did not lessen the workload and
other problems that daily confronted Sedgwick. At their encampment on the Hazel River, two miles from Brandy Station, the 6th
Corps soldiers worked "like beavers on their camps to make themselves comfortable during the cold winter."[48]

Sedgwick had heard about the possibility of a reorganization of
the army, and he wrote to Col. Edward D. Townsend, assistant

adjutant general, on December 16. Declaring that he did not "know or care a straw" whether he was to retain command of the 6th, Sedgwick asked for Townsend's influence to preserve the corps as a unit; he asserted, "there is a great deal of *esprit de corps* in it. I do not believe there is a regiment in it that would leave willingly."[49] (To his satisfaction, the 6th Corps remained essentially intact for the spring campaign — only a few units were transferred.) During December, the reenlistment question and the government's offer of bounties and furloughs to returning veterans became standard subjects of discussion among the men.

As peaceful as the Army of the Potomac winter encampment seemed to be, the enemy continued to disrupt and harass the Union army. Mosby's men continued to carry out raids in the rear of Federal lines. Sedgwick's troops remained on guard and subject to immediate call throughout the winter.

On New Year's Eve, Sedgwick was compelled to react to an emergency. The officers of the 93d Pennsylvania were enjoying a repast at regimental headquarters. At 8 P.M., as Chaplain Lane was preparing to pronounce the benediction, a bugle sounded "pack up." The order to move included all of Sedgwick's 3d Brigade of the 3d Division, commanded by Brig. Gen. Frank Wheaton. After a night march in knee-deep mud, the troops arrived at Brandy Station and boarded open flat-bottom freight cars. The train was destined for Harpers Ferry, where they were to meet an anticipated advance of the enemy through the Shenandoah Valley, and also to guard prisoners quartered there. Not until early spring of 1864 did this veteran division return from its temporary assignment and rejoin Sedgwick's corps.

Feeling the cold, the men picked up bales of hay at the station and spread it over the bottom of the cars for insulation. Nevertheless, they suffered intensely throughout that frosty night; many had frostbitten feet and arms when they arrived. Amputation was necessary in two cases, and one proved fatal.

With the apparent suspension of military operations during the winter, many of the high-ranking officers became unwillingly ensnared in politics, which became more and more pronounced during the long wait for an upcoming spring offensive. The first indication of conflict between Sedgwick and the Lincoln administration had already occurred during the fall. Sedgwick was a conservative Democrat and felt "the greatest regard and admiration" for his old commander, George B. McClellan. Since his removal from the command of the Army of the Potomac, McClellan had become increasingly active in the Democratic Party, and had quickly become an anathema to the Republican administration. On September 1, Sedgwick wrote to his classmate, Maj. Gen. William H. French, and suggested that McClellan's old friends should present Little Mac with "some little testimonial as a pledge of their esteem." To Sedgwick, it was purely a private affair, and nothing more. After all, both Sedgwick and Meade had already received such presentations within their military circle. Soon this idea grew into plans for a "McClellan testimonial," and Sedgwick, Sykes, French, and others felt that it would not be reasonable to limit the affair to just a few friends; they would allow all the old soldiers to join. A circular was proposed, with a rate of subscription for each rank. Sedgwick pledged $20,000 for himself and his corps.[50]

The Radical press, especially the semi-official *Washington Chronicle,* bitterly branded this circular as a political move. Another circular, apparently originating in Washington, was sent to the Army of the Potomac headquarters at Culpeper, denouncing the proposed testimonial "as contrary to Army Regulations" and instructing its supporters "to proceed no further in the matter." On September 25, French wrote to Sedgwick that he had anticipated Washington's reaction, and "would not have advised the 'Round Robin.' " French further confided that "the whole affair, although well meant, was . . . too 'abrupt' " and suggested that the subscriptions be returned in "a quiet way." French thought he would be victimized for his role and could "offer no opposition except that of the 'lamb' for slaughter."[51]

General Meade was persuaded by the Lincoln administration that the testimonial should be quashed; he issued an order to do so, quoting army regulations. Before the whole business was stopped, Sedgwick claimed that 12,000 men in the 6th Corps had subscribed a total of $10,000. It was common talk at Army of the Potomac headquarters that Secretary of War Edwin M. Stanton had actually drawn up an order "summarily dismissing from the service Generals Sedgwick, Sykes, and Hunt, together with a number of other officers, for the part they had taken. Although he remained in the service, Sedgwick must have known that the Radical Republicans would be most happy to dismiss him on any conceivable charge.

In a private letter to Holmes in November, Sedgwick's aide,

Maj. Charles A. Whittier, confided: "I am a copperhead & serve with a man [Sedgwick] proud of McClellan & who thinks he is the man to command this army. Gen. S. is a copperhead. I am sure too that he has done & will always do all possible to stop the war."[53] As copperheads were Northerners who sympathized with or openly supported the Confederate cause to the extreme of demanding that the Lincoln administration sue for peace, Whittier's remark about his superior is inaccurate. But Sedgwick's Democratic Party affiliation, coupled with his conscientious refusal in avoiding bloodbaths for his corps, made him vulnerable to such assumptions during this period of Northern war weariness.

Within a short time, still another crisis drew Sedgwick into an ugly controversy. As the press and Washington officials speculated about Meade's performance at Mine Run, they began to question the conduct of General French. French certainly was guilty of bungling his work. The prevailing belief, even among some of the high-ranking officers such as General Patrick and Colonel Wainwright, was that French had been drunk during the movement, and this had caused him to lose his way twice. This talk soon reached the ears of a *New York Tribune* correspondent who publicly charged in an article that French was indeed intoxicated and was the cause of the Mine Run blunders.

When Sedgwick learned that his close friend was being slandered, he broke his habitual silence. In a letter to French on January 12, 1864, Sedgwick stated that the accusation was "grossly unjust" not only to French, but also to Meade. Recalling that he had observed French on numerous occasions during the campaign, Sedgwick wrote, "During all this time I saw nothing in your manner . . . to give ground for the suspicion that you were . . . under the influence of liquor." The whole charge, he insisted, was "wantonly false in every particular."[54] This letter — perhaps supplied by French to bolster his declining reputation — was soon reprinted in a newspaper.

General French replied that the letter had reconciled him "to the calumny and slanders — no generous, brave, or honorable man would have stated such gross charges to strangers against a brother officer, with whom he had been on terms of friendship for twenty years." French charged that Meade was attempting through his aides to create trumped-up charges against him "for future use and reference."[55] Despite fairly conclusive evidence of French's intoxication, Sedgwick defended his West Point classmate through blind allegiance, not sound judgment. Sedgwick was in error, but the incident blew over.

On January 9, 1864, Meade left for Washington for a few days, and Sedgwick again assumed command of the army. While on leave, Meade became seriously ill with pneumonia and inflammation of the lungs. It was not until February 16 that he had recovered sufficiently to resume his duties. For over a month, Sedgwick was left to deal with the problems of the army. He thoroughly disliked the daily ride to his troops and "looking over papers, sometimes called 'redtapism.' " Patrick commented, "Sedgwick does not run the Army with much vim! Why should he?"[56]

Administrative problems were heaped on the general's desk. One in particular required immediate attention. Many destitute people, including women and children, lived in the vicinity of the Union encampment. Maj. Gen. George Sykes explained, "Common humanity requires that they should be fed."[57] On January 27, Sedgwick advised Sykes that all those who could afford payment should send their orders to the provost marshal; penniless citizens would be issued food and supplies on approval of corps commanders and the taking of an oath of allegiance. General Patrick was in charge of this relief operation. The Northern press assured the public that there would be no malappropriation of property.

A quick solution was also needed concerning furloughs. Many officers and soldiers had not yet returned from winter leaves. For his own 6th Corps, Sedgwick submitted a field report for January 25, 1864, which disclosed that more personnel were away than were in camp. Over 10,000 men were absent. The problem of absent men, the general admitted, was "beyond my control." Sedgwick wrote again to Col. E. D. Townsend, the assistant adjutant general, and suggested that all men on leave be returned immediately: "If this is not done, I fear it will not be possible to furlough before the season for active operations commences all the enlisted men now here awaiting furloughs and those who will re-enlist if they can be furloughed." To promote reenlistments, inducements were necessary. Thousands ultimately did reenlist, and nearly all claimed that they cared little for large bounties, but that the thirty-five days' furlough was their chief consideration.[58]

Many officers took advantage of their friendship with the good-natured Uncle John to make special demands. Maj. Charles P.

Adams desired a seventy-day furlough to visit his mother in London, and the application was sent to Sedgwick for his signature. Lyman commented, "A lucky thing that Gen. Meade is not here."[59]

Throughout the time Sedgwick was in command, President Lincoln sent him many messages suspending executions of Union soldiers. Deserter Joseph W. Clifton, for example, escaped the gallows as the president commuted his sentence to imprisonment at Dry Tortugas, Florida. Sedgwick sent the records and court transcripts in these cases to Washington for further study.

On the evening of February 3, while in the midst of his paper work, Sedgwick received a startling message in cipher from Maj. Gen. Benjamin F. Butler, commander of the Army of the James. Butler had devised a desperate plan, and having political influence in Washington, he had cleared his arrangements through General in Chief Henry W. Halleck. Butler wanted Sedgwick to make a forward movement within two days toward Richmond and engage Lee's troops so that Butler's army could attack the Confederate capital in a surprise move up the peninsula from Fort Monroe. Replying the next morning, Sedgwick disagreed with Butler's strategy, citing the unfavorable weather and bad roads. He flatly stated, "The Rapidan in my front is so strongly intrenched that a demonstration upon it would not disturb Lee's army." Both Sedgwick and Humphreys were privately disgusted with the whole business, "looking on it as childish."[60]

Butler ignored this response. He immediately informed Secretary of War Stanton, "I can get no co-operation from Sedgwick."[61] Soon Sedgwick received orders from Halleck and, under direct pressure from Washington, consented to make a vigorous demonstration regardless of weather. There was no choice in the matter; Butler's political machinations outweighed the military and strategic considerations.

On Saturday, February 6, Sedgwick began his advance to the Rapidan in the rain and deep mud with the 1st and 2d corps and sufficient artillery. At Morton's Ford, the main force waded across the stream, with frigid water up to their waists, and managed to surprise the Confederates temporarily. But with extensive earthworks and increasing fog, Lee's soldiers easily fought off the attack. General Warren was almost killed. Sedgwick lost 200 men before tramping back ten miles to camp. With the aid of lanterns, the staff rode back in three hours.

Through official reports and an official despatch, the head-quarters of the Army of the Potomac learned that Butler had suffered but nine casualties in his great move on Richmond; he was stopped by some trees felled across the road at Bottom's Bridge. One of Butler's enlisted men, held in a stockade for some offense, had escaped from his guard, deserted to the enemy, and informed them of the intended movement.

Humphreys was "very mad" about the whole affair. In a telegram to Halleck on February 7, Sedgwick showed his disgust, stating, "One result of the co-operation with General Butler has been to prove that it has spoiled the best chance we had for a successful attack on the Rapidan."[62] At the president's urging, Halleck demanded a point-by-point explanation of this statement. Sedgwick replied in detail. The impression in Washington, however, was that the Army of the Potomac had not done its job in supporting Butler.

On February 13, Meade spent the entire day at the War Department and the White House. Stanton told Meade that several officers in his army "did not have the confidence of the country."[63] Without mentioning names, Stanton indicated these officers were injuring the army and Meade should not retain them. A general "sweeping out" would be forthcoming.

Meade returned to Culpeper on February 15 to resume command, which undoubtedly pleased Sedgwick. He had learned in the last month that there was much more to running an army than fighting battles: the constant bickering between military and civilian authorities, the day-to-day administrative work, and the problems associated with feeding and quartering an army had frustrated him. Soon after Meade's return, there was talk about changes at headquarters. Sedgwick wrote his sister, "We hear that there is to be a reorganization of this army, probably for the purpose of getting rid of some obnoxious Generals. I shall not be sorry to hear that I am one of them. . . . I could even leave altogether without many regrets."[64]

During the winter of 1863–64 there were occasional moments when Sedgwick could relax along with the other 100,000 men in the encampment. The officers and men devoted themselves to debating societies, horse races, cock fights, contests with greased pigs and poles. Checkers, chess, and cards were favorite pastimes. The Christian Commission assisted the soldiers in building chapels, and many grizzled veterans felt a change of heart. Everyone looked forward to occasional trips to Washington. Regiments built amusement halls, and amateur troupes gave entertaining performances. Many wives came for visits; in early February, nearly a thousand were in camp. Some of Sedgwick's young lady relatives and friends made the trip from Connecticut, and the general's staff gave up their own quarters temporarily to assure them a comfortable stay. The corps vied to present the most glittering balls in improvised ballrooms for the ladies and for guests from Washington. On one occasion, Sedgwick attended an affair given by the 2d Corps at which Vice President Hannibal Hamlin, a senator, a cabinet officer, and four members of the British legation were present.

Sedgwick's greatest pleasure was to remain at his Welford House headquarters, playing his favorite game of solitaire or occasionally cribbage. He enjoyed watching his staff officers play dominoes or poker, but declined to join in himself. With indulgence, the general permitted his men to bet on horse racing and cock fighting in camp. On one race, the 6th Corps backed its fastest horse very heavily in a match against the favorite of the 2d Corps. The result reduced the general's gambling officers to "absolute penury until the next arrival of the paymaster."[65]

As the winter passed, Sedgwick became something of a celebrity. Little girls wanted his autograph. After sending a few in care of Maj. Gen. Henry J. Hunt, Sedgwick wrote, "I hope they will bring something, as they never have to me." The public also requested photographs. Sending "two poor photos" to some young ladies, Uncle John sadly noted, "They make me both much too old, but somehow I cannot have one taken without that fact appearing."[66] Humorous stories were told around camp about "Old Sedgwick." Once a lady on a religious mission appeared at the Army of the Potomac headquarters. She claimed to have direct communication with God, who gazed down with approval on the efforts of the army. Receiving two documents from this lady, Sedgwick read a letter of introduction from Secretary Stanton, but declined to examine the other, purporting to be from the Savior. Sedgwick solemnly explained that the secretary's letter represented enough authority for him, and that it would not be proper for him to receive communications from higher sources except through official channels. The religious lady remained in camp for a few days as Sedgwick's guest.

Other humorous incidents broke the routine. One day a Virginia matron arrived at Welford House with a number of turkeys for sale. She had reserved an especially large one as a gift for the general. Uncle John was on the porch in his usual informal attire without any insignia of rank. Realizing that he was not recognized, he assured the lady that the general hated turkey and would not accept it. Finally he consented to buy it and signed his name on an order for the purveyor. As Sedgwick walked away, the Virginia dame read the signature and exclaimed to a staff officer who had overheard the conversation, "There! Why did you let me make such a fool of myself?"[67]

The Army of the Potomac veterans assumed they would spend the rest of the winter in their warm, comfortable encampment, awaiting the spring offensive. The earlier cooperation with Butler seemed to indicate that more winter movements were unlikely. Then, on February 11, in an apparently routine request, Lincoln asked Sedgwick to send Brig. Gen. Judson Kilpatrick to Washington for two or three days. "Kill-cavalry," as he was nicknamed, proceeded to Washington, where he proposed a daring raid on Richmond. Lincoln approved the plan, in which Kilpatrick and Col. Ulric Dahlgren were to free Union prisoners as they swept through the Confederate capital. Authorized from Washington, the raid did not have the endorsement of either Meade or Sedgwick.

To support Kilpatrick's daring scheme, Sedgwick and his 6th Corps found themselves on February 27 once again breaking camp and marching toward the Rapidan. Nothing was done to conceal this movement; their job was to create a diversion with Brig. Gen. George A. Custer's cavalry in the direction of Madison Court House so that Lee would be given the impression that his left flank was in danger of being turned. On February 28, Sedgwick reached Robertson's River, built a bridge, and crossed for an overnight bivouac. Custer and his men rode southward, and the dashing cavalry officer explained that if he did not return by Wednesday, March 2, Sedgwick should withdraw. Sedgwick checked with Humphreys, however, who told him "to remain until directed to return."[68]

The 6th Corps soldiers remained in position in the rain and mud for two days. They heard gunfire in the distance after Custer advanced; then the sounds died away. After anxious waiting, the soldiers saw Custer return to their line at about 5:30 P.M. on March 1, a day earlier than planned. He and his entire command had almost been captured through the treachery of a guide who had attempted to lead them directly into Lee's main body of infantry.

Custer had discovered this plot in time and retreated on the same road. At 6 P.M., Sedgwick reported Custer's safe return and notified Humphreys that he was withdrawing all his troops, as "the river is rising rapidly" and his men could be isolated on the southern bank by the swollen stream.[69] After crossing to the north side of the river, the men of the Greek Cross spent another miserable night. Through a mixup, the wagon containing their blankets could not be found. The soldiers gathered around large fires, told stories, and passed around bottles of whiskey as they whiled away the hours until dawn.

After two sleepless nights and a twenty-three-mile march through the mud, the men of the 6th Corps arrived back at their old quarters. Their feint had been successful and well carried out; Kilpatrick's bold and foolhardy dash, on the other hand, had resulted in the death of Dahlgren and in no material gain. Sedgwick felt, "The great raid was a great failure. It does not seem to have been made with any judgment."[70]

Troubles were again brewing in Washington. Sedgwick was upset by the Joint Committee on the Conduct of the War, which opened its hearing on February 26. The first witnesses, Maj. Gen. Daniel E. Sickles and Maj. Gen. Abner Doubleday, were most critical of Meade's generalship at Gettysburg, contending that he wanted to retreat. On March 3 and 4, Brig. Gen. Albion P. Howe, one of Sedgwick's division commanders, attacked both Meade and Sedgwick, charging them with lack of vigor and alertness in both the Gettysburg and Mine Run campaigns.

Since the Battle of Gettysburg, both armies had maneuvered and fought to a stalemate. Sedgwick had seen many situations requiring professional military judgment left to the discretion of amateur soldiers and the civilian authorities in Washington. The results were often costly. Time and time again, it seemed that the professional soldier's career was not necessarily based on his ability, but his political allegiance and influential friends. As spring approached, rumors circulated within the Army of the Potomac that Maj. Gen. Ulysses S. Grant was coming to take command. Everyone felt there would be changes.

CHAPTER 6

A NARROW ESCAPE
IN THE WILDERNESS

DURING EARLY MARCH 1864, Sedgwick and his corps settled down into a familiar routine at Brandy Station. The general dutifully paid attention to his paperwork and arranged for his diseased and incapacitated men to be assigned to the Invalid Corps. On March 9, the Army of the Potomac received the long-awaited news that President Lincoln had presented Ulysses S. Grant with the recently restored rank of lieutenant general—he was to command all the Union armies. On the following day, Grant and his staff visited Brandy Station to confer with the generals of the Army of the Potomac. Sedgwick, who had known Grant during the Mexican War, went to see his old army friend.

Along with other high-ranking officers, Sedgwick spent part of the evening with the "Hero of Vicksburg" and discussed the upcoming campaign. The 6th Corps commander "was most agreeably disappointed, both in his [Grant's] personal appearance and his straightforward, common-sense view of matters. . . . Good feeling seemed to exist between him and General Meade." Sedgwick was surprised at Grant's presentable appearance, so much in contrast with that of the old army days. As Sedgwick rode back to his corps headquarters with Brig. Gen. Henry Prince and Colonel Whittier, Prince remarked, "The last time I saw Grant was in St. Louis. I was breakfasting at the Planters Hotel and I was told a man was waiting to see me. I went down and found Grant, who asked me to lend him

143

a quarter of a dollar. I asked him why he hadn't come to the breakfast table. He said, 'Oh, I am too filthy and wretched to be seen among decent people.' "[1] The three riders were amazed at Grant's subsequent career.

Everyone, from Sedgwick to his lowest private, indulged in intense speculation and comment on Grant's recent elevation to such a high position. Soon after returning to Washington, Grant decided to accompany the Army of the Potomac in the field, and he gave his orders to Meade for execution. Sedgwick's veteran soldiers held a mixed opinion of this Western general. Col. Selden Connor, recently transferred to another corps, wrote, "There is no enthusiasm for Gen. Grant; and on the other hand, there is no prejudice against him. We are prepared to throw up our hats when he shows himself the great soldier in Virginia against Lee and the best troops of the rebels." Pvt. Edwin Wentworth of the 37th Massachusetts Regiment explained to his wife, "We shall whip the rebels now we have Grant to lead us. Meade was a good general, but he was subject to the order of Halleck. Grant outranks Halleck and is subject only to the President." Sedgwick's associate, Brig. Gen. Joseph Bartlett, commented, "Grant, I am told, says he will not move in one month, two months, or three months, unless he is more than reasonably sure of success and that all the clamor of newspapers in the North will not have any effect at all upon his movements."[2] Everyone watched Grant closely.

Sedgwick was on good terms with Grant and wanted to serve under him, but he soon learned that his reputation among his West Point comrades did not ensure his retention. In consultations with General Meade in Washington, Secretary of War Edwin M. Stanton decided to remove Sedgwick as a corps commander in the Army of the Potomac. Still convinced that Sedgwick was to blame for Butler's failure during the abortive operation against Richmond in February, Stanton also had other reasons he felt to be valid: Sedgwick's allegiance to the Democratic Party, his friendship with General McClellan, and the presence of Maj. Arthur McClellan, the general's brother, on his staff created a feeling of uneasiness in Stanton's mind. The only solution was to demote the general to a less important command.[3]

Meade protested vigorously at the suggestion that Sedgwick be replaced. He insisted that "he did not know what General Sedgwick's politics were; that probably they were the same as his . . . but he was sure of his [Sedgwick's] loyalty and efficiency." Meade insisted that Sedgwick was "more necessary" to his army "than any other man."[4] Stanton remained undaunted. He told Meade that he would give Sedgwick an even better assignment — an independent command in the Shenandoah Valley, comprising 40,000 men. Meade, finally worn down, consented and recommended Brig. Gen. John Gibbon to command the 6th Corps. Meade and Stanton parted with the understanding that orders would be issued the next day. But higher authority intervened. Lincoln directed that Maj. Gen. Franz Sigel should be assigned to the army in western Virginia. So the whole arrangement fell through, and Sedgwick remained with the 6th Corps.

The entire matter was disturbing to Sedgwick, who believed that Meade's appeal to the president had secured his retention. Halleck, who often overemphasized his role, declared after the war that he had intervened to prevent Sedgwick's dismissal.

Although Sedgwick was retained, important changes were made that affected the 6th Corps. The reorganization of the Army of the Potomac was announced to the officers and soldiers on March 24. The army's five corps were consolidated into three. Corps commanders George Sykes, William French, and John Newton left Grant's army for new assignments. The 3d Division of the 3d Corps was transferred permanently to the 6th Corps and became the 3d Division under the Greek Cross. The 6th Corps now consisted of three divisions, comprising eleven brigades. Two veteran soldiers, major generals Winfield S. Hancock and Gouverneur K. Warren, commanded the 2d and 5th corps respectively.

Brig. Gen. Albion P. Howe, who had criticized Meade and Sedgwick severely for their alleged lack of leadership and judgment at Gettysburg, was one of the displaced officers and did not return to the 6th Corps. Sedgwick wanted, and finally secured in April, Brig. Gen. George Washington Getty for the post of commander of the 2d Division. Getty's previous assignment had been acting inspector general of the Army of the Potomac. Getty "soon won the absolute respect and confidence of all under him, and his men came to believe . . . that they had about the best division commander in the army."[5]

Sedgwick saw his corps "considerably increased" and wrote to his sister, "I hope when the campaign opens to have twenty-five thousand men and forty-eight pieces of artillery — a small army in itself."[6] Through a month of rebuilding, Sedgwick satisfactorily achieved his goal by April 30, when he signed his "consolidated morning report." He submitted detailed lists of figures, revealing that the strength of his command aggregated 24,413 men, including staff, cavalry escort, engineer detachment, infantry divisions, and an artillery brigade. His corps included 942 "serviceable horses" and forty-eight guns.

The largest command ever led by Sedgwick included many old subordinates, along with some new officers. Brig. Gen. Horatio G. Wright — on whom the general relied with such confidence that he designated Wright as his successor — commanded the 1st Division of four brigades. The first, second, third, and fourth brigades were led, respectively, by colonels Henry W. Brown and Emory Upton and brigadier generals David A. Russell and Alexander Shaler. The four brigades of Getty's 2d Division were commanded by Brig. Gen. Frank Wheaton, Col. Lewis A. Grant, Brig. Gen. Thomas H. Neill, and Brig. Gen. Henry L. Eustis. The newly assigned 3d Division, with Brig. Gen. James B. Ricketts commanding, comprised only two brigades, commanded by brigadier generals William H. Morris and Truman Seymour. The men of the latter unit, known in both armies as "Milroy's weary boys," endured a dubious distinction. Beaten by Jackson in 1862 and again by Ewell in 1863, they had never done well. Sedgwick's artillery brigade commander, Col. Charles H. Tompkins, had eight batteries of six guns each, totaling twenty-four Napoleons, eighteen three-inch ordnance, and six ten-pound Parrot guns. Sedgwick had a full-time job preparing his corps for the work ahead.

March was a stormy month. Rain, hail, and snowstorms followed each other to create swollen streams and bottomless mud. Grant and his army simply had to wait. On March 22, six inches of snow lay on the ground at Brandy Station, and two Vermont regiments engaged in a snowball battle. Through early April, the crests of the Blue Ridge Mountains were white with snow.

On one occasion during this disagreeable weather, Sedgwick displayed his concern for the welfare of his men. After being stationed temporarily in West Virginia, Wheaton's brigade returned to Brandy Station in the midst of a driving rainstorm. Debarking on the soaked and muddy ground, Wheaton saw all the available groves of trees occupied with troops and could find no bivouac area except open, muddy fields. While Wheaton's officers were looking around disconsolately, "a large, stalwart horseman, in a plain cavalry overcoat" rode up in the mud, and said, "General Wheaton, you may put your men in those woods." The soldiers recognized Sedgwick, who pointed to a grove of pines already occupied by a brigade commander monopolizing a choice area with widespread huts, horse sheds, and quarters for guards, orderlies, cooks, and servants. Placing the interests of his men above the cozy comfort of this subordinate, Sedgwick quietly suggested that he vacate a greater part of the grove so that Wheaton's deserving brigade could make shelters. The soldiers blessed the "Old General" for his order "to go for the trees." They cut off the tops of the fine ornamental trees and used the pine boughs to keep themselves out of the mud and water.[7]

The first half of April "was almost one continual succession of snow or rain storms." Capt. Philip Schuyler, on the staff of the provost marshal, noted on April 10, "The country here is impossible — everything flooded streams and rivers most dangerous objects — three horses were drowned last night in a torrent which a few days ago was a driblet of a stream. It is again today — I do not think we will move for a fortnight yet."[8] Yet Grant and Sedgwick had to keep their troops busy during this monotonous period of waiting.

Interested in the health of his men, Sedgwick issued a directive to determine the number of sick soldiers who could not march; many had been weakened by measles, pleurisy, fistulas, arthritis, and pneumonia. On April 16, Sedgwick released a circular pertaining to the establishment of field hospitals for the divisions. The surgeons were instructed "to design the location of the hospital, anticipating the encampment of the troops . . . and will on reaching camp, have the tents pitched using the stretchers for beds."[9]

That month Sedgwick was again called to Washington and ordered to testify before the Joint Committee on the Conduct of the War. He offered his explanation of the events at Chancellorsville and at Gettysburg. Defending his own performance at those two battles, Sedgwick related the facts as he remembered them without harsh criticism of Hooker or undue praise of Meade. After this ordeal, Sedgwick was glad to return to Brandy Station, well away from Congressmen and the press.

Throughout March and April, Grant, Meade, and their corps commanders conducted reviews of the troops. To Pvt. Edwin Wentworth of the 37th Massachusetts, these grand occasions were distasteful. "I don't like these reviews," he wrote. "They are hard exercise, all 'fuss and feathers.' " Another 6th Corps soldier, Pvt. Wilbur Fisk of the 2d Vermont, enjoyed them, especially when he saw Sedgwick review his brigade. When Fisk noticed Sedgwick talking excitedly with some officers, he "couldn't tell what he said exactly, but I knew well enough he was telling them how quick he could take Richmond if he only had Vermonters enough to do it."[10]

As the weather improved, Grant personally reviewed his various corps. April 18 was devoted to reviewing the 6th Corps. Grant was mounted on a fine chestnut and was well dressed. Col. Theodore Lyman commented, "The Corps seemed an endless affair; there were upwards of 20,000 men in line, battalions massed. Grant gave some offense by receiving Gen. Sedgwick's salute with a cigar in his mouth, a fault partly to be laid on Gen. Meade's shoulders, who told him there was no harm in it; for the good general has the failing of nine tenths of our officers — a disregard of formal details that brings more trouble than one would think."[11]

With the many reviews, everyone sensed the spring campaign was about to begin. Pvt. S. F. Hildebrand of the 139th Pennsylvania Volunteers wrote, "I suppose our next Review would be by General Lee on the other side of the Rapidan."[12] Tenseness and anticipation prevailed in the minds of Sedgwick and his men. No one knew what Grant's plans were. The rumors and speculation continued. During March, Grant ordered all ladies from camp; by April 18, the sutlers and Federal citizens left the Culpeper encampment, not to return before the fall.

As uninformed as any common soldier in his corps, Sedgwick reflected in a March letter, "The truth is, we are on the wrong road to Richmond." Instead of remaining on the Orange and Alexandria Railroad, Sedgwick believed a shorter and more practical route to be the old Fredericksburg approach with access to the Richmond, Fredericksburg, and Potomac Railroad. But changing the lines of communication for the Army of the Potomac would require a two-day march southeastward through the Wilderness. On April 26, Sedgwick wrote home for the last time, explaining that "we have been engaged in winning political victories, when we should have been engaged in preparing for the rebels." The general also expressed no confidence in Butler's Army of the James being assembled on the Peninsula. Doubts always haunted him before every campaign.[13]

By the spring of 1864, the Army of the Potomac had lost much of the enthusiasm of the previous three years — a much grimmer mood prevailed. Adj. Anthony M. Martin of the 87th Pennsylvania believed, "If Congressmen at Washington or the Rebel Congress at Richmond were required to endure the hardships of a soldier's life during one campaign, the war would then end." One of Sedgwick's old soldiers, Col. Selden Connor, correctly gauged the army's spirit, saying, "We are stripping for work, and we anticipate plenty of it — hot and heavy. You don't hear any big talk in the army now."[14] After the ordeals of Chancellorsville, Gettysburg, and Mine Run, Sedgwick struggled to maintain his corps' fighting spirit.

To break the monotony of camp life, many of his soldiers walked across the railroad tracks at Brandy Station to have their photographs taken by a tintype artist. The photographer was doing a "rushing business." Everyone wanted to send home a picture before starting out on a campaign from which many would not return. Preparations continued; Corporal Horton wrote, "We are preparing for a battle. . . . We practis target shooting every day now."[15]

On April 22, 1864, Sedgwick received a confidential telegram from the assistant adjutant general, Col. Seth Williams. Grant gave his 6th Corps commander orders to "immediately draw the supplies of ammunition, subsistence and forage required by existing orders to be kept on hand in your command." After impressing on Sedgwick "the necessity of making every preparation," Williams asked for an acknowledgment. Sedgwick complied.[16]

On April 28, Sedgwick relaxed at a sumptuous dinner given by John Minor Botts. Practically all the generals, including Grant, attended. This was the last of the social affairs. All that remained now was for Grant to issue the order.

During his stay at Culpeper, Grant had attempted to formulate a satisfactory plan in which four Federal armies would move in concert against the Confederacy. Maj. Gen. Henry W. Halleck, the deposed general in chief, was stationed in Washington with the new title of chief of staff of the army; he was to coordinate matters between Grant in the field and President Lincoln. By remaining with the Army of the Potomac, Grant planned to advance against Lee's Army of Northern Virginia, destroy it in the field, and then capture Richmond. To accomplish this task that had eluded all previous Union commanders, Grant had assembled an immense aggregate of infantry, cavalry, artillery, and other special details — some 118,000

men. Despite the complicated logistical and topographical problems, Grant decided to cross the Rapidan in hopes of turning Lee's
right. With his preponderant forces, the Federal commander hoped
to maneuver through the Wilderness without a fight, move to the
left, and bring his lines into fairly open country. This plan corre-
lated with Sedgwick's own private thoughts expressed in his letter
home in March; capture of Fredericksburg and seizure of its railroad
lines would be the direct route to Richmond.

With his headquarters at Orange Court House, General Lee
had gathered together about 62,000 men to oppose Grant's invasion. Grant outnumbered Lee by about 57,000 troops and almost a
hundred field guns. The enterprising Confederate leader, however,
decided to assume the counteroffensive and to concentrate his forces
in the Wilderness. Lee would fall on Grant during his march and
hold him in the tangled labyrinths of the forest, thus rendering
Grant's artillery and cavalry virtually useless. Unlike Grant, Lee
knew the terrain well; he chose the Wilderness as an ideal place to
defeat the Army of the Potomac as he had done a year before at
Chancellorsville.

All the plans devised at Union and Confederate headquarters
remained unknown to Sedgwick and his 6th Corps. On May 3, Maj.
Gen. Andrew A. Humphreys, chief of staff of the Army of the
Potomac, released an operational plan to the corps commanders.
Humphreys's orders concerning the men of the Greek Cross read,
"Major-General Sedgwick, commanding the Sixth Corps, will move
at 4 A.M. of the 4th instant, by way of Stevensburg and the Germanna Plank Road to Germanna Ford, following the Fifth Corps,
and after crossing the Rapidan, will bivouac on the heights
beyond." At 3 P.M., the 6th Corps received the news. First Lt. James
W. Latta, of the 119th Pennsylvania, noted in his diary, "Camp in
confusion, packing up, etc." — the 6th Corps had thirteen hours to
prepare for its long-awaited march. All the soldiers were issued 50
rounds of cartridges and 6 days of rations. Sedgwick soon received
an order from Col. Seth Williams, stating, "Your pickets are to be
withdrawn soon after dark." The rumors at last had become a
reality.[17]

At 2:30 A.M. on May 4, the 6th Corps broke camp at Hazen
Run. In the faint light of the coming dawn, bands of the different
regiments sounded reveille and various calls. The corps began to

form. Private Hildebrand remembered that it was a moment of "intense interest and excitement to every man. . . . The beginning of a march toward the Rapidan was of itself sufficient to cause one's pulse to get a rapid 'move on.' "[18] Sedgwick and his staff rode along the lines at 6 A.M.; it was foggy, but the troops recognized "the old rooster" by his well-known figure and familiar straw hat.

The day grew hot. Many of the raw recruits had loaded themselves down with excessive equipment, and they threw away much of it. Long before reaching the river, the 6th Corps had littered the sides of the road with thousands of overcoats, blankets, knapsacks, and articles of clothing. Some men exchanged their old equipment for new items when they found them. Straggling developed, as many soldiers still carried great loads on their backs. Many became lame. Capt. Oliver Wendell Holmes, Jr., commented, "Almost everyone including me had a headache by the end of the march."[19] But Sedgwick kept his troops moving to the Rapidan.

As the 6th Corps approached Germanna Ford, the men saw "a squad of Union Scouts on horseback clad in complete Confederate uniforms." To the amazement of the new recruits of the Greek Cross, these scouts filed off into the woods undisturbed by the Union soldiers. Sedgwick led his men across a bridge over the 200-foot Rapidan River without incident. On the south bank, on top of a bluff, was the temporary headquarters of General Grant. Relaxing with a cigar on the porch of an abandoned farmhouse, Grant watched Sedgwick's men pass, and remarked, "Well, the movement so far has been as satisfactory as could be desired."[20]

Sedgwick arrived at his designated bivouac area, about three miles south of the bridge, and halted at 5 P.M. The 119th Pennsylvania camped in a grove of pine woods. With six of its companies out on the picket line, the 15th New Jersey bivouacked near a secessionist's sawmill and helped themselves to the lumber for fires. The regiment cooked supper and boiled coffee. Despite their fatigue, a few soldiers could not resist filling up a boiler and starting up an old steam engine. One of Sedgwick's brigade commanders, Gen. Alexander Shaler, lodged at a fine old Virginia mansion occupied by a strong Southern sympathizer. Shaler remembered the presence there of "two pretty girls but awfully down on all Union officers." Throughout the encampment, everything was "quiet and peaceful, as if there was not a reb within a hundred miles, or ever had been."

But Sedgwick and his veterans felt uneasy. As Lt. James W. Latta predicted before he went to sleep on that peaceful night, "We are on the eve of a great battle."[21]

After their sixteen-mile march on the first day of the campaign, the 6th Corps was in the heart of the Wilderness. Grant decided to let his wagon trains come up and to allow his troops sufficient rest so they would be fresh if they met the enemy the next day. The Wilderness is ten to twelve miles across in any direction and is characterized by many low ridges alternating with swampy swales. The area was thickly wooded, in 1864, with but an occasional field, and intersected by only a few narrow roads. The region was rich with iron deposits, and extensive mining had been carried on. For the operation of the mines, much of the original timber had been cut down, and a dense second growth of low-limbed and scraggly pines, chinquapins, scrub oaks, and hazel had arisen. Soldiers could see only twenty yards ahead in the undergrowth. Old mining pits were everywhere, and winding rivulets added to the complex topography. The average soldier in Sedgwick's command had little knowledge of the roads or the topography and could easily get lost. Sedgwick prepared to maneuver his troops in precise tactical situations through the most impenetrable woods.

The few roads that traversed this gloomy area were narrow tracks in the forest. Germanna Plank Road extended from the Rapidan in a southeasterly direction, where Brock Road intersected it. The two other major roads in the area, the Orange Turnpike and Orange Plank Road, extended to Fredericksburg in an east-west direction and intersected the Germanna Plank and Brock roads at right angles.

Commanding the Union right, Sedgwick held Germanna Plank Road to a point just west of the Wilderness Tavern. Maj. Gen. Gouverneur K. Warren deployed his 5th Corps to secure the Union center. On the left, Maj. Gen. Winfield S. Hancock of the 2d Corps originally formed the Union line at Chancellorsville, but soon moved southward to take up a position on Brock Road. Still in reserve, Maj. Gen. Ambrose E. Burnside's 9th Corps was preparing to cross the Rapidan.

During his uneventful bivouac, Sedgwick received instructions for the next day, May 5. Issuing his orders in a most routine manner, Meade stated, "General Sedgwick . . . will move to Old Wilderness Tavern, on the Orange Court-House Pike Road as soon as the road is clear. He will leave a division to cover the bridge at Germanna Ford until informed from these headquarters of the arrival of General Burnside's troops there."[22] At daybreak on May 5, Sedgwick's troops pushed out to obey these instructions. The general extended flankers out to his right.

Suddenly, at about 8 A.M., firing was heard in the area where Warren's troops were known to be posted. Sedgwick and his staff rode over to Meade's headquarters, now located at Lacy House, and had a short conference. Col. Thomas Hyde of Sedgwick's staff was asked to act as messenger between Meade and Grant for part of the day. Although the firing continued in the distance, Meade remained calm. He reported to Grant at 9 A.M., "Warren is making his disposition to attack, and Sedgwick to support him. . . . I think, still, Lee is simply making a demonstration to gain time." Unknown to Meade and Sedgwick, however, Lee had advanced his troops eastward on the Orange Turnpike and Orange Plank Road to attack in full strength the unsuspecting Union forces.[23]

With the ability he had displayed at Gettysburg, Meade decided to improvise and rearrange his army to best possible advantage. Once again he called on Sedgwick. Allowing his 6th Corps to serve as a manpower pool, Sedgwick supplied men to fight in critical areas. To bolster his left flank, Meade ordered Sedgwick to send his 2d Division, commanded by General Getty, to march eastward to Todd's Tavern and join General Hancock's 2d Corps.

At 10:15 A.M., Getty's division (except Neill's brigade) left to close a gap in the Union line. This reduced Sedgwick's original force by about one-fourth, and he did not see this detached unit again for almost forty-eight hours. Only vague rumors indicating terrible fighting and heavy losses reached him periodically. Soldier Wilbur Fisk of the 2d Vermont, a member of the Getty contingent, participated in the two days of fighting; he wrote in his diary:

> Before light the next morning [May 6] I heard an aide tell Captain Bixby who now was ranking captain and had charge of the regiment that we were to advance down into the same place again and meet the enemy once more on the same ground. I am willing to admit I dreaded it. The officers, too, thought that they were asking us to do more than our share of the bloody work. . . . But not a man flinched. There was no skedaddling to the rear.[24]

Sedgwick and his remaining troops heard the firing in the distance and were filled with terrible anxiety, but they concentrated on defending their own sector of ground.

At 11 A.M., Sedgwick and his other two division commanders, Generals Wright and Ricketts, left the Wilderness Tavern to support Warren's 5th Corps, then engaged on the Orange Court House Pike. Although the distance was only two miles, the 6th Corps was considerably delayed in reaching the scene of the fighting. Col. Emory Upton, commanding one of Wright's brigades, noted, "It was impossible to march in line of battle on account of the dense pine and nearly impenetrable thickets which met us on every hand."[25]

Taking advantage of the thinly defended Union position, Confederate troops had forced back the Federals, captured their line, and entrenched. When most of Sedgwick's force arrived, at about 2:30 P.M., Warren decided to counterattack and ordered Brig. Gen. John C. Robinson's men to make the assault. The 6th Corps was to join in this attempt, but Upton refused to move, saying, "It is madness." A brigade of Robinson's division bravely charged, but "the plain was swept by canister at 350 yards."[26] The attack failed with heavy Union losses. Anxious to hold this strategic terrain, the Confederates fired on Union stretcher-bearers who advanced to bring in the wounded.

A short time later, the 6th Corps veterans counterattacked successfully, charged the hill, and captured about thirty Southerners. Although 200 yards in advance of the 5th Corps line, Wright established his position there, as the hill was strategically important. To prevent any further Union advance, the Confederates set the woods on fire, especially in front of and around Upton's position. The ground was strewn with the wounded of both armies, and many perished in the flames.

By mid-afternoon, Sedgwick arrived with the rest of his forces. He set up headquarters near the front lines close to the crossroads of the Orange Turnpike and the Culpeper Mine Road. Cannon balls from hidden Confederate batteries were landing in range of the camp. Two war correspondents were advised to go to the rear. By then Hyde had been released from his temporary assignment and rode up on horseback to report to his commander. As he dismounted, Hyde was immediately knocked down. A shell had decapitated a New Jersey soldier, and the flying head struck Hyde, covering him with brains and blood. Sedgwick was but a short distance away. Although physically unhurt, Hyde was upset and was useless as a staff officer for fifteen minutes. Other cannon balls struck near a number of mounted troops and bounced under the horses. Fragments were thrown in the air, but Sedgwick escaped unhurt. Realizing the critical state of the fighting, the general sent a messenger to Burnside for assistance. Burnside had crossed the Rapidan with his 9th Corps and was willing to send a division, but Grant made another disposition of this unit. Left virtually alone, Sedgwick was dependent on his staff to convince Meade and Grant that he needed additional support.

During the late afternoon, heavy skirmishing continued on Sedgwick's line. The soldiers heard the Confederates felling timber and covering it with earth as they prepared defenses. The opposing lines were on two slopes of a ravine, with a swamp in the middle. Although the chopping was often done less than a hundred yards away, a dense thicket hid the enemy soldiers. The skirmishing continued and soon a battle raged furiously along the entire Union front. The wild yells of the Southern charge were interrupted by the cheers of Northern soldiers. Artillery was of little use in the forest, and the rifle replaced it in the work of destruction. Some soldiers fired so many rounds of ammunition that their Springfields became too hot to hold. Two 6th Corps brigades charged up a strongly defended slope. The fighting continued after dark until, having lost heavily in killed and wounded, Sedgwick recalled his troops.

The action for May 5 finally ended long after dark. Both sides had suffered great losses. Many men from both armies looked for water during the night and found themselves along the five-mile battlefront within opposite lines. Latta reflected on the day, commenting, "The regiment behaved gallantly. . . . We still remained in the front with no prospect of being relieved."[27] Hampered throughout the day by the terrain — thick underbrush entwined with vines — and the burning woods, Sedgwick had accomplished as much as he could with his reduced force.

Nightfall brought no relief to Sedgwick's exhausted men. A hundred yards away were enemy pickets, within pistol-shot range. Sentinels on either side challenged each other sharply, and fired when a "halt" was disregarded. The enemy was heard chopping, working, and fortifying along Sedgwick's front, and soon thereafter dragging artillery into position. Col. Clinton Beckwith of the 121st New York heard horrible sounds in the night. "We lay in line of battle upon our arms," he wrote, "and shortly after dark when the firing slackened, the cries of the wounded between the lines . . . was something terrible to hear. Some prayed, some cursed, some cried, and some asked to be killed and put out of their misery."[28]

To establish contact between the 5th and 6th corps that night, Col. Mason Whiting Tyler of the 37th Massachusetts selected one of his sergeants, an experienced backwoodsman and surveyor. Leaving their sleeping comrades in a thickly wooded ravine, these two soldiers, with four others, managed to feel their way through the woods until they found the 5th Corps encampment.

That evening Grant and Meade conferred at Lacy House headquarters. Grant remarked, "I feel pretty well satisfied with the result of the engagement; for it is evident that Lee attempted by a bold movement to strike this army in the flank before it could be put into line of battle and be prepared to fight to advantage, but in this he failed." Receiving intelligence reports that Lee was reinforcing his lines with 12,000 fresh troops, Grant decided to seize the initiative before they arrived. He ordered an assault along the whole Union line at 4:30A.M., on May 6. Meade and Grant disagreed about the time of the attack, and Grant modified his original plan. Humphreys sent identical orders to Hancock, Warren, and Sedgwick: "The attack ordered for tomorrow will begin at 5 A.M., instead of 4:30 A.M."[29]

As dawn approached, Sedgwick and his troops on the Federal right prepared to strike at the designated time. But, anticipating the Union plans, Confederate Lt. Gen. Richard S. Ewell launched a spoiling attack at 4:30 A.M. Swarming out of their trenches and advancing across swampy ground, the Southern troops vigorously pressed their attack. Although the assault was launched without warning, it did not maintain momentum. Sedgwick's men were ready, held their lines, and prepared to counterattack.

Sedgwick's counterthrust produced heavy fighting. Many volleys were fired at point-blank range. About one-third of a mile behind the battle line, Sedgwick stood along in the middle of an old road. First Lt. James H. Smith of the 43d New York hobbled to the rear with a wounded leg, using a stick as a cane. Smith noted that the general wore an earnest and anxious expression on his face. After saluting each other, Sedgwick sympathetically inquired about Smith's wounds, and added, "How is it at the front?"

"There is very hard fighting, sir," Smith said, "but we will whip them sure."

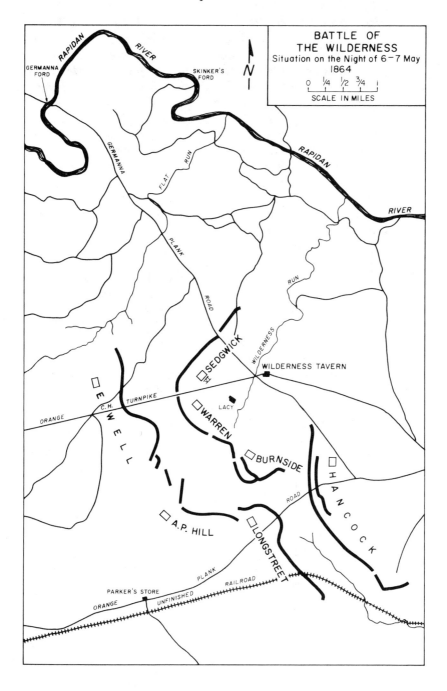

BATTLE OF
THE WILDERNESS
Situation on the Night of 6–7 May
1864

SCALE IN MILES

With a smile, Uncle John answered, "I should think by the sound that there was some fighting; of course we will whip them." He directed Smith to a field hospital behind the lines.[30]

In spite of his optimism, Sedgwick's drive failed. The Confederate defenses — combined with natural obstacles of a marsh covered with a heavy growth of thorn bushes — held its ground. Beaten back with heavy losses, the general retreated to his original line.

Two hours later, at 9 A.M., Sedgwick again sent his two divisions to crack the Confederate line. Brig. Gen. Truman Seymour commanded his men that not a shot should be fired until the enemy's works were reached. "We must find where those rebels are," he said, "and give 'em the bayonet."[31] Then he waved the signal for the charge. Bitter resistance was encountered. Twice Sedgwick's determined troops fought their way to the parapets of the Confederate trenches, only to break before the intense fire. The advance was held to only 200 yards and did not dislodge Ewell.

Meade was greatly concerned about developments on the Union left, which had become the key area of the battle. Seeing that Sedgwick and Warren were not denting the Confederate line, he ordered them at 10:35 A.M. to suspend their attacks. Humphreys notified Sedgwick, "You will at once throw up defensive works to enable you to hold your position with the fewest possible number of men, and report at once what number of men you will have disposable for an attack upon Hancock's right." Sedgwick reported back at 11:30 A.M., "I am afraid that as soon as the work is commenced, they will annoy us with shells and delay the work. They have four batteries in front of my line." An army engineering officer and his party of pioneers supervised the work of entrenching. With a skirmish line out in front to give warning of attack, the 6th Corps stacked its rifles and set to work. The general discussed the situation with his officers and reported to Humphreys: "My breast works are nearly up. . . . I think I can dispense with Morris's and Upton's brigades. I do not think it would be safe to reduce more. General Wright is strongly of that opinion."[32]

To hold the Union left, Sedgwick supplied Morris's brigade of 4,000 men and Upton's force of 1,000. With this troop reduction and with partially completed field works, Sedgwick's right flank lay exposed in a most vulnerable position. To compound his worries, Sedgwick kept receiving news during the day about the terrible losses of Getty's division. Anxious about his right, he sent Colonel

Hyde scouting to the river and back to see if there were any signs of the enemy. Hyde returned, reporting that he had seen nothing. Although Sedgwick had requested troops thirty-four hours before to protect the Union right, he discovered that Meade and Grant planned to strip his corps further.

On the very day Sedgwick was facing this crisis, the *New York Tribune* commended the general: "It is a great tribute to Gen. Sedgwick that he has been longer in this army with high command than any other officer and has had the unshaken confidence of every Commanding General. His record would make a French soldier Marshal of the Empire." It was Sedgwick's nature to cooperate with and adjust to occasional overbearing demands by his superiors. In this instance, however, his willingness to supply troops had resulted in a critical weakening of his line.

Sedgwick's 6th Corps remained entrenched throughout the afternoon. The losses suffered in the early morning caused a considerable contraction of the line to the left. Drawing his forces closer together, General Seymour abandoned some high ground in the woods and stationed his men in the bottom of a ravine. This new position was dangerously overlapped by the Confederate front and was continuously subjected to an enfilade fire of both infantry and artillery. Ordered to strengthen the line at the extreme Union right, Gen. Alexander Shaler was dismayed to discover its vulnerability. He was alarmed "that an army of 100,000 men had its right flank in the air with a single line of battle without entrenchments and ⅔ of that flank not even advised. I lost no time informing Genl Seymour that I would not be held responsible for any disaster that might befall the troops at this point, calling upon him for at least 4,000 or 5,000 more men to properly defend that point." Seymour's brigade had only recently joined the 6th Corps and, in Shaler's words, "Seymour was a stranger to me, and my troops to him." But Seymour apparently did nothing; he did not even post pickets on the road that led to Germanna Ford. Sedgwick was not notified of this gross neglect.[33]

Shaler's and Seymour's troops were reasonably well entrenched by late afternoon. Both these generals decided to report to 6th Corps headquarters to confer with Sedgwick. As commander of this sector, Seymour gave his men permission to make small fires and cook coffee, a privilege they had not enjoyed since the morning of May 5. Then, with the situation apparently under control, both generals rode off. The troops quickly started fires. Without warning, Confederate troops led by Brig. Gen. John B. Gordon dashed down the slopes at 6 P.M. "with the force of a thunderbolt." Col. Matthew R. McClennan, commanding the 138th Pennsylvania, reported that "before the men were properly under arms, the Fourth Brigade of the First Division was hurled upon us in confusion by an overwhelming enemy, and soon the panic spread, resulting in a disorderly and hasty retreat to the Chancellorsville road." The veterans of Gordon's Georgia brigade charged "with their peculiar yell and a withering volley . . . and 'sent us whirling.' " Panic-stricken soldiers ran empty-handed down the narrow wagon road in the woods. Company commanders shouted angrily at their men, charging them with cowardice and dishonor. "Milroy's weary boys" had disgraced themselves again. The 6th Corps sustained four hundred men killed and several hundred taken prisoner; Gordon's loss amounted to about fifty.[34]

At 6th Corps headquarters, Generals Seymour and Shaler had finished talking with Sedgwick and were preparing to return to their commands when the attack began. As Seymour mounted his horse, he said, "Well, General, we have repulsed two attacks today, but my men are pretty shaky, and I should be very fearful in case of another attack." Whittier recalled the incident: "Just as he [Seymour] said these words — bang, bang, bang — the attack came, and the division at once melted into thin air." Shortly thereafter, the startled general and his aides saw "throngs of excited men pushing through the bushes for the rear." Without a moment's hesitation, Sedgwick rode straight down the road himself. Oblivious of his personal safety, he rushed here and there, urging the fugitives to halt. Boldly throwing himself "into the breach, and on the very front of the line," Uncle John swung his hat in the air. "Stand! Stand, men! Remember you belong to the Sixth Corps," he shouted to his veterans. Everywhere he went he held the line by his personality.[35]

Seymour and Shaler also rushed into the heart of the stampede and attempted to stem the retreat. Other courageous officers tried to rally their men: Col. Benjamin F. Smith of Seymour's brigade shouted, "Shoot them, bayonet them, stop them any way you can!" A short time later, Seymour was captured. As Shaler rode into the streams of fleeing men, he pleaded, "For God's sake, men, make a stand on this road, if you think anything of the Army of the Potomac, make a stand on this road! If you think anything of your country, for God's sake, make a stand on this road!" Recognizing the colors of a regiment, Shaler urged, "The 61st Pennsylvania, why sergeant, advance with those colors and Pennsylvanians don't you desert them." The Confederate momentum was too strong, however, and Shaler and a small number of brave men were overwhelmed. To his disgust, Shaler found himself "in an instant surrounded by a dozen or more butternuts, each having his gun pointed in the direction of my innocent carcass."[36]

In spite of the initial shock, the situation of the Union right was not as hopeless as it had originally seemed. General Wright kept his men in order. Sedgwick notified Meade of the crisis and requested reinforcements. Continuing his personal reconnaissance, Sedgwick soon discovered himself trying to maintain order in the darkness of the forest; trees, shadows, and men became difficult to distinguish. An officer whose voice he recognized told the general that he was going to investigate some moving objects on one of the narrow roads. This captain advanced, and Sedgwick followed rapidly, to make his own observations. Convincing the general that he should wait in this hazardous situation, the captain moved forward and discovered the flitting shadows to be moving men. Loud voices rang out, "Surrender, you Yankee son of a bitch!" The captain hastily retreated, and Sedgwick returned to his own lines. If not stopped by the captain, Sedgwick would have ridden about fifty yards ahead into a group of forty Confederates. Certain capture would have resulted.[37]

At about 7 P.M., two of Sedgwick's aides, Col. E. B. Beaumont and Capt. J. Ford Kent, galloped up in a great flurry to Meade's headquarters. They exclaimed to Meade and Colonel Lyman that "the 6th corps was broken and driven back . . . and that we had better look out not to be captured." Both aides were practically hysterical.

Meade asked calmly, "And where are Upton's and Shaler's brigades that Sedgwick said he could spare me this morning?"

"I don't know, sir."

Meade retorted, "Do you mean to tell me that the Sixth Corps is not to do any more fighting this campaign?"

"I am fearful not, sir," Kent answered.[38]

Wild rumors that both Sedgwick and Wright had been captured were soon circulating around Meade's headquarters. Meade immediately reported the situation to Grant, who was temporarily away from Lacy House: "General Sedgwick has just reported the enemy having vigorously assaulted his line and turned his right flank. I have sent the Pennsylvania Reserves to him." He added in a postscript, "Another officer just reported that Sedgwick's whole line has given way." Within a half hour, Humphreys, Meade's chief of staff, notified Hancock of Sedgwick's situation and ordered him "to send all the troops you can spare up here as soon as possible." In the excitement and panic of the moment, Meade and Lyman were disgruntled by the 6th Corps' performance; the latter called it "a most disgraceful stampede."[39]

The rumors about Sedgwick's plight continued. At 7:30 P.M., Lyman relayed these reports to Grant, who was in a nearby hollow. The usually imperturbable general was more disturbed than Meade about the news. Soon afterward the two harried commanders met to discuss the situation. Listening to the report of one hysterical officer, Grant said, "I don't believe it." Meade ordered the officer under arrest for spreading false rumors. Later reports convinced Humphreys that the crisis was over and the whole affair exaggerated.

Meade and Grant had acted promptly to divert disposable reserves to Sedgwick's line. The two brigades led by Upton and Russell, which had been detached in the morning for Hancock, were now called on to return and restore order. They hurried on the double-quick to Sedgwick's battered lines.

Arriving near 6th Corps headquarters, Upton reformed portions of the two regiments at the rifle pits. Sedgwick quickly consulted with him and ordered that he endeavor to regain the lost ground. Upton displayed no hesitation. Using the North Star for direction, he began his reconnaissance in the dark. His troops expected a volley at any moment from the enemy concealed in the thicket. The skirmishers of the 95th Pennsylvania could hear the dry leaves and brushwood cracking under their feet as well as the groans and sighs of the wounded still in the weeds.

Finally reaching the scene of the earlier rout, Upton's men discovered "little pots of coffee on smouldering embers, and pans of meat in process of frying, side by side, all undisturbed. . . . Knapsacks, haversacks and canteens were scattered around in every direction, guns and accoutrements lay beside the killed and wounded, tin plates and cups lay all about, and shelter tents, which had been stretched from the breastworks, remained intact, while those in the rear were partly knocked down in the hurry to leave them. The whole scene was infinitely awful."⁴⁰ After moving through a mass of fallen timber and abatis (timber with sharpened sticks set up as defenses), Upton's troops secured a favorable position.

Federal troops kept arriving. The Pennsylvania Reserves had been eating their supper on Lacy's Farm when they received Meade's order to fall in and march to support of the 6th Corps. In the darkness, they found their way more by the roar of the battle than by knowledge of the country. After a long march through the woods, the reserves arrived at Sedgwick's headquarters only to have the general tell them that he did not require additional troops. They returned to the farm for the night.

At 10 P.M., the strongly entrenched 61st Pennsylvania Regiment easily beat off a Confederate night attack in its sector. With his own regrouped veterans and new troop additions, Sedgwick worked to strengthen his position as the night continued. In a new headquarters at the extreme end of the Union right, Sedgwick and his aides worked by lantern light to devise a new position for the corps. This defensive line crossed the Germanna Plank and Culpeper Mine Ford roads in the vicinity of the old gold mine mill. Here men began throwing up entrenchments around midnight, and gradually the defenses became solid. Satisfied that the peril was over, Sedgwick sent Grant and Meade the laconic message, "I have re-established my lines."⁴¹ Sedgwick had turned the near defeat of the early evening to a formidable position as dawn approached. His leadership had contributed much to the reversal of events.

Fighting all along the Union line had been heavy the day of May 6. The soldiers sent letters to assure their families of their safety; quickly penciled notes described their terrifying ordeal. Brigadier General Webb wrote, "I have lost most of my brigade, have had a fearful battle. . . . Lee is very strong. God alone saved me. . . . I had a terrible defeat." Perhaps Colonel Lyman had the most succinct summation of the last two days: "In truth, this whole Battle of the Wilderness was a scientific 'bushwhack' of 200,000 men."⁴²

May 7 dawned hot and sultry. After finishing its entrenching, the 6th Corps worked to clear the roads for the supply and hospital trains. No one was able to find time for sleep. During the early morning, Sedgwick sat with his aides on the pine-needle-strewn roadbank with the freshly spaded line of entrenchments behind them. A long, black smudge was visible on his left cheekbone where he had been brushed by a charred limb.

The tired general was soon notified to prepare for a night's march to Spotsylvania. Grant had decided to move out of the Wilderness. Realizing that the Confederates would be difficult to dislodge because of their fortifications and their knowledge of the area, Grant planned to move eastward, outflank Lee, and prevent him from falling back to Richmond. At 6:30 A.M., he ordered Meade to make all preparations during the day for this movement. The orders concerning the 6th Corps stated, "Sedgwick can move along the pike to Chancellorsville, thence to Piney Branch Church and on to his destination."[43] Sedgwick was the oldest corps commander, and it took all his energy to keep his stubby body going during these emergencies. The younger Meade and Grant were pushing "Old Sedgwick" to his physical and mental limit.

The day was quiet except for minor skirmishing and sharpshooters, but the mental tension remained. After a brief encounter with an enemy battery, Sedgwick probed in front of his lines. He notified Humphreys that "the cavalry find nothing as far as they have been out to the left of the Germanna Plank road." A little later, Sedgwick again reported, "My infantry pickets now reach from the Rapidan to General Warren's right." In front of the 87th Pennsylvania, skirmishers were actively engaged the entire day. These 6th Corps veterans heard the "zip, zip of the minie balls above and around them." Being so near the enemy skirmish line, they could hear the conversations of the Confederates, although they could not see them because of trees and smoke. "Hello, Yank, how are you?" asked the Southern pickets. The answer was "All right, Johnnie, look out or you'll get hurt."[44]

Sedgwick kept busy, sending reports and supervising entrenching. At noon, he sent Hyde with some cavalry on a reconnaissance to see if the Confederates were endeavoring to cut the 6th Corps off at the river. There was no serious attempt.

A more rewarding event greeted Sedgwick. General Getty's contingent, comprised mainly of Vermont troops, returned to the 6th Corps during the afternoon. When the Vermonters saw their commander, they broke out into wild cheering. Sedgwick blushed as he saluted their colors. This tired and decimated unit managed to build some fine earthworks by evening.

At 3 P.M., Meade issued the final orders of the day, which slightly changed Sedgwick's itinerary: "At eight and a half o'clock P.M., General Sedgwick, commanding Sixth Corps, will move, by the pike and the plank road, to Chancellorsville, where he will be joined by the authorized trains of his own corps and those of the Fifth corps; thence, by way of Alrich's and Piney Branch Church, to Spotsylvania Court House, and the road from Alsop's to Block House."[45] The long and circuitous march would begin in the darkness and continue throughout the night.

At 6 P.M., Sedgwick ordered his corps to fill canteens and be ready to move at a moment's notice. It was a sultry night with no cooling breeze. No rain had fallen for several days and the soil was bone dry. The wagon trains moving along the Germanna Plank Road and Orange Pike created a cloud of dust that soon rose hundreds of feet into the air. The Federal uniforms were gradually changing to the color of Confederate garb. To the east, the 6th Corps heard the wild cheering of Hancock's men as they recognized General Grant riding along the ranks. The men waited for an hour, as the orders to march had been postponed an hour to 9:30 P.M. Then Upton's brigade, which had performed so much fighting, marching, and countermarching during the last three days, led the 6th Corps out of the Wilderness on its way to Spotsylvania. The ordeal in the Wilderness was over. The cry was "On to Richmond!"

The Battle of the Wilderness proved costly to both the Army of the Potomac and the 6th Corps. The Union force of 118,000 men suffered a total of 17,666 casualties. The losses of the 6th Corps during the battle aggregated 5,035; some 719 were killed. The Confederate losses are not known, but Lee's casualties are thought to be in the same ratio to his total force — an estimated 8,700 killed, wounded, and missing. William Swinton, a war correspondent who accompanied the Army of the Potomac, asserted, "There is something horrible, yet fascinating, in the mystery shrouding this strangest of battles ever fought — a battle which no man could see, and whose progress could only be followed by the ear, as the sharp and crackling volleys of mystery, and the alternate Union cheer and Confederate yell told how the fight surged and swelled."[46] Both armies paid a staggering price for a tactical impasse.

Sedgwick's generally competent performance during the Battle of the Wilderness was marred by his shaky situation during the evening of May 6. Grant, however, gave him full credit in his official report for holding his lines. On the Union right, almost broken by Gordon's attack, Sedgwick was plagued by many cumulative factors: mediocre troops at a critical point, the stripping away of many of his veteran units, and the lack of awareness and military leadership on the part of several subordinate generals. But Sedgwick reacted promptly to the emergency. As he had done at Antietam, Salem Church, and Manchester, the general threw his whole energy, regardless of personal safety, into solving the crisis. His men responded to his leadership with renewed vigor, as they had always done; in times of danger, veterans often told one another, "It must be all right. Uncle John is there." Sedgwick performed as well as he could in the Wilderness. In any case, the wild nature of the land prevented spectacular results.

Sedgwick had no time to think about the past as he started to lead his corps southeast toward Spotsylvania on the evening of May 7. His destination was sixteen miles away. The task was still unaccomplished. The soldier's job was to fight, rest, march, and then fight another battle.

Sedgwick's friend, Brig. Gen. Alexander S. Webb, typified the attitude of Grant's troops, writing during early May, "I am sick & worn out. This cannot last many days longer. . . . There will be no drawn battle. One or the other will be destroyed."[47] All the guns, equipment, and numerical superiority are worthless in war unless soldiers want to fight. These thoughts occupied Sedgwick's mind as he forced himself forward again.

CHAPTER 7

A SHOT
AT SPOTSYLVANIA

As SEDGWICK LED his exhausted corps toward Spotsylvania Court House during the warm evening of May 7, 1864, he did not know that he was racing against time. Confederate troops on the way to Richmond were marching at the same moment along a parallel road to reach the same junction. Lt. Gen. "Jeb" Stuart reported that Federal wagon trains were moving toward Spotsylvania and Gen. Robert E. Lee, sensing the significance of the quiet that day, was determined to reach the crossroads first to block Grant's move around his right flank. Hearing the noise of moving Northern columns and being unable to find a suitable bivouac area in the burning woods, Maj. Gen. Richard H. Anderson asked Lee's permission to move. Whether by accident or by strategy, Anderson conducted an all-night march to Spotsylvania. On arrival at 8 A.M. on May 8, the Southern general wisely began to throw up defenses. Sedgwick and the other Union generals had lost the race. This development sidetracked Grant's Overland Campaign. The Army of the Potomac would have to fight again.

The 6th Corps had a much longer distance to tramp than both the Confederate army and most of the Union corps. The heat, dust, and lack of sleep caused many men to fall by the wayside. As one of Sedgwick's veterans, S. F. Hildegrand, recalled, "We were so overcome by weariness and lack of sleep that we in the ranks neither knew, nor cared much where we were." The march seemed to be the hardest the 6th Corps had ever undertaken. Near the historic ruins of the Chancellor House, at dawn on the morning of May 8, Sedgwick stopped the corps for a half hour for breakfast. His aide, Col. Thomas Hyde, remembered being "positively lightheaded as well as ragged and dirty, hungry and thirsty." The men wolfed down some food. The general's decision to halt probably saved his corps from collapse. After a brief rest, and leaving his trains in charge of Burnside's 9th Corps, Sedgwick continued his march.[1]

Passing Piney Branch Church, Sedgwick heard gunfire as he approached Spotsylvania. Maj. Gen. Gouverneur K. Warren's 5th Corps had already arrived near the crossroads and was engaging Anderson's forces. As Grant was anxious to crush Anderson before Lee could come up in force, he was resolved to assault and overwhelm the Confederate defensive line. At 1:30 P.M., Meade instructed Sedgwick "to join General Warren in a prompt and vigorous attack on the army now concentrating there. Use every exertion to move with the utmost dispatch." Shortly thereafter Sedgwick reported back to Meade's chief of staff, Humphreys: "I sent Lieutenant-Colonel McMahon to say that General Warren, having examined the ground, had formed a plan of attack and is about to carry it out. A division and brigade of the Sixth will commence on the left, to be followed up if any impression is made. There is a very thick tangle to get through before reaching them."[2]

At 3:30 P.M., Col. Theodore Lyman joined Generals Sedgwick, Warren, and Wright in a clearing near Piney Branch Church. The observant Lyman

> . . . was struck by their worn and troubled aspect, more especially in Sedgwick, who showed its effect more from contrast with his usual calmness. In fact the sudden transition from the long winter's rest to hard marching, sleepless nights, and protracted fighting with no prospect of cessation, produced a powerful effect on the nervous system of the whole army. And never, perhaps, were officers and men more jaded and prostrated than on this very Sunday. Artillery was planted here and there had been cannonading. Gen. Sedgwick said, "Where is the Vermont Brigade? Not up yet. Just when I wanted it. Everything unlucky."[3]

After virtually no rest, the 6th Corps was again about to go into battle. When the men of the Greek Cross saw their commander, they were upset by his appearance. Sedgwick's clothes were covered with dust; his face was sunburned and scratched by thorns and vines; his felt hat crushed from contact with brush. He proceeded slowly on horseback, guiding his mount among the trees, saying half to himself, "We'll get through here after awhile, boys, this won't last always. The enemy has been fearfully punished, so we'll get out into the open country and have a better chance."[4] The troops cheered Uncle John as he rode alongside them.

The region into which Sedgwick was leading his corps was forbidding. The terrain at Spotsylvania was similar to that of the Wilderness. Narrow streams and abrupt banks were bordered by heavily timbered country with occasional clearings. It was an ideal area for a defensive campaign, and already the Confederates were waiting behind breastworks. Sedgwick passed to the rear of Warren's men to take up a position on the left.

The terrible strain of the last several days had affected the nervous Warren. When Meade told him, "Warren, I want you to cooperate with Sedgwick and see what can be done," Warren had burst out, "General Meade, I'll be God-Damned if I'll cooperate with Sedgwick or anybody else. You are the commander of this army and can give your orders and I'll obey them; or you can put Sedgwick in command and he'll give the orders and I'll obey them, or you can put me in command and I'll give the orders and Sedgwick shall obey them, but I'll be God-Damned if I'll co-operate with General Sedgwick or anybody else."[5]

The situation looked ominous. Huge trees were felled across the road, halting Sedgwick's troops temporarily. They saw dead men along the roadside. Some of Warren's wounded were being carried to the rear on stretchers. Lt. Oliver Wendell Holmes, Jr., "found woods afire & bodies of Rebs & our men just killed & scorching."[6] Having just delivered a message to Sedgwick to inform him that he was wanted at the front, Holmes was so tired that he could hardly sit up. The soldiers of both armies were spent before the battle began.

During the halt, the brigade butchers of the 139th Pennsylvania killed some cattle to issue fresh meat to the men. While they were skinning them, lively enemy firing suddenly broke out in front. Private Hildebrand remembered the moment: "As there was no telling where we would be the next hour, and the skinned beeves yet lying there the butchers told the men to help themselves, and at the beeves, the hungry soldier went, worst than a pack of hungry wolves, every man that had a knife, and every man for himself or his mess.

The intestines had not yet been taken out of the beeves where they lay and soon scores of soldiers were hurriedly cutting off hunks of beef wherever they got a chance."⁷ The prolonged ordeal had reduced the tired soldiers to beasts surviving on instinct.

The 6th Corps was driven from its first position by fire in the woods; blasts of hot air swept over the men. Sedgwick finally deployed his troops on Warren's left at Alsop's Farm. Soldier Philip Cooke of the 151st New York Regiment noted in his diary, "We form a line of battle in the afternoon on a piece of bottom land near a branch. In our front is a wooded hill and we can hear the rebels chopping trees and building breastworks."⁸ At 6:30 P.M., about half of the 6th Corps attacked the Confederate defenses, and three Pennsylvania units were extended to the left to prevent the enemy from flanking the assault column. A New Jersey brigade led the advance.

But the ground was new to the tired troops. Sedgwick's attack faltered as darkness began to fall. His men finally carried an important crest of a hill; he instructed Brig. Gen. Thomas H. Neill "to keep it at all hazards," and sent entrenching tools to him. During the fighting, Sedgwick had exposed himself needlessly near the front lines; he was hit in the stomach by a spent ball, but was uninjured.⁹

Just before darkness, the Vermont brigade (which had brought up the rear of the corps) arrived after a forced march. Reduced to half its normal strength by the Wilderness fighting, the Vermonters moved into line. Sedgwick's veterans broke out in spontaneous and hearty cheers for this welcome arrival.

Confident now that his line would hold, Sedgwick rode with Major Whittier to General Meade's headquarters for a conference. The 6th Corps remained in place. Lt. James W. Latta noted, "The sun has just set as volley after volley is delivered on the left; we do not, however, advance. The firing continues incessantly after dark. . . . . Got a partial night's rest." Brig. Gen. Frank Wheaton, one of Sedgwick's 2d Division brigade commanders, summarized the military impasse: "The nature of the position, its proximity to a swamp, the dense woods, the darkness of the night, and the entire ignorance of the relative position of the enemy made it useless to do anything until morning."¹⁰

During Sedgwick's absence, scattered 6th Corps troops kept arriving at Alsop's Farm. The 139th Pennyslvania Regiment waited for two hours during the hot, muggy night, and finally lay down to rest alongside the road to allow some Union cavalry to pass. Many soldiers fell asleep. They were suddenly awakened by a loud clamor, and instantly believed that "Jeb" Stuart with all his cavalry was charging down the road. "Steady, men! Don't shoot!" shouted the officers to their frightened men. It was soon learned that the panic was caused by a runaway "Jackass Battery," with its load of shovels, mess pans, and coffee pots banging against the sides of the mules. One observer wrote, "It was a laughable affair, but had but one scared Yank fired his gun, our two lines of men would have been firing into each other in a jiffy." The muleteers finally stopped the stampede that had almost resulted in a tragic accident. The intermittent firing throughout the night prevented the 6th Corps veterans from sleeping. They tried to take short naps, but the fierce crash of musketry prevented rest. Morning found the men more tired than ever.[11]

At Army of the Potomac headquarters, General Meade had finished his late dinner and was in a testy mood as he awaited the arrival of his corps commanders. Lyman remembered that "the General let out. Burnside, he said, was too late in the Wilderness to do any good. . . . Sedgwick was constitutionally slow. The men were now very tired. 'I told Warren today,' continued he, 'that he had lost his nerve; at which he professed to be very indignant.' " When Sedgwick and Whittier arrived, Meade pointedly told Sedgwick, "I desire you to take command of your own corps."[12] This sarcastic comment indicated that Meade believed Sedgwick was disposed to lean on the opinion of General Warren, whose corps was first in position.

The conference lasted far into the night, and General Meade's irritability continued. It was after midnight when Sedgwick and Whittier returned to corps headquarters. Although Warren had invited Sedgwick to spend the night at his headquarters, he declined. Because of the tense feelings among the Union generals, Uncle John preferred the company of his own staff. With a few aides, he rode out into an open field. No tents or blankets were available, so Sedgwick lay down on the grass beside a haystack and slept until morning.

Monday, May 9, 1864, was destined to be a day of entrenching and adjusting of lines, with a minimum of fighting. Sedgwick awoke at daylight to learn that General Neill had abandoned his position. Whittier was there when Sedgwick was notified of this completely unforeseen development. The aide recalled, "Inquiry

developed an unsatisfactory condition of things — the fact that
Gen. Neill, who had been an excellent brigade commander, had
entirely lost his nerve, and from this time on was not good for
command. A wreck from no fault of his, simply tension too great
for him to bear."¹³ Without breakfast and dressed in plain clothes
without even a sword, Sedgwick immediately went to the most
critical location and supervised the digging of rifle pits and en-
trenchments.¹²

With this accomplished, Sedgwick sat down on a hardtack
box, his back resting against a tree, near a recently pitched headquarters tent at a crossroads at Alsop's Field, some hundred feet
from the front line. He was in excellent spirits and began joking
with his aides. Grant's aide and brother-in-law, Lt. Col. Frederick
T. Dent, stopped by momentarily. Enemy sharpshooters were an-
noying Sedgwick's men. As he left, Dent remarked, "Uncle John,
your tent is too near to the battle-line for the comfort of your
visitors."¹⁴

Meade notified his corps commanders that the day would be
one of rest. Through McMahon, Sedgwick informed his officers,
"It is intended to remain in position by intrenching." Another
order came from Humphreys directing that in the event of
Meade's absence, "in any combined operation on the left by both
sides the Fifth and Sixth Corps, General Sedgwick will take command of both corps besides commanding his own."¹⁵ Meade evidently reasoned that if an emergency were to require his attention
away from his headquarters, he wanted Sedgwick as senior in rank
to direct the left wing. Sedgwick, however, rode over to Warren's
breastworks to speak with him. The general encountered Maj.
W. A. Roebling, Warren's aide-de-camp.

"Where is General Warren? I want to see him."

"Right here."

"Well, he has just showed me the order putting me in command of the two corps; just tell General Warren to go on and
command his own corps as usual. I have perfect confidence that he
will do what is right, and knows what to do with his corps as well
as I do."¹⁶

Sedgwick then returned to his own headquarters. Generals
Grant and Meade and their staffs came by on a reconnaissance of
the enemy's line. Grant complimented Sedgwick on his recent services and mentioned all the hardships that the 6th Corps commander had encountered. Sedgwick acknowledged Grant's words

and "expressed every confidence in the abilities of his troops to respond heroically to every demand made upon them." When Grant and Meade asked him to accompany them on their tour, Sedgwick excused himself, saying he was busy at the moment. Riding toward the enemy's line by mistake, the two Union generals turned around before they were fired on.[17]

Noticing that some of his troops had been filing from the left into the rifle pits, had halted, and were lying down, Sedgwick said, "That is wrong; those troops must be moved further to the right; I don't wish them to overlap that battery." Colonel McMahon started out to execute the order, but Sedgwick decided to go out to the position himself. About a half hour before, McMahon had mentioned the danger of exposure to sharpshooters at that location, as Brig. Gen. William H. Morris had already been wounded there. But this earlier conversation had escaped their memories. Sedgwick and McMahon walked to the front line.[18]

Major Whittier had gone ahead to check on the regiment of infantry that was too close to the artillery battery. He returned and reported his findings to the general. Sedgwick continued on toward the 14th New Jersey. For part of the morning this regiment had been molested by Confederate sharpshooters firing from a tree on higher ground to the east. Lt. John G. Fisher of this unit saw the general walk up to the line and stand in open view. During a temporary lull, McMahon and Sedgwick examined the exposed angle between the 5th and 6th corps. McMahon then gave the necessary order to move the New Jersey regiment to the right to allow a clear line of vision and of fire for one of the batteries of the 1st Massachusetts.

As the soldiers moved, the enemy opened fire. Bullets whizzed by, and many veterans dodged for their own safety. "What! what! Men, dodging this way for single bullets," laughed Sedgwick. "What will you do when they open fire along the whole line? I am ashamed of you. They couldn't hit an elephant at this distance!"

Another sharpshooter's bullet passed by with a long, shrill whistle. A soldier in front of Sedgwick fell to the ground. Sedgwick laughed again and repeated, "They couldn't hit an elephant at this distance." Standing beside Sedgwick, McMahon heard a third shrill whistle that interrupted his conversation with the general. Sedgwick turned to speak, and in the next moment, blood spurted from his left cheek under the eye. He fell in McMahon's direction and, as the aide attempted to support him, the two men fell together.[19]

Sedgwick toppled flat on his back among the undergrowth. McMahon tried to raise the general's head and placed his handkerchief over the wound. Sedgwick did not speak. His staff gathered around; Hyde hurried over when he heard someone cry out, "The general!" A corps doctor poured water from a canteen over the general's face as blood still spurted upward in a little fountain. Medical aid was useless. Sedgwick was dead.

Picking up Sedgwick's limp body, his aides carried him through the woods to the rear. The officers at the angle told their men that Sedgwick was only wounded. For a short time, an effort was made to keep the depressing news from the 6th Corps.

Immediately after the incident, a detail from the Vermont brigade went to the front to look for the sharpshooter. Sgt. Sanford Grey and D. R. Sanborn discovered a dummy soldier — a red shirt stretched over a crossbar. Waiting near the rifle pit, Grey saw a man approach and shot him. The sharpshooter tumbled back into another pit. On examining the body, the Vermonter found it to be that of a man about fifty years old with a rifle clasped in his right hand. It was felt by many that this unknown Confederate soldier was the individual who shot Sedgwick.

The killing of this sniper was slight revenge for the loss of the general. Most Union observers believed that the sharpshooter used a telescopic rifle to fire the fatal shot; this weapon was, ironically, newly issued Union equipment. Southern forces had evidently captured a few of these rifles in the recent fighting. After the war, many a surviving Confederate sharpshooter boasted that it was he who had picked off the Union general. Sedgwick's death resulted from his own carelessness and negligence; his aides had repeatedly warned him to be more careful. Throughout the Army of the Potomac, he had acquired a reputation of needlessly exposing himself to danger.

Despite his personal grief, Colonel McMahon realized that his next responsibility after ordering an ambulance to pick up the general's body was to report the news to Meade so a successor could be designated to command the 6th Corps. He started on horseback down a road through the woods; Lyman saw him approach, "looking haggard and distressed." McMahon exclaimed, "General Sedgwick is shot through the head, and my God! I'm afraid he is killed!" He almost bowed over in the saddle. Lyman accompanied McMahon to Army of the Potomac headquarters. Meade had already heard the news and had sent an order to Brig. Gen. Horatio

G. Wright — long Sedgwick's own choice for the position should anything happen to him — to assume command of the 6th Corps. When Grant heard about the loss of his corps commander, he found it difficult to accept the news. He twice asked his aide, Col. Horace Porter, "Is he really dead?" Grant said to Porter, "His loss to this army is greater than the loss of a whole division of troops."[20]

Sedgwick's body was taken to Meade's headquarters. With a solution of arsenic salt, Dr. Brinton embalmed the corpse as best he could. The general lay in state on a rustic bier over which soldiers built a bower of evergreens. Two Zouaves kept guard with their arms reversed. Throughout the rest of the day (May 9), officers and soldiers passed by the bier, mourning their beloved Uncle John, many of them weeping. Meade was especially upset, telling Lyman, "I feel the more grieved at his death because we had not parted entirely in good feeling."[21] In the evening, Major Whittier, in charge of the general's body, left for Fredericksburg with two other aides, Capt. E. B. Beaumont and Capt. Richard F. Halsted.

Secretary of War Edwin M. Stanton issued an official dispatch, announcing the distressing news to the nation. The *New York Times* editorialized, "The grief of this sad event intensifies as it becomes known throughout the army." In the general's home state of Connecticut, its leading newspaper, the *Hartford Courant* commented, "His loss at this juncture is a sad national calamity." The general's popularity reached even to his former acquaintances in the Confederate army. Col. Charles S. Venable of Lee's staff wrote, "He was much liked and respected by his old West Point comrades in the Confederate army, and his death was a real sorrow to them."[22]

But the statements of Sedgwick's own associates in the army showed most vividly the loss so many felt. To Whittier, Sedgwick was "one of the truest and whitest souls ever known to any army." McMahon believed the 6th Corps "seemed like an orphaned household."[23]

At Washington, the embalming was completed and the body of the general was placed in a coffin. Many citizens and soldiers passed by the bier. One lady, anxious to obtain souvenirs, had to be restrained from clipping two buttons from the uniform. On May 11, Whittier left Washington with the remains and stopped at New York for similar ceremonies and military honors. Two days later, Gov. William A. Buckingham of Connecticut and other dignitaries boarded an express train in New York to convey the dead soldier to Bridgeport. Amid the firing of cannon, the coffin was transferred to a car draped in mourning for the final journey to Cornwall Hollow. Some patriotic citizens desired further homage at New Haven and the governor's presence at the funeral. But Sedgwick's family rejected more display. Buckingham explained in a public letter that "I should lay aside every other duty to be present; but as his family friends desire a more private and unceremonious burial, it is not so important."[24]

On Sunday, May 15, 1864, more than 2,000 of Sedgwick's family, friends, and neighbors gathered at his old residence at Cornwall Hollow. A simple ceremony — not a military funeral, as Buckingham had originally suggested — marked the occasion. The Rev. Charles Wetherby, pastor of the village church, delivered the discourse. At the village graveyard, less than a half mile from his house, the general was buried in the family plot.

The grisly business of the war continued. The battles at Spotsylvania had not yet begun in earnest when Sedgwick was killed on May 9. The following day, the 6th Corps resumed fighting. General Wright sent Col. Emory Upton with twelve regiments to attack the Confederate lines during the late afternoon. Upton's well-planned and executed probe achieved a partial success. Suffering terrible losses at Spotsylvania for ten days, the morale of the 6th Corps was shattered. On May 19, Hyde explained in a private letter, "My ambition fled with the General's death. . . . I do not care to stay in the service now the General is no more. Our fighting yesterday was bloody, but futile. Do not people have enough of the slaughter? . . . It has been simply give & take — we in the open, the enemy behind breastworks, no skill on our side."[25]

Despite his misgivings, Hyde did remain in the service. Although Sedgwick had fallen on the way to Richmond, the 6th Corps continued to follow the bloody road until victory was achieved. The men of the Greek Cross fought at Cold Harbor, defended Washington in July, and were sent to support Maj. Gen. Philip H. Sheridan in the Shenandoah Valley of Virginia during the fall of 1864. Returning to the entrenchments at Petersburg, the 6th Corps awaited the coming of spring and the resumption of Grant's grinding offensive. Included in the long line of Federal siege works outside Petersburg was Fort Sedgwick, named for the general. This Union stronghold was known to the enemy in opposite Fort Mahone as "Fort Hell" because the Confederates dreaded its artillery fire.

On April 2, 1865, the 6th Corps joined in the general Union

assault and penetrated the enemy lines. After fighting at Saylor's Creek and tramping to Appomattox Court House to receive the surrender of Lee's Army of Northern Virginia on April 9, the corps marched southward to occupy Danville. On May 23, at Washington, 12,000 veterans of the 6th Corps passed in review before President Andrew Johnson and shortly thereafter journeyed to their home states for discharge. The 6th Corps passed into history. Sedgwick was not there, but he remained in the thoughts of his soldiers for the remainder of their lives.

A memorial to Sedgwick was discussed even before the war ended. In November 1864, Maj. Gen. Horatio G. Wright called together his chief officers at 6th Corps headquarters on Cedar Creek, Virginia. It was proposed to erect a statue of Sedgwick at the U.S. Military Academy, West Point, New York. Soldiers donated funds for this tribute. On October 21, 1868, the statue was dedicated with many civilian and military leaders attending. The life-size statue of the general, standing and in uniform, was cast in bronze obtained from three Confederate cannon captured by the 6th Corps in battle. Prominently located near the commandant's quarters, the bronze Sedgwick looks over the drill and parade grounds he knew as a cadet.

The U.S. Military Academy continues to honor Sedgwick in other ways. The West Point Museum preserves the saddle, pistol holsters, and saddle bags owned by the general on the day he fell. In a case in the museum, Sedgwick's Class of 1837 ring, the oldest the Academy has obtained, is on permanent display.

There were other tributes to John Sedgwick. Officials named new counties in Kansas and Colorado after the general. In 1887, many 6th Corps veterans traveled back to Spotsylvania — where they had fought twenty-three years before — for a soldiers' reunion. There they dedicated a simple monument that stands on the exact spot where Sedgwick fell. In 1900, Carl and Ellen Battelle Stoeckel subsidized the construction of an impressive memorial across the road from the Cornwall Hollow cemetery. Interested in preserving Sedgwick's letters, in 1902 and 1903, the Stoeckels privately published his correspondence in two volumes. On July 4, 1913 — the centenary of Sedgwick's birth and the fiftieth year since the Battle of Gettysburg — some surviving 6th Corps veterans assembled on the ground just to the north of Little Round Top. There, on Sedgwick Drive, an equestrian statue was dedicated to the general's memory.

In Cornwall Hollow, the general's birthplace and his later residence across the road still stand. A Connecticut State picnic area in the village bears the Union soldier's name. The town library preserves his papers and a dress sword. In addition, the Connecticut Historical Society at Hartford has another Sedgwick sword on permanent display. At the state capitol, Connecticut has honored him as one of its most illustrious sons who served the Union cause. A triumvirate of stone statues — Sedgwick, Secretary of the Navy Gideon Welles, and Gen. Alfred H. Terry — occupy three niches in a portico above the south entrance.

But the modest Sedgwick did not seek fame. He felt himself to be merely one of thousands of Northern men who were simply responding to a sense of duty during these critical years of the nation's history. A soldier's general, his home was in the field with his men.

John Sedgwick was not a military genius. Brilliance alone, however, does not win wars. Many Civil War generals — Lee, Jackson, Stuart, McClellan, and others — had genius, but this quality lost its initial import as the war became prolonged. Sedgwick's endurance and steadfastness were appropriate strengths for a long struggle.

Sedgwick survives in legend as a colorful personality as well as a general. There exists to this day at the U.S. Military Academy at West Point a custom, concerning Sedgwick's statue, that captures the spirit of the man. Tradition has it that a cadet who is in danger of being found deficient in his academic courses will pass his final examinations if he sneaks out of the barracks after taps and twirls the rowels of Sedgwick's spurs. Uncle John would have laughed. As a cadet, he would have done it himself.

Notes

Chapter I
From the Plains to the Peninsula

1. Sedgwick, Correspondence, II:30.
2. Ibid.
3. Cullum, I:533–34; Welch, p. 16.
4. Sedgwick, Correspondence, II:31.
5. Sedgwick Memorial Assoc., p. 28; Headley, p. 432; US War Dept., Series I, Vol. III, p. 377; Funeral Services, p. 14.
6. Sedgwick, Collection, February 20, 1861.
7. Sedgwick, Correspondence, II:32–33.
8. US War Dept., Series I: Vol. II, p. 439 and Vol. V, pp. 418, 714; Small, p. 30.
9. Sedgwick, Collection, September 2, 1861.
10. Ibid., March 3, 1862; Higginson, I:179–81.
11. US War Dept., Series I, Vol. V, pp. 414, 418. An excellent drawing of Sedgwick's winter headquarters appears in Johnson and Buel, II:163; Small, pp. 30–33.
12. Sedgwick, Correspondence, II:37.
13. McClellan, Own Story, pp. 81, 140.
14. Sedgwick, Correspondence, II:38.
15. Ibid.; US War Dept., Series I: Vol. XI, pt. 1, p. 280, and Vol. V, p. 48.
16. Ford, pp. 137–38; Ward, p. 25.
17. Sedgwick Memorial Assoc., pp. 26–27.
18. Bruce, pp. 78–79; Sedgwick, Correspondence, II:40.
19. Hassler, McClellan, p. 62; Walker, pp. 3–8; US War Dept., Series I, Vol. V, pp. 748–55; Webb, McClellan's Campaign, pp. 10–34.
20. US War Dept., Series I: Vol. VI, p. 254, and Vol. XI, pt. 3, pp. 12, 16, 41; Sedgwick, Collection, March 24, 1862; Abraham Lincoln, Papers, Nathaniel P. Banks to Seth Williams, March 24, 1862; Bruce, p. 80; McDermott, p. 10.
21. Heintzelman, March 29, 1862.
22. Johnson and Buel, II:170–71; Webb, McClellan's Campaign, p. 26fn; Sedgwick, Correspondence, II:42.

23. Ward, pp. 36–38; Aldrich, p. 64; Searles and Taylor, pp. 104–105.
24. Howe, Touched with Fire, pp. 38–39.
25. Ford, pp. 150–51.
26. Sedgwick, Correspondence, II:43.
27. Aldrich, pp. 70–71.
28. Biddle, William F., April 15, 1862; Sedgwick, Correspondence, II:44.
29. US War Dept., Series I, Vol. XI, pt. 3, p. 101; Bruce, pp. 83–84.
30. Barlow, April 23, 1862.
31. McClellan, Own Story, p. 286.
32. Adams, pp. 28–29; Nevins, p. 44.
33. Ward, p. 43.
34. Sedgwick, Correspondence, II:45–46.
35. Adams, p. 29.
36. Sedgwick, Correspondence, II:46–49.
37. Ibid.
38. Biddle, William F., May 21, 1862.
39. Sedgwick, Correspondence, II:48–49.
40. NY Times, May 21, 1862.
41. Dwight, p. 176.
42. Bruce, pp. 94–95; Howard, Autobiography, I:237.
43. Sedgwick, Correspondence, II:52–53, 58, 60; US War Dept., Series I, Vol. XI, pt. 1, p. 795.
44. Ward, pp. 53–54.
45. Higginson, I:230.
46. Sedgwick, Correspondence, II:54, 61–62.
47. Aldrich, p. 94; Freeman, II:69–72.
48. Howe, Touched with Fire, p. 51.
49. Sedgwick, Correspondence II:60.
50. Ibid., pp. 55, 60–61.
51. NY Times, June 2 and 3, 1862.
52. Sedgwick, Collection, June 7, 1862.
53. Ford, p. 166.
54. Sedgwick, Correspondence, II:63.
55. Ropes, H., June 11, 1862.
56. Johnson and Buel, II:373.
57. US War Dept., Series I, Vol. XI, pt. 2, pp. 90–93.
58. McDermott, p. 13.
59. Searles and Taylor, p. 159; Howe, Touched with Fire, p. 59.
60. McClellan, Own Story, p. 439.
61. Dwight, pp. 214–15.
62. Barlow, July 4, 1862.
63. Ibid., July 4 and 8, 1862.
64. Sedgwick, Correspondence, II:70–71.

Chapter 2
Agony at Antietam

1. NY Times, July 7, 1862.
2. Ibid., July 8, 1862.
3. Ibid., July 11 and 12, 1862; NY Tribune, July 11, 1862; Sedgwick, Correspondence, II:74.
4. Sedgwick, Correspondence, II:73–74.
5. Sedgwick, Collection, letter from William Hillhouse, August 9, 1862.
6. NY Tribune, July 28, 1862.
7. Heintzelman, July 31, 1862.
8. McClellan, Report, p. 287; Hebert, p. 91.
9. NY Tribune, August 8, 1862.
10. McClellan, Own Story, p. 495.
11. NY Tribune, August 13, 1862.
12. Ibid., August 21, 1862.
13. Ibid., August 23, 1862.
14. Larned, letter to Henry Larned, July 25, 1862.
15. Dwight, p. 276.
16. Sedgwick, Correspondence, II:78–79.
17. Gardner, August 31, 1862.
18. Sedgwick, Correspondence, II:79–80.
19. Nevins, p. 91.
20. Sedgwick, Correspondence, II:80.
    Howard, Autobiography, I:272.
22. Howe, Touched with Fire, pp. 61–62.
23. NY Times, September 5, 1862.
24. Biddle, September 6, 1862.
25. Barlow, September 6, 1862; NY Tribune, September 17, 1862.
26. Sedgwick, Correspondence, II:81–82.
27. Gibbon, pp. 73–74.
28. US War Dept., Series I, Vol. XIX, pt. 2, p. 283; Whittier, p. 5.
29. US War Dept., Series I, Vol. XIX, pt. 1, p. 275; Whittier, p. 5.
30. Searles and Taylor, p. 197.
31. Ibid., p. 199.
32. Walker, p. 104.
33. Whittier, p. 5.
34. US War Dept., Series I, Vol. XIX, pt. 1, p. 311; Howard, Autobiography, I:297.
35. Searles and Taylor, pp. 213–14; Walker, p. 106.
36. Quaife, p. 135; Whittier, pp. 5–6.
37. Aldrich, p. 140.
38. Higginson, I:189.

39. Rhodes, William, September 18, 1862; Ford, pp. 198–99.
40. Gardner, September 18, 1862.
41. McClellan, Own Story, p. 612.
42. Ropes, Letters, September 20, 1862.
43. Gardner, n.d.
44. Sedgwick, Collection, October 1, 1862.
45. Welch, pp. 23–24; Sedgwick, Collection, September 20 [?], 1862 and October 6, 1862.
46. Sedgwick, Collection, October 12, 1862.
47. Walker, p. 138.
48. Description of Statue Dedication, p. 30.
49. Sedgwick, Correspondence, II:87.
50. Rhodes, John, p. 148.
51. Holmes, Jr., Papers, December 29, 1862.
52. Walker, p. 198 and 198fn.
53. Ibid., pp. 199–200; Barton, January 25, 1863.
54. NY Times, February 12, 1863.
55. Poore, p. 202.

Chapter 3
Storming Over Marye's Heights

1. US War Dept., Series I, Vol. XXV, pt. 2, pp. 109, 580–81.
2. Hebert, pp. 178–84; NY Tribune, March 3 and 26, 1863.
3. Sixth Corps, letter of March 20, 1863; Hyde, Letters, February 23, 1863.
4. Hyde, Greek Cross, p. 117; NY Times, February 19 and March 1, 1863.
5. Murphy, diary entries of February 24 and March 6, 1863.
6. NY Times, April 8, 1863.
7. Sedgwick, Correspondence, II:89–90; Fisk, W., April 8, 1863; Johnson and Buel, III:120.
8. NY Times, April 8, 12, 19, and 28, 1863; NY Tribune, April 27, 1863.
9. Sedgwick, Correspondence, II:90–91; Hyde, Greek Cross, p. 121.
10. Johnson and Buel, III:155; Sedgwick, Correspondence, II:92.
11. Wentworth, letter to his father, April 17, 1863; Fisk, W., diary entries of April 15 and 23, 1863.
12. Stevens, Sixth Corps, pp. 188–89.
13. Pearson, pp. 178–80.
14. NY Times, May 2, 1863.
15. McMahon, Recollections, pp. 165–66; Latta, Papers, diary entry of April 28, 1863.
16. Weld, pp. 199–200.

17. Pearson, pp. 181–82.
18. US War Dept., Series I, Vol. XXV, pt. 2, pp. 288, 336–41, 409.
19. Abbott, letter to his parents, April 29, 1863.
20. Hebert, pp. 194–95; US War Dept., Series I, Vol. XXV, pt. 2, p. 309.
21. US War Dept., Series I, Vol. XXV, pt. 2, p. 322.
22. Hebert, p. 203; NY Tribune, May 5, 1863.
23. Nevins, p. 190.
24. Dodge, pp. 163–65.
25. US War Dept., Series I, Vol. XXV, pt. 2, pp. 365–66.
26. Bigelow, p. 382.
27. Sedgwick, Correspondence, II:117; McMahon, Recollections, p. 168.
28. Hutchinson, p. 143.
29. US War Dept., Series I, Vol. XXV, pt. 2, p. 336; Hyde, Greek Cross, p. 125.
30. Hutchinson, p. 143.
31. Hyde, Greek Cross, pp. 125–26.
32. Brewer, p. 53.
33. US Congress, I:38–40; Johnson and Buel, III:228–29.
34. Stine, pp. 372–73.
35. Sedgwick, Correspondence, II:119.
36. Benedict, I:364–66.
37. Hyde, Greek Cross, p. 128; Stevens, Sixth Corps, p. 200.
38. Connor, letter to his father, May 10, 1863.
39. Bigelow, pp. 394–96.
40. Sedgwick, Correspondence, II:121.
41. Bigelow, p. 400.
42. US War Dept., Series I, Vol. XXV, pt. 2, p. 396.
43. McMahon, Vermont Address, pp. 21–22.
44. McMahon, Recollections, p. 175.
45. Tyler, p. 87.
46. Hicks, pp. 141–42; Nevins, p. 199.
47. Hyde, Greek Cross, pp. 131–33.
48. Fisk, W., letter of May 9, 1863.
49. US War Dept., Series I, Vol. XXV, pt. 2, p. 412.
50. Johnson and Buel, III:232; Tyler, pp. 88–89.
51. US War Dept., Series I, Vol. XXV, pt. 2, pp. 418–19.
52. Sedgwick, Correspondence, II:127–28.
53. Ibid, p. 109.
54. US Congress, I:101.
55. Sedgwick, Correspondence, II:125–26; Nevins, pp. 213–14.
56. US Congress, I:146.
57. McMahon, Vermont Address, p. 24.
58. Tyler, p. 91.

Chapter 4
A Night March to Gettysburg

1.   Trobriand, p. 472; Gibbon, pp. 122–23, 425.
2.   Hebert, p. 226.
3.   Sedgwick Memorial Association, p. 84.
4.   Sedgwick, Correspondence, II:161–62.
5.   Meade, G., I:372 and II:7.
6.   Sedgwick, Correspondence, II:127
7.   Latta, Papers, diary entry of May 24, 1863.
8.   Sedgwick, Correspondence, II:131.
9.   US War Dept., Series I, Vol. XXVII, pt. 3, p. 7.
10. Ibid., p. 13.
11. Hyde, Greek Cross, p. 138.
12. US War Dept., Series I, Vol. XXVII, pt. 1, pp. 677–78; Stevens, Sixth Corps, p. 220.
13. Meade, G., I:383; Pearson, pp. 193–94.
14. US War Dept., Series I, Vol. XXVII, pt. 2, p. 73.
15. NY Tribune, June 16, 1863.
16. Coffin, pp. 258–59; NY Tribune, July 1, 1863.
17. Tyler, pp. 94–95.
18. Hyde, Greek Cross, p. 140.
19. Description of Statue Dedication, p. 25; New York Monuments Commission, II:622–23.
20. Commonwealth of Pennsylvania at Gettysburg, I:187; II:29–30.
21. Cleaves, p. 134.
22. US War Dept., Series I, Vol. XXVII, pt. 3, p. 465.
23. Hyde, Greek Cross, pp. 142–43; US War Dept., Series I, Vol. XXVII, pt. 3, p. 467.
24. Latta, Address, p. 19.
25. Commonwealth of Pennsylvania, I:377.
26. Tyler, p. 102.
27. New York Monuments Commission, II:623.
28. Tyler, p. 103; Mark, p. 213.
29. Coffin, p. 286.
30. Sedgwick, Correspondence, II:133.
31. Hyde, Greek Cross, pp. 148–49; Commonwealth of Pennsylvania, I:506 and II:654.
32. Mark, p. 233; Hyde, Greek Cross, pp. 149–50.
33. Sedgwick, Correspondence, II:134; Coddington, p. 481.
34. Johnson and Buel, III:313–14; Gibbon, pp. 138–45.
35. US Congress, I:461.
36. Sedgwick, Correspondence, II:134.

37. Hyde, Greek Cross, p. 155.
38. US Congress, I:640.
39. US War Dept., Series I, Vol. XXVII, pt. 1, p. 690.
40. Ibid.
41. Nevins, p. 249.
42. Stevens, Sixth Corps, p. 253.
43. Tyler, pp. 109–110.
44. US War Dept., Series I, Vol. XXVII, pt. 3, pp. 530–31.
45. Ibid., p. 535.
46. Ibid., p. 555.
47. Hyde, Greek Cross, p. 159.
48. Brewer, p. 69.
49. McMahon, Vermont Address, p. 26.
50. US Congress, I:463.
51. Sedgwick, Correspondence, II:132.
52. Cleaves, p. 182.
53. US War Dept., Series I, Vol. XXVII, pt. 3, p. 687; Nevins, pp. 261–62.
54. Pearson, p. 236.
55. Sedgwick, Correspondence, II:136–37.
56. Meade, G., II:134.

Chapter 5
Stalemate at Mine Run

1. Connor, letter to his sister, July 18, 1863.
2. Sedgwick, Correspondence, II:137.
3. Murphy, diary entry of August 21, 1863.
4. NY Tribune, August 31, 1863.
5. Freeman, III:172–73.
6. NY Tribune, August 31, 1863.
7. Sedgwick, Correspondence, II:156.
8. Ibid., p. 157.
9. NY Times, October 3, 1863.
10. Abbott, letter to his parents, October 7, 1863.
11. Stevens, Sixth Corps, pp. 278–79.
12. US War Dept., Series I, Vol. XXIX, pt. 2, p. 917.
13. Ibid., p. 273.
14. Murphy, diary entry of October 12, 1863; Stevens, Sixth Corps, p. 281.
15. Meade, G., II:154; Sedgwick, Correspondence, II:160; Freeman, III:183.
16. Agassiz, pp. 36–37.
17. Abbott, letter to his parents, November 4, 1863.
18. Cleaves, pp. 202–203.
19. Holmes, Jr., Papers, letter from Whittier, November 10, 1863.

20.   Johnson and Buel, IV:86.
21.   Clark, p. 47.
22.   Best, p. 102.
23.   US War Dept., Series I, Vol. XXIX, pt. 2, p. 924.
24.   Johnson and Buel, IV:87.
25.   Holmes, Jr., Papers, letter from Whittier, November 10, 1863; Nevins, p. 299.
26.   Freeman, III:192.
27.   Holmes, Jr., Papers, letter from Whittier, November 10, 1863.
28.   Lyman, diary entry of November 14–16, 1863; NY Tribune, November 18, 1863.
29.   Sparks, pp. 308, 310; Lyman, diary entry of November 20, 1863.
30.   Meade, G., II:156.
31.   Sedgwick, Collection, Halsted to Emily Sedgwick, December 13, 1863.
32.   Hyde, Greek Cross, p. 174.
33.   Stevens, Sixth Corps, pp. 295–96.
34.   Sedgwick, Collection, Halsted to Emily Sedgwick, December 13, 1863; Horton, letter to his wife, December 4, 1863.
35.   US Congress, I:323.
36.   Sedgwick, Collection, Halsted to Emily Sedgwick, December 13, 1863.
37.   US War Dept., Series I, Vol. XXIX, pt. 2, p. 928.
38.   Sedgwick, Collection, Halsted to Emily Sedgwick, December 13, 1863.
39.   Horton, letter to his wife, December 4, 1863; Haines, p. 120.
40.   Sedgwick, Collection, Halsted to Emily Sedgwick, December 13, 1863; Goss, pp. 249–50.
41.   Cleaves, pp. 212–13.
42.   Sedgwick, Collection, Halsted to Emily Sedgwick, December 13, 1863; US War Dept., Series I, Vol. XXIX, pt. 2, p. 929.
43.   Stevens, Sixth Corps, pp. 298–99.
44.   Horton, letter to his wife, December 4, 1863.
45.   Tyler, p. 129.
46.   NY Times, December 3, 1863, excerpted from the Washington Star; Sparks, p. 320; NY Tribune, December 9, 1863.
47.   Agassiz, pp. 58–59.
48.   NY Tribune, December 9, 1863.
49.   Sedgwick, Correspondence, II:168.
50.   Ibid., p. 155; Nevins, pp. 282, 284.
51.   Sedgwick, Collection, letter from French, September 23, 1863.
52.   Nevins, p. 286.
53.   Holmes, Jr., Collection, letter from Whittier, November 10, 1863.
54.   Headley, pp. 428–29.
55.   Sedgwick, Collection, letter from French, January 13, 1864.
56.   Sparks, p. 331.

57. US War Dept., Series I, Vol. XXXIII, p. 398.
58. Ibid., pp. 410, 439.
59. Lyman, diary entry of January 14, 1864.
60. Agassiz, p. 72.
61. Butler, III:369–70.
62. Ibid., pp. 396–99.
63. Meade, G., II:165.
64. Sedgwick, Correspondence, II:165.
65. McMahon, Vermont Address, pp. 28–29.
66. Sedgwick, Two Letters.
67. McMahon, In Memoriam, pp. 21–22.
68. US War Dept., Series I, Vol. XXXIII, p. 616.
69. Ibid., p. 628.
70. Sedgwick, Correspondence, II:177.

Chapter 6
A Narrow Escape in the Wilderness

1. Sedgwick, Correspondence, II:177; Whittier, p. 8.
2. Connor, letter to his father, April 16, 1864; Wentworth, letter to his wife, April 17, 1864; Howland, letter from Joseph Bartlett, April 8, 1864.
3. Gibbon, pp. 209–210.
4. Whittier, pp. 8–9; Meade, G., II:185.
5. Benedict, I:412–13.
6. Sedgwick, Correspondence, II:179.
7. Military Historical Society, IV:178–79; Hildebrand, n.p.
8. Schuyler, letter to his father, April 10, 1864.
9. Sixth Corps, directives for April 19, 1864.
10. Wentworth, letter to his wife, March 20, 1864; Fisk, W., letter of March 14, 1864.
11. Lyman, diary entry of April 18, 1864.
12. Hildebrand, n.p.
13. Sedgwick, Correspondence, II:179, 181–82.
14. Prowell, p. 115; Connor, letter to Will Connor, April 14, 1864.
15. Horton, letter to his wife, April 29, 1864.
16. Sedgwick, Collection, letter from Williams, April 22, 1864.
17. US War Dept., Series I, Vol. XXXVI, pt. 2, p. 332; Latta, Papers, diary entry of May 3, 1864; Johnson, Papers, Seth Williams to Sedgwick, May 3, 1864.
18. Hildebrand, n.p.
19. Howe, pp. 103–104.
20. Porter, p. 43.

21. Shaler, diary entries of May 3, 4, 1864; Latta, Papers, diary entry of May 4, 1864.
22. US War Dept., Series I, Vol. XXXVI, pt. 2, p. 371.
23. Ibid, p. 404.
24. Fisk, W., diary entry of May 6, 1864.
25. Michie, p. 92.
26. Ibid.; Military Historical Society, IV:212–13.
27. Latta, Papers, diary entry of May 5, 1864.
28. Best, p. 120.
29. Porter, pp. 53–54; US War Dept., Series I, Vol. XXXVI, pt. 2, p. 415.
30. Gold, p. 35.
31. Lewis, p. 83.
32. US War Dept., Series I, Vol. XXXVI, pt. 2, pp. 451–52, 459–60.
33. Shaler, diary entry of May 6, 1864.
34. US War Dept., Series I, Vol. XXXVI, pt. 1, pp. 751–52; Lewis, pp. 88–89.
35. Whittier, p. 10; Stevens, pp. 315–16; Schaff, p. 318.
36. Brewer, p. 85; Shaler, diary entry of May 6, 1864.
37. Sedgwick Memorial Association, pp. 39–40.
38. Lyman, diary entry of May 6, 1864.
39. US War Dept., Series I, Vol. XXXVI, pt. 2, pp. 438, 448.
40. Michie, p. 92.
41. Sedgwick Memorial Association, p. 39.
42. Webb, letter to his wife, May 6, 1864; Lyman, diary entry of May 6, 1864.
43. US War Dept., Series I, Vol. XXXVI, pt. 2, p. 481.
44. Ibid., pp. 500, 507; Prowell, p. 127.
45. US War Dept., Series I, Vol. XXXVI, pt. 2, p. 484.
46. Swinton, pp. 438–39.
47. Webb, letter to his wife, May 9, 1864.

Chapter 7
A Shot at Spotsylvania

1. Hildebrand, n.p.; Hyde, Greek Cross, p. 325.
2. US War Dept., Series I, Vol. XXXVI, pt. 2, p. 545.
3. Lyman, diary entry of May 8, 1864.
4. Brewer, p. 89.
5. Wilson, I:396.
6. Howe, pp. 108–109.
7. Hildebrand, n.p.
8. Howell, p. 65.
9. Whittier, p. 11.
10. Latta, Papers, diary entry of May 8, 1864; US War Dept., Series I, Vol. XXXVI, pt. 1, p. 683.

11. Hildebrand, n.p.
12. Lyman, diary entry of May 9, 1864.
13. Whittier, p. 11.
14. Sedgwick Memorial Association, pp. 13–14.
15. US War Dept., Series I, Vol. XXXVI, pt. 2, pp. 574, 579.
16. Ibid., p. 574.
17. Sedgwick Memorial Association, p. 89.
18. Johnson and Buel, IV:175.
19. Ibid.
20. Lyman, diary entry of May 9, 1864; Porter, p. 90.
21. Lyman, diary entry of May 9, 1864.
22. NY Times, May 13, 1864; Hartford Courant, May 11, 1864; Johnson and Buel, IV:242.
23. Whittier, p. 11; Johnson and Buel, IV:213–14.
24. Hartford Courant, May 14, 1864; Litchfield Enquirer, May 19, 1864.
25. Hyde, Letters, Letter of May 19, 1864.

Bibliography

Books

Adams, John G. B., *Reminiscences of the Nineteenth Massachusetts Regiment.* Boston: Wright and Potter Printing Company, 1899.

Agassiz, George R., ed., *Meade's Headquarters, 1863–1865: Letters and Colonel Theodore Lyman from the Wilderness to Appomattox.* Boston: The Atlantic Monthly Press, 1922.

Aldrich, Thomas W., *The History of Battery A, First Regiment, Rhode Island Artillery in the War to Preserve the Union, 1861–1865.* Providence: Snow and Farnham, 1904.

Basler, Roy P., ed., *The Collected Works of Abraham Lincoln.* Vol. III. New Brunswick, New Jersey: Rutgers University Press, 1953.

Benedict, G. G., *Vermont in the Civil War: A History of the Part Taken by the Vermont Soldiers and Sailors in the War for the Union, 1861–1865.* Vol. I. Burlington, Vermont: The Free Press Association, 1886.

Best, Isaac O., *History of the 121st New York State Infantry.* Chicago: Published by Lieut. Jas. H. Smith, The Hammond Press, W. B. Conkey Company, 1921.

Bicknell, George W., *History of the Fifth Regiment Maine Volunteers.* Portland, Maine: Published by Hall L. Davis, B. Thurston and Co., Printers, 1871.

Bigelow, John, Jr., *The Campaign of Chancellorsville: A Strategic and Tactical Study.* New Haven: Yale University Press, 1910.

Boatner, Mark Mayo III, *The Civil War Dictionary.* New York: David McKay Company, Inc., 1959.

Bowen, James L., *Dedication of the Monuments of the 7th, 10th, and 37th Mass. Vols. [Massachusetts Volunteers] at Gettysburg, Pa., October 6, 1886.* Springfield, Mass.: Published for the Committee by James L. Bowen, The Homestead Job Print, 1886.

_____, *History of the Thirty-Seventh Regiment, Massachusetts Volunteers in the Civil War of 1861–1865.* Holyoke, Mass. and New York: Clark W. Bryan and Company, 1884.

Brewer, A. T., *History Sixty-First Regiment, Pennsylvania Volunteers, 1861–1865.* Pittsburgh: Art Engraving and Printing Company, 1911.

Bruce, George A., *The Twentieth Regiment of Massachusetts Volunteer Infantry, 1861–1865*. Boston and New York: Houghton, Mifflin and Company, 1906.

Butler, Benjamin F., *Private and Official Correspondence of Gen. Benjamin F. Butler During the Period of the Civil War*. Vol. III. Norwood, Mass.: The Plimpton Press, Privately Issued, 1917.

Clark, Charles A., *Campaigning with the Sixth Maine: A Paper Read Before the Iowa Commandary, Military Order of the Loyal Legion of the United States*. Des Moines, Iowa: The Kenyon Press, 1897.

Cleaves, Freeman, *Meade of Gettysburg*. Norman, Oklahoma: University of Oklahoma Press, 1960.

Coddington, Edwin B., *The Gettysburg Campaign: A Study in Command*. New York: Charles Scribner's Sons, 1968.

Coffin, Charles Carleton, *Four Years of Fighting: A Personal Observation with the Army and Navy, from the First Battle of Bull Run to the Fall of Richmond*. Boston: Ticknor and Fields, 1866.

Cullum, George W., *Biographical Register of the Officers and Graduates of the U.S. Military Academy, at West Point, N.Y.* Vol. I. New York: D. Van Nostrand, 1868.

Description of the Ceremony of Dedication of the Statue of Major-General John Sedgwick, U.S. Volunteers, Colonel Fourth U.S. Cavalry, at West Point, N.Y., October 21, 1868. Including the Oration of Hon. George W. Curtis on the Occasion. New York: D. Van Nostrand, 1869.

Dodge, Theodore A., *The Campaign of Chancellorsville*. Boston: James R. Osgood and Company, 1881.

Dwight, Theodore A., *The Virginia Campaign of 1862 Under General Pope*. Boston and New York: Houghton, Mifflin and Company, 1895.

Emerson, Edward W., *The Life and Letters of Charles Russell Lowell*. Boston and New York: Houghton, Mifflin and Company, 1907.

[Fiske, Samuel] *Mr. Dunn Browne's Experiences in the Army*. Boston: Nichols and Noyes, 1866.

Ford, Andrew E., *The Story of the Fifteenth Regiment, Massachusetts Volunteer Infantry in the Civil War, 1861–1865*. Clinton, Mass.: Press of W. J. Coulter, Courant Office, 1898.

Freeman, Douglas Southall, *R. E. Lee: A Biography*. Four Vols. New York and London: Charles Scribner's Sons, 1935.

Funeral Services of Gen. John Sedgwick, Cornwall, Conn., May 15th, 1864. Utica, New York: Utica State Hospital Press, 1893.

Gibbon, John, *Personal Recollections of the Civil War*. New York: G. P. Putnam's Sons, 1928.

Gold, Theodore Sedgwick, ed., *Memorial Day Exercises in Memory of Gen. John Sedgwick, Cornwall, Conn., May 30, 1892*. Hartford, Conn.: Press of the Case, Lockwood and Brainard Company, [1892].

Goss, Warren Lee, *Recollections of a Private: A Story of the Army of the Potomac*. New York: Thomas Y. Crowell and Company, 1890.

Grant, Ulysses S., *Personal Memoirs*. Vol. II. New York: Charles L. Webster and Company, 1886.

Haines, Alanson A., *History of the Fifteenth Regiment, New Jersey Volunteers*. New York: Jenkins and Thomas, 1883.

Hassler, Warren W., Jr., *Commanders of the Army of the Potomac*. Baton Rouge: Louisiana State University Press, 1962.

_____, *General George B. McClellan: Shield of the Union*. Baton Rouge: Louisiana State University Press, 1957.

Headley, J. T., [Joel Tyler], *Grant and Sherman: Their Campaigns and Generals*. New York: E. B. Treat & Company, 1865.

Hebert, Walter H., *Fighting Joe Hooker*. Indianapolis and New York: The Bobbs-Merrill Company, 1944.

[Hicks, Josiah D.], *History of the [Pennsylvania] One Hundred and Twenty-First Regiment*. Philadelphia: J. B. Lippincott, 1906.

Higginson, Thomas Wentworth, ed., *Harvard Memorial Biographies*. Two Vols. Cambridge, Mass.: Sever and Francis, 1868.

Howard, Oliver Otis, *Autobiography of Oliver Otis Howard*. Two Vols. New York: The Baker & Taylor Company, 1908.

Howe, Mark De Wolfe, *Justice Oliver Wendell Holmes: The Shaping Years, 1841–1870*. Cambridge, Mass.: The Belknap Press of Harvard University Press, 1957.

_____, ed., *Touched with Fire: Civil War Letters and Diary of Oliver Wendell Holmes, Jr., 1861–1864*. Cambridge, Mass.: Harvard University Press, 1946.

Howell, Helena Adelaide, compiler, *Chronicles of the One Hundred Fifty-First Regiment, New York State Volunteer Infantry, 1862–1865*. Albion, New York: A. M. Eddy, Printer, 1911.

Hutchinson, Nelson V., *History of the Seventh Massachusetts Volunteer Infantry in the War of the Rebellion of the Southern States against Constitutional Authority, 1861–1865*. Taunton, Mass.: Published by Authority of the Regimental Association, 1890.

Hyde, Thomas W., *Civil War Letters*. n.p. Published by John H. Hyde, Privately Printed, 1933.

_____, *Following the Greek Cross or, Memories of the Sixth Army Corps*. Boston and New York: Houghton Mifflin and Company, 1895.

Johnson, Robert Underwood, and Buel, Clarence Clough, eds., *Battles and Leaders of the Civil War*. Four volumes. New York: The Century Company, 1884, 1887, 1888.

Judd, David W., *The Story of the Thirty-Third N. Y. S. Vols.* [New York State Volunteers]. Rochester, New York: Benton and Andrews, 1864.

Jurgen, Robert, and Keller, Allan, *Major General John Sedgwick, U.S. Volunteers (1813–64)*. n.p. Connecticut Civil War Centennial Commission, n.d.

Latta, James William, *Address of Gen. James W. Latta, President, Sedgwick Memorial Association, Thursday, May 12, 1887.* n.p.: n.d.

Leach, Margaret, *Reveille in Washington, 1860–1865.* New York and London: Harper and Brothers, 1941.

Lewis, Osceola, *History of the One Hundred and Thirty-Eighth Regiment, Pennsylvania Volunteer Infantry.* Norristown, Penna.: Wills, Iredell, and Jenkins, 1866.

Livermore, Thomas Leonard, *Days and Events, 1860–1866.* Boston and New York: Houghton Mifflin Company, 1920.

_____, *Numbers and Losses in the Civil War in America, 1861–1865.* Boston and New York: Houghton Mifflin and Company, 1901.

McClellan, George B., *McClellan's Own Story, The War for the Union, The Soldiers Who Fought It, The Civilians Who Directed It, and His Relations to It and To Them.* New York: Charles L. Webster & Company, 1887.

_____, *Report on the Organization and Campaigns of the Army of the Potomac to which is Added an Account on the Campaign in Western Virginia with Plans of Battle-Fields.* New York: Sheldon & Company, 1864.

McDermott, Anthony W., *A Brief History of the 69th Regiment, Pennsylvania Veterans Volunteers.* Philadelphia: D. J. Gallagher and Company, [1889?].

McMahon, Martin T., *Gen. John Sedgwick: An Address Delivered Before the Vermont Officers' Reunion Society at their Sixteenth Annual Meeting at Montpelier, Nov. 11, 1880.* Rutland, Vermont: Tuttle & Co., Official State Printers, 1880.

_____, *In Memoriam: Maj.-Gen. John Sedgwick.* Togus, Maine: Printed at the National Home, 1885.

Mark, Penrose G., *Red: White: and Blue Badge, Pennsylvania Veteran Volunteers: A History of the Ninety-Third Regiment.* Harrisburg, Penna.: The Aughinbaugh Press, 1911.

Meade, George, *The Life and Letters of George Gordon Meade, Major-General, United States Army,* ed. George Gordon Meade. Two Vols. New York: Charles Scribner's Sons, 1913.

Michie, Peter S., *Life and Letters of Emory Upton.* New York: D. Appleton and Company, 1885.

Military Historical Society of Massachusetts, *The Wilderness Campaign, May–June 1864.* Vol. IV. Boston: The Military Historical Society of Massachusetts, 1905.

Murfin, James V., *The Gleam of Bayonets: The Battle of Antietam and the Maryland Campaign of 1862.* New York and London: Thomas Yoseloff, 1965.

Nevins, Allan, ed., *A Diary of Battle: The Personal Journals of Charles S. Wainwright, 1861–1865.* New York: Harcourt, Brace & World, Inc., 1962.

New York Monuments Commission for the Battlefields of Gettysburg and Chattanooga, *Final Report of the Battle of Gettysburg.* Three Vols. Albany: J. B. Lyon Company, 1902.

Nichols, Edward J., *Toward Gettysburg: A Biography of General John F. Reynolds.* University Park, Penna.: The Pennsylvania State University Press, 1958.

Palfrey, Francis Winthrop, *The Antietam and Fredericksburg*. New York: Charles Scribner's Sons, 1882.

Pearson, Henry Greenleaf, *James S. Wadsworth of Geneseo, Brevet Major-General of United States Volunteers*. New York: Charles Scribner's Sons, 1913.

Pennsylvania at Gettysburg, *Ceremonies at the Dedication of the Monuments Erected by the Commonwealth of Pennsylvania to Major-General George G. Meade, Major-General Winfield S. Hancock, Major-General John F. Reynolds and to Mark the Positions of Pennsylvania Commands Engaged in Battle*. Two Vols. Harrisburg, Penna.: Wm. Stanley Ray, State Printer, 1904.

Poore, Benjamin Perley, *The Life and Public Services of Ambrose E. Burnside, Soldier — Citizen — Statesman*. Providence: J. A. & R. A. Reid, 1882.

Porter, Horace, *Campaigning with Grant*. New York: The Century Company, 1897.

Prowell, George R., *History of the Eighty-Seventh Regiment, Pennsylvania Volunteers*. York, Penna.: Press of the York Daily, 1903.

Quaife, Milo M., ed., *From the Cannon's Mouth: The Civil War Letters of General Alpheus S. Williams*. Detroit: Wayne State University Press and the Detroit Historical Society, 1959.

Rhodes, James Ford, *History of the Civil War, 1861–1865*. New York: The Macmillan Company, 1917.

Rhodes, John H., *The History of Battery B, First Regiment, Rhode Island Light Artillery*. Providence: Snow and Farnham, 1894.

Roe, Albert S., *The Tenth Regiment Massachusetts Volunteer Infantry, 1861– 1864: A Western Massachusetts Regiment*. Springfield, Mass.: Press of the F. A. Bassette Co., 1909.

Ropes, John Codman, *The Army Under Pope*. New York: Charles Scribner's Sons, 1881.

Schaff, Morris, *The Battle of the Wilderness*. Boston and New York: Houghton Mifflin Company, 1910.

Searles, Jasper N., and Taylor, Matthew F., *History of the First Regiment, Minnesota Volunteer Infantry, 1861–1864*. Stillwater, Minn.: Easton and Masterman, 1916.

Sedgwick, John, *Correspondence of John Sedgwick, Major-General*. Two Vols. New York: The De Vinne Press, Printed for Carl and Ellen Battelle Stoeckel, 1902– 1903.

Sedgwick Memorial Association, 6th Army Corps, Spotsylvania Court House, Va., May 11, 12, and 13, 1887. *Dedicatory Proceedings*. Philadelphia: Dunlap and Clarke, 1887.

Small, Harold Adams, ed., *The Road to Richmond: The Civil War Memoirs of Major Abner S. Small of the Sixteenth Maine Volunteers, Together with the Diary which He Kept when He was a Prisoner of War*. Berkeley: University of California Press, 1939.

Smalley, George W., *Anglo-American Memories*. London: Duckworth and Company, 1910.

Sparks, David S., ed., *Inside Lincoln's Army: The Diary of Marsena Rudolph Patrick, Provost Marshal General, Army of the Potomac*. New York and London: Thomas Yoseloff, 1964.

Starr, Edward C., *A History of Cornwall, Connecticut: A Typical New England Town*. New Haven: The Tuttle, Morehouse, and Taylor Company, 1926.

State of Connecticut, *Dedication of the Equestrian Statue of Major-General John Sedgwick*. Hartford: Published by the State, 1913.

Steere, Edward, *The Wilderness Campaign*. Harrisburg, Penn.: The Stackpole Press, 1960.

Stevens, George T., *The First Fighting Campaign of the Seventy-Seventh. Address to the Survivors' Association of the Seventy-Seventh Regiment, N. Y. Volunteers at their Forty-Third Reunion Held at Saratoga Springs, June 26, 1915*. n.p., n.d.

———, *Three Years in the Sixth Corps: A Concise Narrative of Events in the Army of the Potomac from 1861 to the Close of the Rebellion, April, 1865*. New York: D. Van Nostrand, 1870.

Stine, J. H., *History of the Army of the Potomac*. Washington, D.C.: Gibson Bros., 1893.

Swinton, William, *Campaigns of the Army of the Potomac: A Critical History of Operations in Virginia, Maryland, and Pennsylvania from the Commencement to the Close of the War, 1861–5*. New York: Charles B. Richardson, 1866.

Sypher, J. R., *History of the Pennsylvania Reserves Corps*. Lancaster, Penna.: Elias Barr and Company, 1865.

Trobriand, Regis de, *Four Years with the Army of the Potomac*. Boston: Ticknor and Company, 1889.

Tyler, Mason Whiting, *Recollections of the Civil War: With Many Original Diary Entries and Letters Written from the Seat of War and with Annotated References*. William S. Tyler, ed. New York and London: G. P. Putnam's Sons, 1912.

U.S. Military Academy, Department of Military Art and Engineering, *Civil War Atlas to Accompany Steele's American Campaigns*. West Point, New York: USMA, 1941.

Walker, Francis A., *History of the Second Army Corps in the Army of the Potomac*. New York: Charles Scribner's Sons, 1886.

Ward, Joseph R. C., *History of the One Hundred and Sixth Regiment, Pennsylvania Volunteers*. Philadelphia: F. McManus, Jr. and Company, 1906.

Webb, Alexander S., *The Peninsula: McClellan's Campaign of 1862*. New York: Charles Scribner's Sons, 1881.

Welch, Emily Sedgwick, *John Sedgwick, Major-General: A Biographical Sketch*. New York: The De Vinne Press, 1899.

Weld, Stephen Minot, *War Diary and Letters of Stephen Minot Weld, 1861–1865*. Cambridge, Mass.: The Riverside Press, 1912.

Wilson, James Harrison, *Under the Old Flag*. Vol. I. New York and London: D. Appleton and Company, 1912.

Public Documents

U.S. Congress, Joint Committee on the Conduct of the War, *Reports.* Vol. I. Washington: Government Printing Office, 1865.

U.S. War Department, *The War of the Rebellion: A Compilation of the Official Records of the Union and Confederate Armies.* 128 Vols. Washington: Government Printing Office, 1880–1901.

Articles and Essays

Finan, W. J., "Major General John Sedgwick: One of Litchfield County's Greatest Soldiers," *The Lure of the Litchfield Hills,* Vol. XIV, No. 1. (June 1957), pp. 17–18.

Holmes, Oliver Wendell, Sr., "My Hunt After 'The Captain,' " *Atlantic Monthly,* Vol. X (December, 1862), pp. 738–64.

McMahon, M[artin] T., "Major-General John Sedgwick," *Personal Recollections of the War of the Rebellion: Addresses Delivered Before the Commandary of the State of New York, Military Order of the Loyal Legion of the United States,* ed. A. Noel Blakeman. New York and London: G. P. Putnam's Sons, The Knickerbocker Press, 1897, Second Series, pp. 159–82.

Manuscript Collections

Abbott, Peter M., Papers. Vermont Historical Society, Montpelier, Vermont.

Barlow, Francis Channing, Papers. Massachusetts Historical Society, Boston, Massachusetts.

Barton, The Barton Family, Papers. Vermont Historical Society, Montpelier, Vermont.

Biddle, James Cornell, Papers. Historical Society of Pennsylvania, Philadelphia, Pennsylvania.

Biddle, William F., Papers. Historical Society of Pennsylvania, Philadelphia, Pennsylvania.

Connor, Selden, Papers. John Hay Library, Brown University, Providence, Rhode Island.

Fisk, Wilbur, Collection. Library of Congress, Washington, D.C.

Gardner, Alfred Gray, "Extracts from Letters and Sketches of his Life by Various Authors" (Typescript). John D. Rockefeller, Jr., Library, Brown University, Providence, Rhode Island.

Heintzelman, Samuel P., Papers and Diary. Library of Congress, Washington, D.C.

Hildebrand, S. F., "Notes and Reminiscences of Service in the 139th Regiment, [Pennsylvania Volunteers] Company E." Unpaginated manuscript. Library of Congress, Washington, D.C.

Holmes, Oliver Wendell, Jr., Collection. Harvard Law School Library, Harvard University, Cambridge, Massachusetts.

———, Papers. Library of Congress, Washington, D.C.

Horton, Edwin, Papers. Vermont Historical Society, Montpelier, Vermont.

Howard, Oliver Otis, Collection. Bowdoin College Library, Bowdoin College, Brunswick, Maine.

Howland, Joseph, Papers. New York Historical Society, New York, New York.

Humphreys, Andrew A., Papers. Historical Society of Pennsylvania. Philadelphia, Pennsylvania.

Johnson, Andrew, Papers. Library of Congress, Washington, D.C.

Larned, Daniel Reed, Papers. Library of Congress, Washington, D.C.

Latta, James William, Papers and Diary. Library of Congress, Washington, D.C.

Lincoln, Abraham, Papers. Library of Congress, Washington, D.C.

Lyman, Theodore, Papers and Diary. Massachusetts Historical Society, Boston, Massachusetts.

Lynch, John Wheaton, Papers. Historical Society of Pennsylvania, Philadelphia, Pennsylvania.

Mead, Walcott A., Collection. Vermont Historical Society, Montpelier, Vermont.

Murphy, Thomas Parish, Diary. Vermont Historical Society, Montpelier, Vermont.

Rhodes, William B., Diary. Sterling Memorial Library, Yale University, New Haven, Connecticut.

Ropes, Henry, Letters. Boston Public Library, Boston, Massachusetts.

Schuyler, Philip, Papers. New-York Historical Society, New York, New York.

Sedgwick, John, Collection. Cornwall Public Library, Cornwall, Connecticut.

———, Commissions. Connecticut State Library, Hartford, Connecticut.

———, One Letter. In possession of Mrs. J. Sedgwick Cooke, Dibble Hill, Cornwall, Connecticut.

———, Two Letters. New York State Library, Albany, New York.

Shaler, Alexander, Diary of Alexander Shaler while Prisoner of War, May 6th to August 9th, 1864, Captured, Battle of the Wilderness, Exchanged at Charleston, South Carolina. New-York Historical Society, New York, New York.

Sixth Corps, Order and Letter Book of the United States Army, Medical Department, Sixth Corps, Army of the Potomac, dated Sept. 24, 1862, to March 13, 1865. Library of Congress, Washington, D.C.

Webb, Alexander Stewart, Papers. Sterling Memorial Library, Yale University, New Haven, Connecticut.

Wentworth, Edwin, Papers. Library of Congress, Washington, D.C.

Whittier, Charles Albert, "Reminiscences of the War, 1861–1865, or Egotistic Memoirs, C. A. W., Feb. 13, 1888, M. Milit. Hist. Sy." (Typescript). Boston Public Library, Boston, Massachusetts.

Index

AUTHOR NOTE

Richard Winslow, a native of Massachusetts, has degrees from Union College, Schenectady, New York, and the Universities of New Hampshire, Pennsylvania State, and Maryland. He has taught American history in Maine, Connecticut, and Pennsylvania, at both the secondary school and college levels. At the present time he is the associate editor of the Papers of Henry Clay, University of Kentucky, Lexington.

His interest in the Civil War is perhaps inherited from the legacy of two great-grandfathers: Lewis F. Powell, a Virginian, who accompanied the Confederate Army as a youth in that state, and Henry E. Fales, a Massachusetts lawyer and politician, who belonged to the state militia and was a friend of Gen. Benjamin F. Butler.

Winslow is the associate editor of Volume 7 of *The Papers of Henry Clay* (University of Kentucky Press). With Dr. James C. Mohr, he is currently editing two Civil War diaries for a forthcoming book, *Northern Family Life During the Civil War: The Cormany Diaries, 1858–1865*. Winslow has also published articles on canoeing, hiking, and American literary figures.

His concern with the common soldier and life in the field originated with his two years' service in the U.S. Army Infantry in Georgia and Germany. A member of the Madison County (Kentucky) Civil War Round Table and other professional organizations, Winslow enjoys tramping around battlefields and visiting historic sites and homes.